My American Life

Also by Price M. Cobbs, M.D.

*Cracking the Corporate Code: The Revealing Success Stories
of 32 African-American Executives*
(with Judith L. Turnock)

Cracking the Corporate Code: From Survival to Mastery
(with Judith L. Turnock)

The Jesus Bag
(with William H. Grier)

Black Rage
(with William H. Grier)

MY

From Rage

AMERICAN

to Entitlement

LIFE

Price M. Cobbs, M.D.

ATRIA BOOKS

New York   London   Toronto   Sydney

ATRIA BOOKS

1230 Avenue of the Americas
New York, NY 10020

ISBN-13: 978-0-7434-9619-3
ISBN-10:   0-7434-9619-1
ISBN-13: 978-0-7434-9622-3 (Pbk)
ISBN-10:   0-7434-9622-1 (Pbk)

First Atria Books trade paperback edition July 2006

10 9 8 7 6 5 4 3 2

ATRIA BOOKS is a trademark of Simon & Schuster, Inc.

Designed by Jeanette Olender

Manufactured in the United States of America

For information regarding special discounts for bulk purchases,
please contact Simon & Schuster Special Sales at 1-800-456-6798
or business@simonandschuster.com

To Rosa Ellen and Peter Price Cobbs

The ledge has been widened.

ACKNOWLEDGMENTS

After finishing this book, I am acutely aware that a memoir, or at least this one, is an incomplete history of a life. Many important parts were necessarily left out, forgotten, or only recalled after this book was completed. The events of my recent life and work are not told here. Also, various people and specific experiences that have profoundly influenced the direction of my life have been excluded from these pages. I wanted this story to capture the theme of rage to entitlement, and this dictated how certain events and people might be depicted. Perhaps the parts that have been left out tell me that if my health and spirit hold out, I should write another memoir or an addendum to this one. Only time and motivation will provide the answer to that question.

While writing this book, I have lived constantly with the difficulty of resurrecting and confronting memories. Whether they are vivid or murky, comforting or unsettling, they are stored in some reservoir of the mind waiting to be called up. Experiences that I felt had been long settled and rendered benign, I found emotionally wrenching. Others that I dreaded might be weighted with the accumulated baggage of many years were brought forth and proved to be neatly closed and sealed.

I have many people to thank for this book and start with my parents and my brother and sister. The many members of my immediate family are obviously an integral part of my life's story. I also thank many friends and colleagues whose lives have connected with mine and contributed immensely to whatever successes I have had. My acknowledgment and thanks to all of them is written as a part of this story. Beyond that, I thank my dear friend Jeffrey Klein. For over twenty years he has prodded me and held to an unwavering belief that the story of my life story was worth telling. I also thank Alan Rinzler for his helpful suggestions as to what form and shape my book would ultimately take. I thank Terence Clarke for his immense help in getting me through the all-important step of writing a first draft. I owe a debt of gratitude to my literary agents, Daniel Greenberg and James Levine. Their advice and counsel throughout this process has been invaluable. My editor at Atria Books, Malaika Adero, has been exceptionally skillful in guiding me through the always challenging part of crafting a final product.

Finally, I thank the accident of birth for placing me in a time and a place and being a member of a unique family that allowed me to live through a period of profound social, political, and cultural transformation in America. I hope my story indicates that I have tried to grapple with the issues of my times. I also hope that reading their grandfather's memoir inspires my grandchildren, Kendall Evadne and Kristopher Price, to grapple with the issues of their times.

CONTENTS

INTRODUCTION

I've lived through extraordinary times. I've met notable figures from the Harlem Renaissance, grown up during the Great Depression, and felt the dramatic effect of World War II on my own consciousness as well as that of all black people. I've witnessed the dismantling of Jim Crow laws that began immediately after the end of the war and continued through the integration of the U.S. Armed Forces. I've seen the impact of *Brown vs. Board of Education* and the end of restrictive voter registration laws in the South. I watched with awe the ascendancy of Martin Luther King Jr., the heroism of Rosa Parks and so many others, and the explosive growth of education at all levels for black people. I followed the life of Malcolm X and searched avidly for what animated the ideas beneath his fiery rhetoric.

I've been there, at the places with the people when very important events were taking place. So I've chosen to write a memoir of the important issues that, thank my lucky stars, I've confronted in my life.

As a practicing psychiatrist, I came to understand what Black Rage is and to help reveal its complexity to people yearning for such understanding. And I have actively participated in the breaking of the so-called glass ceiling by black men and women striving to enter the corporate boardroom on terms of fairness and equal opportunity.

William H. Grier and I wrote about black rage and how it affects all of us who have endured the unremitting acid rain of oppression, and who therefore need to be understood and treated in unique ways. I've spent my adult life studying the phenomenon and working with many patients and colleagues in a quest to understand it, to explain it, and perhaps most importantly, to enable black people to deal with it.

I've studied racism, the ever resilient foe, from the history of slavery through the years of the post-Emancipation nineteenth and twentieth centuries, and through the period of my own life. Far beyond its overuse as a contemporary label, I've come to understand racism as a system of beliefs about individuals and groups built up over centuries. It purports to predetermine who is good and bad, smart and dumb, superior or inferior. I've read about the first Europeans encountering the first Africans and how that most arresting characteristic of skin color began its long and deadly journey. And I've also come to understand that racism looms like an iceberg in the Arctic Sea. It is huge and immobile and what lies above the water must be avoided, but the real danger lies in what is unseen. I've observed the effects racism has had on me, on others, and the changes that racism itself has undergone. I know that when white people say that racism no longer exists in this country, they are wrong. And that when black people say they are still imprisoned by it, they too are wrong.

My parents told me that "it's not what you do that matters. It's what you do with what you do that makes the difference." This advice was given at a time when educated black people could only get jobs as elevator operators, drivers, hairdressers, and so on. There were certain professions we could enter in those times: teaching, for which my mother had received her degree; medicine, my father's chosen vocation; and the ministry, a calling that included many of my mother's relatives. The world of corporate America, where the real power resides, was closed to us except in those rare instances where we ourselves founded, owned, and managed the business. When the thirtieth president of the United States once declared "the business of America is business," he was speaking to this reality. Generations of inventors, merchants, and immigrants have built wealth in this country by founding businesses. The Golden State Mutual Life Insurance Company founded in Los Angeles in 1925 was one such example. Then, there was the often told story of Madame CJ Walker, the first African American woman millionaire in this country. In 1905 she established her own business and began selling a product to soften and straighten the hair of black women.

Times have changed. Legally sanctioned discrimination has been largely eradicated. While the civil rights movement of the 1960s was not the panacea many hoped for, the country was set unalterably on a different path. The weight of government can no longer be used to support and rationalize second-class citizenship for blacks. The succeeding era of equal opportunity and affirmative action, however resisted by implacable opponents, has also contributed immeasurably to our progress. As a result of this, corporate and organizational attitudes toward blacks have been remarkably altered. I've been privileged to have had a hand in this.

There have been far too few black people in the mahogany-paneled grandeur of the corporate boardroom, with its promise of influence and riches. As a consequence, African Americans have only recently begun to participate in these important institutions of capitalism and wealth formation. I've been among many who wanted to change that, and I've helped the guardians of corporate power understand the real talent and ability that blacks bring to decision making, sophisticated management practices, and corporate leadership. And I've helped black people understand that they can walk into that big room and sit down in the chair at the head of the table and succeed.

All Americans have the same birthright and certainly the same civil rights as full American citizens. I have seen in my lifetime black people struggling beyond the legacy of slavery and rage to take their place as equal citizens entitled to the same opportunities and responsibilities as everyone else. One path to accomplishing this is by developing and cultivating a healthy sense of entitlement. I don't mean that we should become a people who are incessantly demanding and constantly exploitative, with a grandiose self-image and a strong sense of deserving special treatment. I also don't mean we should feel that the world and everyone in it owes them something. That sort of "entitlement" is free of the constraints of personal responsibility, and if left to their own designs, such individuals are consigned to lifelong patterns of selfish and destructive behavior.

Nor am I speaking of the type of "entitlement" that has entered the social and political discourse of this country, in which an individual or a group can lay claim to a pension, some sort of veterans' rights, or a special status gained through the previous, collective suffering of generations that went before. No. What I'm talking about is social, political, and cultural entitlement, that is, entitlement that is the fundamental right of everyone: blacks, whites, Asians, Hispanics, Native Americans, the lot of us. For black people this means moving beyond a sense of impotence, victimhood, and rumors of inferiority. It means embracing the legitimacy of one's needs and the right to lay claim to them. At its core this entitlement is the essential vision of the American dream. In my view, it is what the Founding Fathers had in mind when they held "these truths to be self-evident, that all men are created equal." Certainly the Founding Fathers intended this equality only for men, and moreover only for white men. But if an idea is compelling, it cannot be confined to an exclusive group, it inevitably becomes the province of all groups.

I have come to realize that what many successful people—particularly whites—possess is this sense of cultural entitlement. Without thinking about it, most white people in this country have no doubt that they belong to a club where skin color bestows many privileges. They have a sense of ownership of the resources and legacy of this society and will take advantage of whatever it has to offer. It's as simple as that. They accept their entitlement as part of their birthright.

Many black people in this country, though, have not yet allowed themselves to incorporate this kind of cultural entitlement for many reasons, some justifiable and others self-imposed. And even when such entitlement is successfully realized by a black person, I have found that, emotionally, he or she has had to struggle mightily to retain that God-given sense of self. It's beyond what they naturally expect. They often feel that they don't deserve it.

By understanding and incorporating this crucial sense of entitlement, a black person can identify and discard the accumulated detritus of centuries. With a healthy sense of this kind of entitlement, blacks will be free to focus their rage externally on the actual problems that still truly exist and not internally on the emotional problems that accompany perceived victimhood, problems that can only cripple. Worthy at last, they will be free at last.

Consequently, this book is more than a memoir. I offer it as a guidebook to Entitlement as I've come to define it in my life and in my work along my American journey.

My American Life

CHAPTER ONE

Doctor Boswell's first words to my mother, Rosa, after she delivered me, her third child, were "that boy looks just like a bishop." I was born at home, 1531 East Forty-ninth Street in Los Angeles, California, on November 2, 1928. And as I took what no doubt was a noisy first breath, Dr. Boswell's humorous, well-intended depiction of me resonated deeply in some part of my mother's soul. She herself had long-term standing as a leader of the Colored Methodist Episcopal Church, of which the good doctor was also a member. Indeed, back in Birmingham, my mother's father and two brothers had been prominent members of the church and later her brother ran for bishop, which, in the CME Church, is an elected position. My uncle lost that election. But that did not interfere with my mother's certainty that I indeed had the appearance of intelligence, probity, and righteousness that could help me on the path to great expectations. My looking like a bishop was good news to her and fitting as well.

My father, Peter Price Cobbs, would have been pleased too. He wasn't as devoted to the church as my mother, but he attended regularly and appreciated the social and political aspects of being a member of the church community. A thoughtful man of action, he was in 1928 one of the very first black physicians to practice in Los Angeles. He knew that if his newborn son Price truly fit such a description, he was already exhibiting qualities that would serve him well in a world that even my father, "PP" as a few close friends called him, could only imagine was coming. So as I was laid in my mother's arms for the first time that day, I was welcomed with joy to the family of Doctor and Mrs. Peter Price Cobbs, my brother, Prince, and my sister, Marcelyn.

I don't remember the ride, of course, but a few days after my birth, my mother and father drove me in their late-model Reo from our little house on Forty-ninth Street between Hooper and Central Avenue for a ride down Central Avenue. He later only drove either a Dodge or a Chrysler.

In 1928 there were about twenty thousand black people in Los Angeles, and most of them could be found in the neighborhood of Central Avenue, in a corridor several blocks wide and thirty blocks long, just south of downtown. This was, of course, a segregated Los Angeles in which black people were severely restricted in where they could live. Real estate land covenants forbidding the sale of property to black people in most sections of L.A. were part and parcel of the law itself and had been legitimized by a California Supreme Court ruling in 1919. That judgment, which legalized segregation in housing, stood until well after the end of World War II.

The covenants did not stop people from coming, though. There was money in Los Angeles, lots of it, and many black immigrants from the Carolinas, Georgia, Alabama, Mississippi, Tennessee, Florida, Louisiana, and Texas felt that some portion of it could be theirs. Especially in comparison to wages in the South, those in L.A. were high, even for menial jobs. A black janitor in L.A., for example, could make three times what he'd earn working a farm in Georgia, Alabama, or Mississippi. Also, despite the restrictive covenants, there was the important and wonderful possibility of even having a home of your own, although its location may be restricted to a certain section of the city. In 1930, one-third of the black people in L.A. owned their homes, a much higher percentage than in any other city in the United States.

Most of the blacks immigrating to Los Angeles in those days were upwardly mobile people seeking education and good jobs who had the intention of improving their lot financially and every other way. There was also a steady trickle of black professionals like my parents. My father had a thriving practice he had built over the years in Montgomery, Alabama, so the move to Los Angeles was thoughtfully considered.

Something important was apparently missing in Montgomery, and he was looking for a place where he could improve his position. One day when I was in junior high school and riding with my father to his office he mentioned he found Montgomery "too confining." He never explained and I didn't ask whether this meant he wanted to build a larger medical practice or to participate more fully in the political life of a city. He considered Tallahassee, Florida, where he had applied for a position as the infirmary physician at Florida A and M. While he was visiting there though he was treated with all of the rough, backward truculence that the white South reserved for blacks, no matter their talents. Refusals of service. Insults. Degrading indifference or outright hostility. Nothing even in Montgomery had prepared him for this. Life for blacks in Tallahassee was not good.

My father came away from the experience shaken by the way he was treated except, of course, among the students and staff of the college. After living in both Tuskegee Institute and Montgomery, Alabama, the racial hostility of the Deep South was certainly not a new experience for him. Maybe being a part of the medical community in those places cushioned some of the blows. Whatever it was, the sheer intensity of Tallahassee was undoubtedly different. The few days he spent there in 1924 remained symbolic to him for the rest of his life of what the South intended for people like him, my mother, and their family to come. Indeed his description of this visit was one of the few occasions when my father actually uttered the word *racist,* a word that we seldom used in those days. We talked more about "prejudice" when I was a child. But my father said that Tallahassee was one of the most racist places he had ever visited, and I think that experience is what pushed him to go far away, way out west, to the new promised land of California and Los Angeles.

Leaving the South and migrating west was a common theme with a great many of the kids that I grew up with—whether their parents had brought them to L.A. in the 1920s and 1930s or had arrived there before the kids themselves were born. The idea was to move to a safer place with a better social and racial climate—but in reality conditions weren't all that great in L.A. You were, after all, still black, still in America, and change was still a long way off. . . . There was in L.A. a certain "cautiousness" that you had to maintain, a wariness, a constant vigilance. There was the sense that something dangerous was always out there lurking somewhere. It was not the more rigid, precisely defined South where everyone, especially black folks, knew their place. There was capriciousness. This was L.A. where racism was often insidious, not nearly as blatant and outright as it was in the South.

In Los Angeles, you never knew when something might occur that made folks generate their own unique brand of regional prejudice and western-style discrimination. For example, other than one or two downtown cafeterias, most restaurants were reserved for whites. While there were no WHITES ONLY signs posted in the window, a father or mother knew the family wouldn't be served, so why go in and have the children humiliated. At an early age you discovered which neighborhood places to avoid, be they the five-and-dime around the corner, a nearby cleaners, or even a small candy store. If you forgot and wandered in, you were either ignored, stared at, or told, sometimes even politely, that the establishment didn't cater to "colored people." Many public places were off-limits. As a neighborhood turned increasingly black, a swimming pool and park would become available for use. Yet several blocks away in a white area the same black people trying to use similar facilities were chased away. But it was worse elsewhere. Often much worse. So these people came to L.A. because they could not tolerate the raw, naked racism of the South. Or—and justifiably—it frightened them.

Boldness, though, accompanied the fear and caution that came west with these southern blacks. These people were pioneers. They had the courage to pull up their roots and travel far from their families and everything that had been familiar to them. They didn't let the obstacles of continued legal and unyielding segregation stop them from taking what freedom and opportunity there was to make a better place for themselves and their families. With no guarantees of employment, no special prospects in sight, and in most cases very little or no money, these courageous immigrants set forth to make a new life in a New World.

•-•-•

So as they looked at their baby bishop in his home on a November afternoon in 1928, each of my parents had a view of me tempered by their own experiences as black Americans in a society that still bore a heavy burden of racial inequity and enmity. My father no less than my mother.

Peter Price Cobbs was born in Barboursville, Virginia. He was the oldest child, and it's interesting to consider how cultured, well educated, and politically developed a man my father became, coming from a place like Barboursville that was not even a town, barely a village. Once he could, he left. His brothers and sisters left too. They moved to New York; North Carolina; Washington, D.C.

He attended Howard University in Washington, D.C., both as an undergraduate and through medical school, graduating in 1919. Through hard work, intelligence, and determination, he had become a physician, a middle-class profession that was one of the few available for blacks at that time. There was the ministry, of course. Dentistry. Teaching. But medicine was one of the most important professions, and my father was indeed an important man, highly regarded and respected in the community, by virtue of his work and his personality.

My father did not project self-importance. Underneath his self-confident bearing, humility, and lack of pretension, though, my father had an edge, a subtle undercurrent of anger leaking out. Rage bubbling dangerously just beneath the surface. It was this edge that became for me, later, the most important part of his personality. It found much of its expression, when I was a teenager, in his increasing involvement in progressive politics. But at the time of my birth he was not yet expressively political or left-wing. I know just the same that even then, when we were little kids, he had a political viewpoint, because he helped all of us grow up with one of our own. His motivation for moving to L.A. and going into practice there would have been part of it. He wasn't going to tolerate bringing up his kids in the blatant racism of the old South, and we knew that.

L.A.'s version of racial segregation was the development of our Central Avenue neighborhood as a thriving center of black business, culture, and above all, family. The street itself had the same invigorated atmosphere as other such streets in the United States, including 125th Street in Harlem in New York City, Beale Street in Memphis, or "Sweet" Auburn Avenue in Atlanta, Georgia.

Among the many attractions of Central Avenue during that period was the music. Los Angeles was either a significant stopping-off place or a home to many notable black musicians who were able to find work in the new Hollywood talkies as well as the clubs. Jelly Roll Morton regularly played at a club called Wayside Park in nearby Watts in the early 1920s, and he introduced King Oliver to the L.A. audience at that same club in 1922. Morton was so successful at Wayside Park that after a few years there he was able to open his own club near the corner of Twelfth and Central. Buck Clayton arrived in Los Angeles in 1929 and played for years in Central Avenue clubs. He played the trumpet and later became a leading soloist and arranger for the Count Basie Orchestra. Nat King Cole formed his first trio at a Central Avenue club, and in later years, Dexter Gordon, another Los Angeleno (whose father, incidentally, was also a physician), found his first fame on the Avenue. Dexter became a seminal tenor saxophonist of the bebop era and in 1986 was nominated for an Oscar for his role in the film *Round Midnight*. There were hundreds of musicians who were fueling the innovative explosion in jazz in L.A. during that period.

And Central Avenue had some pretty grand buildings too. The same year I was born, a black dentist named John Somerville built The Somerville Hotel on Central Avenue at Forty-first Street, thirteen blocks from where we lived. Four stories high with one hundred rooms, The Somerville opened in time to provide shelter and services to W. E. B. DuBois and James Weldon Johnson, who had come to L.A. to attend the NAACP convention that year. Descriptions of the hotel point out that it contained a barbershop, a beauty parlor, a florist, a thriving restaurant, and other such establishments. It was one of the finest hotels for black people in the country.

The stock market crash in 1929 forced Doctor Somerville to sell the hotel to a group that renamed it The Dunbar Hotel, after the famous Paul Laurence Dunbar, a black American poet born in Dayton, Ohio, in 1872. Dunbar's work was internationally known during his own lifetime. He was praised and personally helped in his career by James Whitcomb Riley, William Dean Howells, and none other than Orville and Wilbur Wright, with whom he attended high school. The Dunbar Hotel remains today at the same address.

Black people lived and worked on Central Avenue, strolled up and down its length, shopped, visited, or simply hung out in its many diners and cafés, on its stoops and corners, nearly twenty-four hours a day.

There were barbershops, funeral parlors, insurance offices, movie theaters, billiard parlors, restaurants, beauty parlors, bookstores … . in short, every kind of activity going on day and night. Central Avenue was the place to be, the center of the community.

•-•-•

Despite all this opportunity for growth and relative freedom, none of the people who lived in my neighborhood were ever emotionally far from the South, and none of them could ever forget the legacy of slavery, the one legacy that all of them shared equally. Like immigrants from Ireland or Italy, my parents and many others referred to the place they left as the "old country," and like every other black person in 1928, whether they were living in Los Angeles, Tuscaloosa, New York, Dallas, or wherever, they knew people in their own families who'd been born slaves or had parents who had been slaves. This was only sixty-five years after Emancipation and even less time since the bad old days of Reconstruction, the Ku Klux Klan, and the continuing abuse of legalized Jim Crow segregation and murderous racism.

Lynchings were still a common event. Between 1882 and 1950 there were more than 3,400 documented lynchings of black people in the United States, according to a study by Tuskegee Institute. The most immediate of these that we knew about took place in August 1935, when a black man named Clyde Johnson was lynched in Yreka, California, for allegedly killing a white man. I was six years old at the time. As sad and grisly as this event was, it is important to remember as an example of the extreme action that could be taken against any black person for any perceived crime.

Although my family was not personally affected in so violent a way, we were certainly aware of what was happening and our lives were still mightily influenced by the legacy of slavery. One's very appearance, for instance, was assessed by values passed down from the slave experience. In the antebellum South, color had been crucial. Field slaves were usually darker, and the more favored house servants commonly used as objects of sexual gratification were usually lighter, since they were often the offspring of white masters. This differentiation went on after Emancipation, and black people's culture and society still continues to be sullied by the influence of a hierarchy based on the subtle gradations of skin color.

My mother, Rosa Mashaw Cobbs, was from a large family in Birmingham, Alabama. Her father was a minister, a presiding elder, of the Colored Methodist Episcopal Church, the CME church, which was the fourth or fifth largest black denomination in the country. So her family was proud to be a member of the small but struggling middle-class black community.

When she was growing up, blacks were the craftsmen of Birmingham: electricians, plumbers, building contractors, and so on. Most of the labor in these professions was black as well. That changed in her lifetime, she recalled, with the introduction of unions. As people began to make more money in those crafts, the crafts themselves became less black. But when she was a girl, there were many such crafts, and also the steel mills, where Birmingham blacks had the opportunity to find good jobs. Nonetheless, my mother described a harsh existence in that city for blacks when she was a child. And there, as everywhere else in black America of the time, color was a powerful factor in how well one did in the struggle for survival.

I'm not speaking of color just as a factor in the relationship between blacks and whites, although that's a central issue, to be sure. I'm also speaking of the issue of skin color among blacks themselves, and the influence it has always had on where you fit within black society.

In Los Angeles, I met several of my mother's friends from Birmingham, several who looked almost white. My mother told me that there had been many light-skinned people in her circle at home, and some of those who came to California quickly discovered that they could now pass as something other than colored or Negro. They could disappear in a crowd. For some, their lives as colored people ended and they were reborn as Greeks, Italians, or some other swarthy skin citizen of the Mediterranean. My guess is that my mother knew of only a few such people, although she often spoke as though there were dozens.

My mother herself was a beautiful darker skin woman, who was shrewd and tough-minded. My father was much lighter. When Dr. Boswell described me as looking like a bishop, it was my complexion that also projected that image. Part of what also pleased her was that like my brother, Prince, I was not "too dark." She knew that lighter skin African Americans always had an easier time in white society, and were also—sad to say—more valued among her own black community. My sister's skin was even lighter than mine. My mother would have wanted all of us to be light, but above all she wanted her daughter to have light skin, since this was a mark of real beauty.

My mother developed an elaborate vocabulary to define different shades of color among black people, and the words she used were not *mulatto, quadroon,* or any of the other formal-sounding terms. Those were not really part of the black vocabulary anyway, but rather a literary sort of terminology or, to be more succinct, a white terminology. My mother used words such as *mariney.* However the word might be officially spelled and pronounced, my mother would always draw out the "a" sound: maaariney—which was a light brown skin with undertones of red. Or *almond, ebony, ashy, high yellow, redboned, blue black.* Vivid words that would enable me to see, on a scale of one to ten, white to black, exactly where some particular individual belonged in my mother's skin-color consciousness.

My mother was more outspoken and very early in life I knew that both my parents' views about skin color and hair were complex and often conflicting. As a young kid, it seemed these matters just hung in the air like the smell of roast beef cooking in the oven, neither questioned nor debated, just commented on. Most black adults and even kids shared such confusion. From my earliest recollections, embedded somewhere in many conversations, was something called "race talk." Sometimes implied and guarded, at other times open and direct, such talk covered much more than skin color and hair. It might include how certain black people looked and talked, or how others might dress, smell, and act with one another and around white people.

In our neighborhood, we were free to walk up and down the block, play in the street, and even venture around the corner. That was safe, well-known territory. But whenever I roamed too far beyond the safety of Trinity Street, I was bombarded by furtive glances, outright stares, or barely heard comments. These were times of early, uneasy integration, and walking in a strange neighborhood, particularly several blocks west of Main Street, presented a certain danger of the unknown. At these times, I forced myself to act as if I were oblivious to whatever was going on around me, a survival technique practiced from time immemorial by most black folks. At that time I didn't know I was practicing what is called "being cool."

In my childhood, black kids faced monumental psychological challenges, and over seventy years later, the task remains ever formidable. In order to remain healthy through the many stages of development from infancy to childhood and later into adolescence, these kids must learn how to select what to keep or discard, listen to or ignore, of the many messages they receive about themselves. I learned quite early that the society in which I lived considered people like me lazy and dumb, loud and violent, irresponsible and dishonest. Such notions seemed to come from everywhere. My parents and other black adults assured us that all these negative things were what white people said about us. While I had no reason to dispute this, I knew such opinions were also a part of the first street-corner conversations I heard among young black boys and the first jokes I tried to understand. At about age five the first joke I remember was told by a kid about seven or eight years old: "Niggers and flies I do despise and the more I see Niggers, the more I like flies."

Although stated differently, such ideas were always lurking somewhere in the booming sermons delivered each week by our pastor Reverend Cleaves as he admonished the congregation to prove white (and black) folks wrong. And what was supposed to be proved wrong was always spelled out in some new and often funny homily about a wayward brother who exhibited all or most of these racially undesirable characteristics. Even in the Saturday movies seen in the theater around the corner, usually in the second or the B picture, the same unspoken themes were expressed in the occasional black face. Whatever the role, male or female, the black character had to walk slowly, roll their eyes, and somehow display the stereotypic characteristics whites wanted to see. My parents thought that it was the lifelong responsibility of kids like me to dispel these notions and be the opposite. With heroic help from them and others, I learned early on the importance of knowing lies from the truth and

to note down to the smallest deta[...]
ductive stereotypes being promote[...]

This meant I was engaged in [...]
ing, deflecting, or ignoring a c[...]
times this noise was hidden in th[...]
Sunday visitor who dropped by [...]
obviously did not mention "Ni[...]
scribing a particular foible of a [...]
people are storytellers. Since [...]
South, there were other storie[...]
someone white by getting out of town, being [...]
viving. Rather than a story about a "stupid Negro," these were depic[...]
of us outsmarting the white man. In my young mind white people and
what they thought of us were a constant unseen presence whenever black
people gathered. For me, it meant that there was always something else
to discard and I had to be ever ready to identify yet another undiscovered
falsehood about people like me.

Whether shopping for groceries or walking in the neighborhood together, my mother was quick to describe in expansive terms the people
we saw. She immediately described, in words she frequently used, who
"had class"—who she thought was pretty or handsome, who had a certain style or walked or talked in a particular way. She also did not hesitate
to make ready determinations about the intellectual capabilities of people making appearances in our small world. When we had a visiting minister, she might whisper to me about "big preachers" and "little
preachers" and I learned early that these descriptions had nothing to do
with physical size. They were her way of signaling to me who she thought
properly used "the king's English" or in a fiery sermon, who "split verbs."
After all, only a refined and proper-speaking preacher was capable of
ministering to a congregation such as ours at Phillips Temple CME
Church.

Mother always described in vivid detail how a person looked, whether
the nose was flat or aquiline, what the color of a shirt or a dress might be,
and how well the person looked in that particular color. She would describe "good" posture and "bad" posture, and how to move or sit down.

sual seat next to her in church or attending an
everal women's clubs, on the way home she would
e she thought particularly beautiful.

ack people of the time, my mother made immediate and
ons about the hair of black folks. If you had straight hair like
erson's, as Cab Calloway—a singer and band leader popular at
me—did, hair that you could flip back away from your eyes, do
gs with, move around . . . that was good hair. If you had kinky hair,
commonly called nappy, that was bad hair. She took great pains to improve the texture of her own hair with an army of brushes and combs. It
never grew quite long enough for her liking but instead would break
when it reached a certain length. I accompanied my mother to the
beauty parlor many times and overheard countless conversations she had
with Mrs. Mortenson or Miss Florence or whoever it was who owned
the shop, about what she could do to get her hair to glisten and be
straighter.

Mrs. Underwood, who came by the house periodically and cooked
catfish for us, also worked hard so that her hair glistened. My mother described her as "stunning," and as I grew older and came to appreciate
such things, I knew what she meant and agreed wholeheartedly with her
conclusion. In this instance the lady she was describing was "ebony" in
my mother's lexicon of colors. As mother talked about other friends and
acquaintances, I sensed at a young age that she was trapped in many of
the intolerant beliefs and outright prejudices that prevailed in that post-
Victorian time. After all, she was born just thirty-nine years after the end
of slavery. She made snap judgments about people based on bits and
pieces of information about them—a piece of clothing worn, a particular word used (or misused), or a choice about which hymn to sing in Sunday school. Her judgments were swift, decisive, and often negative.
Above all one had to be respectable, and that was a constantly moving
definition. While I would never describe her as stuffy, mother only let
down her guard in the privacy of her own home.

When I grew up and became more aware of what motivated these
things, I realized the terrible irony in thinking that being closer to white
would bring you closer to beauty. Freud wrote about how victims will

sometimes identify with the aggressor, how in ways both conscious and unconscious we identify with aspects of the aggressor's being, yet come nonetheless to hate those things when they appear in ourselves. However much many blacks think progress has been made in this regard, this is one of the false and seductive notions that continues to fragment many of our psyches. Black people to this day maintain a painful ambivalence about skin color.

A business acquaintance told me a story once about a woman who had consulted with her firm. The consultant was a light-skin black woman—politically aware, an intellectual, and very much in touch with contemporary black thinking. She was an astute observer of the cultural scene and never hesitant to voice her opinions about the treatment of blacks in this country. In my work I would describe her as "super black," ever militant and outspoken about all matters of race. On many occasions she lamented to my friend what she called "the goddamned slave owners" who raped her great-great-grandmother. "Why do you think I look the way I do?" she asked. I frequently encounter very light-skin blacks, men as well as women, who are supermilitant in this way. Their very skin color drives them to constantly prove that they are authentically black.

This same woman called my friend on one occasion to ask to reschedule a meeting because she had just made plans to attend a reunion of the descendants of Sally Hemings. She made a point of the fact that she is descended from Thomas Jefferson. So on the one hand, as my friend observed, she hated what happened to the women of her family, raped by slave owners and their ilk, while on the other hand she made sure that others understood that being a descendant of Thomas Jefferson put her a step above everybody else. The act that she was talking about was the same act in both instances, and she voiced both hatred and acceptance, even pride, in the same breath.

•◆•

My mother conveyed to the world that she would not be pushed around or taken advantage of by anybody. She made sure, in those days, that everything she, her husband, and her three children did was prepared for and accomplished with exquisite care. This was the case for many of my peers as well, and such care for the children may be interpreted as simply proper concern on the part of good parents.

For example, the "exquisite care" with which they prepared us—and themselves—to go shopping, to go to a movie, to go for a Sunday drive . . . much of that was intended for protection. This was especially true if we were going anywhere outside those parts of the city that we knew for certain to be safe for blacks. My parents would somehow have scouted that place out or at least learned from others what kind of treatment could be expected there. Otherwise, we would not go. Sometimes the advance information would be wrong, and we'd learn that their practice was to not "serve colored here." But usually my parents knew what to expect whenever they took us somewhere, and it was my mother who would have done the prior research to make sure it was all right for us.

Our parents spent a good deal of time protecting us.

The period when I was growing up in Los Angeles was relatively benign. I did not suffer from the kinds of overt racist hostility that have been so well chronicled by blacks raised in places like Mississippi, Alabama, or Georgia. We were not treated as Clyde Johnson had been treated in Yreka. I did not have to jump off the sidewalk if a white man or woman were coming in the opposite direction, as friends of mine who were raised in the South have told me they had to do. But make no mistake, from our earliest years there were thousand of ways, direct and indirect, in which we were informed about how "Negroes" were regarded.

Whenever my mother advised or warned us about anything concerning the world outside of Central Avenue, she spoke of "The Other Group." And there was never any doubt in my mind, when she used the term, that she was alluding to white people. She would lower her voice on these occasions as if a secret was being shared. "Honey, you have to be careful how you talk around the other group." . . . "Your father can't go to the medical society dinner at the Biltmore; it's a place where only the other group goes." . . . Etc.

Referring to white people as "The Other Group" made it possible for us children to use a term that we could use in mixed company. My mother's words were never spoken with rancor or hostility. They were merely terms of description aimed at pointing out a very important difference between them and us. We believed that to ignore the difference was to invite trouble. The term also served, maybe unwittingly, to define the way in which the treatment of black people by whites so often took on a faceless but nonetheless powerful implacability. Bank loans would not get approved. Attempts to buy a house would go unheeded. Common goods and services would, for some reason, be unavailable. Police would either not come at all or would take much, much longer to respond. Any number of bureaucratic devices were used to restrict blacks, and usually there was no particular reason given. Or the reason was a pleasantly expressed, Kafka-like, featureless lie: "I'm so sorry. The hotel is full."

Opportunities for blacks were very limited when I grew up. If a job involved more than manual labor, it was called a profession. And there was euphemistic language intended to elaborate on those professions in a way, to make them sound more important than they were. For example, most women who worked were house servants. A white person for whom you worked might refer to you as a "maid" or a "cook." But as far as you and the black community were concerned, you were "in service," a fine distinction. If you cooked for someone, you were a "caterer," or a "chef." The guy who cleaned up was a "custodian." A driver was a "chauffeur." If you had been in the military, you were thereafter known by your last, highest rank. Sergeant Brown. Corporal Lewis. Titles were all-important.

But the words connoted more than importance. They were used to preserve one's dignity and place in the world, particularly the black world. They were used to convey to one's family and children, to the people in the church and community, that the job involved was more than just being a servant of some white family in Beverly Hills or West Los Angeles.

So, to their friends and associates my father was always Doctor Cobbs. My mother was always Mrs. Cobbs. At church, in deference to her status, she was sometimes Mrs. Doctor Cobbs. This was also the result of simple post-Victorian politesse. But like the phrase The Other Group, these polite euphemisms also served to remind us of the differences between us and The Other Group itself.

•◆•

My father always made a quick reading of who was friendly and who was not. He could make the subtlest distinctions about just who might be hostile or who might show the slightest signs of friendship. He understood the legacy of slavery and was acutely sensitive to its manifestations, explicit or subtle, wherever he was. His reaction, to be sure, was always muted, always oblique, and usually nonconfrontational, especially in a situation where it might be dangerous to himself or his family. No doubt that control, that bottled rage, was the source of his edge.

As we got older, my father became close to several of the few black politicians in L.A., such as Augustus F. "Gus" Hawkins. Hawkins was a member of the California State Assembly from 1935 to 1962 and elected as a Democrat to the U.S. House of Representatives in 1963. He remained active in the House until his retirement in 1991. He gained international fame as the coauthor of the Full Employment and Balanced Growth Act of 1978, the Humphrey-Hawkins Bill, that sought to establish goals of full employment and production plus increased real income, balanced growth, a balanced federal budget, and reasonable price stability. Mr. Hawkins and his wife rented a home from my parents at one time because he wanted to have a house in the district he represented.

I became aware at an early age that, because of this kind of connection, my father had a broader view of what was happening beyond L.A., whether it was a cultural issue or something taking place in city government or in L.A.'s dealings with Sacramento or Washington, D.C. He always gave us a personal view of his involvement in and understanding of political issues that was borne out by our own personal experience.

He would explain to us, for instance, that one of the reasons the Los Angeles Police Department treated black people so harshly was that many of the white officers had been recruited from the South. I never knew this to be true or untrue, never saw any documentation to corroborate it. But many years later my wife and I were traveling by car in Alabama. We stopped in Auburn, Alabama, to get gas, and the man pumping the gas was elderly and white. When I explained that we were from California, a big smile broke out on his face and he said, "California? Sure, I know California. I used to be a cop in L.A.!"

Though the religious fires did not burn as hot in my father as they did in my mother, he was nevertheless a churchgoing man. He enjoyed the community that church and its related activities provided. For us the church was the center of an organized, self-respecting, and thoughtful cultural milieu that was also peopled by those who were groundbreaking. The first black physicians in L.A. The first black dentists. Plumbers. Politicians. Business owners. Store managers. My family moved easily within this milieu. We were by no means wealthy the year I was born. If most blacks were either poor or one step from poverty, my parents and their friends were a step and a half away, maybe two. But they were accomplished and were churchgoing.

It would be in such a milieu that my father would meet people like W. E. B. DuBois, Langston Hughes, or a visiting CME bishop. On Sundays after church, Dr. and Mrs. Bledsoe, for example, would have a tea in their home. Churchgoers would go to the Bledsoes', the men and boys still dressed in coat and tie, the women and their daughters in beautiful dresses. In fact, my father would be wearing clothing that had been made by a Los Angeles tailor named Mr. Glover who was a member, as was my father, of the Tuskegee Club, the alumni association of Tuskegee Institute.

One summer something happened in the Glover family that was both a personal tragedy and a lesson to me of how much people respected my father. The Glovers had three sons who were approximately the same ages as my siblings and I. Their youngest, Carl, at about the age of ten, developed a case of acute appendicitis. In those days, which were of course preantibiotic, appendicitis was a much more dangerous issue than it is now and could worsen very quickly. In this case, the boy's appendix burst over the weekend, and he developed peritonitis from which he subsequently died a few days later. This was the first death I was to experience among friends my age, and I remember the profound sadness we all felt with the passing of a boy who was both a close friend and so young.

We spent our summers at Lake Elsinore, a resort area about seventy miles from L.A., and my father would come up to the lake on weekends. For many years after, Mr. Glover would say that if only Doctor Cobbs had been in L.A. that weekend, his son would still be alive. The comment was both a sad-hearted lamentation for his lost boy, and also a statement of Mr. and Mrs. Glover's high regard for my father as a physician.

It was a mark of my family's position in the church and community to have been invited to the Sunday teas. Often there was entertainment offered by some of the guests of the tea. People would read poetry by Paul Laurence Dunbar, read a speech by Frederick Douglass, or read the Twenty-third Psalm. The speaking styles of the presenters were always dramatic. People would show off their oratorical skills, slowing down and then speeding up their cadence and modulation, mimicking the style of the minister of whatever church they attended. If they caught fire and touched the holy spirit of one of the adults, then the recitation would be interrupted by numerous loud "amens" and shouted hosannas. While the CME Church to which we belonged was not a foot-washing-and-speaking-in-tongues kind of place (my mother wouldn't have belonged to such a "primitive" church), the joint could sometimes rock with the precious noise of Jesus being discovered. Even when in later years I was reciting a poem or speaking in church, I was one for whom there was always a lot of amens. After all, "that boy looks just like a bishop."

My father was noted for his singing voice. I remember one afternoon when we children were playing outside and the entertainment had begun. We hurried to put on our own little jackets and made sure our shirts were still clean, pressed, and tucked in, and our ties properly straight and quietly went in and listened. Dressed as always in his tailor-made suit, white shirt, and tie, he stood at the piano, accompanied by someone, and sounded out:

"Oh promise me that someday you and I
Will take our love together to some sky . . ."

His gestures while he sung, the way he formed the words and delivered them, the very stage presence that he had and the warm applause he received, impressed me greatly that afternoon.

"Where we can be alone and faith renew
And find the hollows where those flowers grew.
And on many such afternoons."

•◆•

In retrospect I was a very lucky little black boy in the early 1930s. I had a wonderful childhood. My parents' "exquisite care" included their preparation of me, my brother and sister, for most of the things that adolescence and adulthood would bring to us. We were being prepared to deal with the issues that would come because of our blackness. Certainly they could not possibly prepare us for everything; the world was too complex and fast moving for that to occur. Yet they offered us every shred of their memories and experiences in order to help us grow up and survive in a world they knew would not always make us feel welcome. We were taught the lessons of caution as well as those of boldness. In a world in which there were few privileges, I knew that I had some of them. I had been given them by my parents and came to understand this through what my mother said and what my father did.

We were never allowed, though, to forget that the Civil War had ended just a short time earlier, and that the residual effects of slavery and all that it meant still existed. On one occasion, in which my mother could not possibly have explored the terrain beforehand, we found out how true that was.

My father was a "Chrysler man," meaning he bought automobiles only from that manufacturer. There were frequent discussions among the men at church or at the barbershop about others, such as Mr. Smith being a "General Motors man" or Mr. Pillors a "Ford man." These arguments were serious but included all kinds of jokes and ribbing about which cars were better and why. Someone would always be able to come up with an obscure—and often hilarious—automotive reason why one brand was better than the other.

"Man, how come you bought that Chevy? Can't get no pickup with a Chevy!" "I saw you drivin' that 'Bewrick'." The mispronouncing of the word *Buick* of course was essential to the disrespect you were showing to the car. "When you gonna turn it in for a good car like my Packard?" This was classically male competition among car owners, with a black cultural slant. The serious aspect of the competition was rooted in real issues, especially when the discussion turned to which auto company had first hired blacks, for example.

When I was five, my father owned a 1932 Dodge four-door sedan. It was a dark color, as were all our cars, and he kept it up meticulously. We were all very proud of it and enjoyed going on excursions every chance we could.

One weekend we went to visit a friend of my father's, a man we called Uncle Will. He lived in the Temple district of L.A., about seven miles from our home. He was a veteran of World War I and must not have attained any rank because we just called him Uncle Will. I believe he had once come to my father for medical advice, but as a veteran, he undoubtedly almost always went to the nearest V.A. hospital. He was more my father's friend than my mother's. She disapproved of his habit of always having a glass of water at his side, from which he frequently took a sip. At least it looked like water to me. I didn't understand her attitude until later when I found out that the water was actually gin.

My father liked him, though, and they were longtime friends who enjoyed conversing with each other.

On our way back home from Uncle Will's that Sunday, we came to an intersection where there were several cars approaching in all directions. It was seven o'clock in the evening in winter and raining. Visibility was poor. The other cars appeared like wet, rounded boxes, one after the other waiting for the light to change. My father's hands were on the wheel and his shoulders hunched as he surveyed the traffic ahead. My mother was seated in the front with him, while we three children were in back. All of us were dressed as though we had been to church. We were a family enjoying the outing but looking forward to getting home out of the storm. When the light changed, my father let the clutch out, and we moved ahead.

We heard a loud horn, then the ugly screech of braking tires, then a quick, very loud crack of noise as another car hit us. All of us were tossed around, and there was a good deal of shouting and screaming among us children. My father got out of the car to see what had happened. He was then confronted by a quickly gathering group of onlookers and witnesses, all of whom were white. The other car had run the red light, but both cars were damaged.

My mother gently, but firmly, got us children out of the car and over to the sidewalk, to make sure we were out of any possible danger from the cars themselves. Fortunately, none of us was hurt, just shaken up. After a moment, a white man and woman got out of the car that had hit us. From the wobbly and unbalanced manner in which they walked, it was obvious that they had been drinking. Even I as a child was aware that we as a family looked far better off than this fellow and his companion. They were not dressed well. The man started to survey the damage to his car, and when he looked up finally and saw us, he turned to the woman with him and said, "We don't have to worry, Helen. They're just niggers."

The moment was surreal for us, standing in the rain, hearing this man's words above the sounds of traffic and the murmurs of the growing crowd. We were the only blacks in sight. I imagine that the man got some comfort from this, and that the composition of the crowd made it easy for him to say what he said. He probably felt that, if trouble were to come because of his remark, he would have plenty of help from the others. They were the dominant group, in this particular scene and in every other social respect as well. These were the kind of people who had owned slaves or refused rooms to people like us. The managers of and the beneficiaries of all those rules and laws that had been set up to keep us from competing with them. In short, even I as a child could tell that we were now surrounded by The Other Group.

The man who had hit us broadside while running a red light was acting upon the prevailing notion of the time, a clear legacy of slavery itself, that if you are white and the other person is black, you can act with impunity and you will be absolved. He chose the one word that could put him in a position of power over us, the one implacable idea that had so informed the history of this country. He chose the word *nigger* and assumed that he was right to do so and that the surrounding witnesses would back him up.

My mother was fearless in such situations. She was always the more vocal of my parents on occasions like this. I never thought of my father as hiding behind her in any way because I too often saw him do things, say things, and act in ways that I knew required courage. My father's very stoicism in this moment was a heroic response. There was no muscle flexing, no shouting, nothing that could have put him or his family in danger. And I know that the heroism was in the restraint that he showed. But my mother spoke out.

"Shut up!" she said to the white drunk. "Who do you think you are?"

There was silence for a moment, then a woman finally spoke from the crowd, addressing the rest of the onlookers, and gesturing toward the man who had hit us.

"That guy may be white, but his heart's as black as tar."

• ◆ •

Many years later, I thought about such occurrences when Bill Grier and I were writing our book *Black Rage*. Listening to the story of a patient, talking with a Civil Rights leader visiting San Francisco, or interviewing someone about a confrontation brought back memories of a little boy's anger that had been submerged and forgotten.

We wrote in that book: "The problem [of the Negro family today] is a latter-day version of the problem faced by the slave family. How does one build a family, make it strong, and breed from it strong men and women when the institutional structures of the nation make it impossible for the family to serve its primary purpose—the protection of its members?"

My parents were facing that problem. That car collision and its aftermath formed an iconic moment that has influenced a great deal of my life and work ever since. I've thought of my parents' bravery in that moment and the protection they gave our family. I've thought of the power that The Other Group had over us then and now in varying degrees. The power they still have, if we let them, especially when we have not exorcised the demons. I've thought as well about the white person in that crowd who understood the situation in its entirety and refused to agree that in this case The Other Group should prevail.

There was agreement from others in the crowd, by the way. So by the time the police came, the white man had backed off, and he was cited. My parents behaved with great care combined with the edge that comes from slavery and its legacy. I think this combination speaks to a good deal of what I've tried to do with my own life.

I've always tried to pay keen attention to the situation around me and to understand what it truly is about. Then I try changing that situation if change is warranted, as it so often has been. It's like standing on the ledge of a high building. You have a clear view, but the view can hold dangers. The ledge I stood on, of course, was wider than the ledge upon which my parents stood. But I owe my position on that ledge in many respects to them.

Anxiety, fear, and rage are all legacies of slavery. There was no closure on them when I was six and we were being insulted in that intersection. There is no closure on them now. Given the changes with regard to laws, land covenants, basic civil rights, representation in government and business and even simple behavior, I think black people can move beyond the emotional remnants of slavery. We can make a psychological transformation from rage to entitlement.

CHAPTER TWO

When I was five years old, my mother took her three children on a month-long summer trip to the South and Midwest to visit our family. My grandfather was still alive and still living in Barboursville, Virginia. My mother's extended family was in Birmingham, Alabama, and elsewhere. She especially wanted me to meet her brothers and sisters and their children. We were so separated from them geographically that the children from the various branches of the family had not actually all met before. My parents wanted us to see how much larger a family we really were.

I also have the sense that my parents wanted to introduce us to the South, to give us the chance to see what the "old country," as they called it, was really like. The gap between the South and L.A. was more than geographical, and I suspect that my parents wanted us to understand it.

This trip was very special for many reasons, among them being that the summer of 1934, five years into the Great Depression, was so difficult for most people. My parents were well aware that anything affecting America economically affects black people in specific and usually more negative ways. There's a famous phrase: "When America gets a cold, black folks get pneumonia." When there is a boom we may be better off than in normal circumstances, but we don't enjoy the full benefits of the dominant group. In lean times, though, we take a bigger hit than others.

One of the things that helps me understand what the Depression was like for blacks was my father's use of the word *hustler.* In 1934, *hustler* was not a pejorative term. A hustler was, for example, Mr. Jones, who had a good steady job but moonlighted somewhere else on the weekends. Or sold some legal product like hair pomade on the side. A man like that was admired because he was working hard for his family during Depression times.

The kinds of jobs open to blacks were limited. A job in a warehouse was considered a good job, for example. Unloading trucks was considered a good job. Mr. Barker, a friend of ours, ran the elevator at L.A. City Hall. Then he moved on and became a messenger for the mayor. He didn't do that because it was all he was qualified or able to do. He did it because that was what he could get. If a job was steady, as Mr. Barker's was, it was a good job. But if a man were a "hustler" as well, he was a special sort of man. So that word was an unalloyed, positive term that my father would have applied even to some of his peers who were doing well by their families during the Great Depression.

As a child, I had no idea that there was anything special about a trip to visit family around the country like the one our parents had arranged. I was too young to be aware that such a journey was not simply available to everyone. Later I realized that there was a kind of glow, a kind of aura, about this trip, simply because we were in an economic position that allowed us to take it. This was an act of affluence, and my parents would have thought of it as such.

My father didn't make the trip that year because he had to keep working. As was true for most women in those days, my mother had no driver's license. But my father hired a young patient by the name of Frank to drive us in the same 1932 Dodge, now again in pristine condition, in which we had had the fateful accident. Also a member of our church, Frank was in his early twenties and was chosen to help us because he was "a good driver," as the phrase went. He was careful, stayed within the speed limit, and knew how to drive safely.

The choice of a driver was an important decision and meant more than just a consideration of careful driving habits. We were black people driving across many states in which attitudes toward people of color were quite antagonistic and abusive. You could make such a trip, but you had to be cautious, knowing where you were going and the care with which you had to go. Frank was an important element in this strategy, and my parents would have made sure that Frank would do nothing in his driving that would call attention to us in that car.

We traveled the southern route on our way east, which meant a lot of hot weather. I remember the excitement of our first overnight stop in Tucson, Arizona. We'd start very early in the morning, to beat the heat and put in as many miles as possible on any given day. It was a great deal of fun for a five-year-old. An open-eyed, curious kid watching the scenery go by . . . the deserts of Arizona and New Mexico, with their endless variety of yellow, brown, and red colors that extend far into the clear distances; high mountains that appeared so far away at first, so majestic, which we approached, skirted, and sometimes traversed; the changes in view, from desert to forest, blue lakes, wide brown rivers crossed by great bridges. Little towns, big towns, seeing Native Americans for the first time, seeing actual cowboys, rolling farmland and open wilderness. . . . It was a new view of a large world for me, and very, very thrilling.

We didn't have the choice of hotels and motels that we might enjoy on a similar journey today. For not only did they not exist in such numbers as now but those that were available usually practiced racial segregation, honoring laws that prohibited blacks from receiving most services. My mother would not have been able to assess which did and which didn't ahead of time. We wouldn't be able to know whether we'd be welcome or not. Unless the hotel was a black-owned one, and they were rare.

As a consequence, we stayed in private homes with friends, or friends of friends, relatives, colleagues of my father, or church people we knew or who had been told of us. Sometimes we would be asked to pay, sometimes not. It just depended on the nature of the people in the "network." Did they know my parents? Were they people who rented rooms to make extra money? Did they come recommended by black people whose opinion we trusted? The network was well established in African American neighborhoods across the country. All black people knew about it. It is a classic example of how marginalized people found alternative ways of maintaining a quality of life denied them by the dominant culture.

When white society said no room at the inn, We said, we'll make an inn of our own.

When we got to Hillsboro, Alabama, we met my mother's older brother Reverend Samuel Mashaw. Uncle Sam was a prominent minister in the CME church. He took us to a place where they processed sugar, and I got to chew on raw cane for the first time in my life. I remember a boiling pot and someone handing me a fresh piece. There were also enormous horses, huffing and snorting. I especially enjoy thinking about Uncle Sam and that sugarcane now because they were both so much a product of the South, to which I was then getting my first introduction.

Like my mother, who had graduated as a teacher, Uncle Sam was an alumnus of Miles College in Birmingham, Alabama, which had been founded in 1905. Miles was the only two-year college (then called a Normal School) open to black students in Birmingham at that time. It had been founded as a CME church-related institution, and its curriculum was notable for its attention to morality, Christian ethics, and the furthering of Christian values.

Now a four-year institution, Miles College has always also been a major "teaching institution" in Alabama and is involved to a large extent in providing community services to the black population. A high percentage of Birmingham's leaders were educated at Miles. Uncle Sam became a presiding elder of the church like his father and an older brother and a pastor of large CME churches in Alabama and Kansas City. He was a vibrant man who, in his early eighties when I last visited him, appeared to be in his early sixties. He had once run for bishop in the church but lost. He later became the chief justice of the supreme court of what, by then, had become the Christian Methodist Episcopal Church. For over thirty years he adjudicated cases of ministerial malfeasance and other problems in which ministers had gotten into trouble. An important man in the church, he once said to me, "Price, I have more trouble going on in my choir than they have in the average pool hall." He was a man of humor as well.

Uncle Sam showed me that I had come from a family of some prominence in the South. My roots were there, represented by people like him. Later in the trip, we went to Barboursville, Virginia, where we visited my father's father. He was by then blind. Born in the early 1850s he was in his eighties. I recall seeing him for the first time on a sunny day, sitting beneath a tree in a rocking chair. This was the only time I ever met my grandfather, a man who had been a slave.

This was a fact that I don't recall my father ever having spoken about. In 1934, in the polite black society of our home, one did not bring it up. This is understandable, since the memory of slavery was so fresh and its legacy was looked upon with profound sadness.

But the legacy did not go away. Black people are forever reminded that they are black, that their people were brought here in captivity and their ancestors were slaves. Now we realize that it's important—both for the rage we may feel and also for the sense of entitlement toward which we are now moving—that we remember the truth of our past. Yes, we live with the legacy of slavery, and many of us have direct memories of relatives who were indeed slaves. Fresh memories. And even for very young black people these memories have been fueled and amplified by new access to the emerging legacy of oral history, music, traditions, and literature of black slavery in this country.

The entitlement that I'm advocating in this book contains the memory of slavery and is realized in the context of that legacy. In fact, the memory of slavery, among other things, does much to legitimize that entitlement. The history of black people in this country is unique. Without that history, the United States would be a very different place. Slavery, in fact, may be the most important institution in this country's collective memory. The United States wouldn't be what it is today, economically and politically, for better and for worse, if it hadn't been for slavery. So while any American may have the knowledge of this legacy, we in fact have a very direct memory of it, and that's key to our sense of personal entitlement as Americans. I cherish the memory of my grandfather beneath that tree when I was five years old.

After our East Coast visits with family, we headed back on the northern route, stopping at Springfield, Ohio, to visit my mother's older sister Babe. Aunt Babe had actually raised my mother after their mother had died and their father had remarried. She was very religious, quite strict, with a forbidding quality of disapprobation in her personality that I was very well aware of even at the age of five.

There were occasions during this trip on which our behavior—our

California behavior—was viewed as being a little too free by our more conservative relatives. My sister Marcelyn was seven years old at the time and came down to breakfast one morning wearing a pair of shorts and a blouse. This was an outfit that, in summertime in L.A., would be *de rigueur* for girls my sister's age. But Aunt Babe rose up and chastised my mother for allowing Marcelyn to wear those shorts. There was something sinful about them, something just too revealing for a good Christian girl, albeit one who was only seven years old.

But mother, who was otherwise very proper, was offended by her sister's disapproval and may also have thought of that disapproval as being somewhat unsophisticated. No one in L.A. would have been offended by Marcelyn's shorts. These different levels of caution and boldness informed mother's and Babe's contrary views on child rearing.

As we traveled, so did the famous bank robber John Dillinger, though under different circumstances. His many heists and jail escapes were at that time the stuff of legend. He was at large in the summer of 1934, and the F.B.I. was after him. The authorities were not happy with press coverage of the Dillinger gang and the Robin Hood–like reputation they had earned stealing from the rich and never from the poor. The legendary bandits were unfailingly polite to the common man and ever humorous and inventive when it came to avoiding arrest or hoodwinking the law. Or so the myth went.

Dillinger's days were numbered though, and he met his end on July 22, 1934, having been betrayed by the famous "Woman in Red." Anna Sage, a Chicago tavern owner, one-time prostitute and brothel owner, had fingered Dillinger to the F.B.I., helping to arrange for his arrest outside the Biograph Theatre in Chicago on that evening. She, Dillinger, and another woman named Polly Hamilton had gone to see Clark Gable's new gangster picture *Manhattan Melodrama*, and F.B.I. agents were lying in wait as they came out of the theater. Dillinger attempted an escape and was gunned down by the authorities in an alleyway to the side of the theater. Anna Sage's orange skirt apparently glowed a kind of bloodred in the lights from the theater marquee, and for that reason she was named "The Woman in Red" in newspaper reports about Dillinger's demise.

Dillinger's death in 1934 had a lasting effect upon our family. From that time on, my mother never wanted us to wear red. It was an exotic color that she associated with ladies of the night, especially Anna Sage. Years later, when Oklahoma Senator Fred Harris was chairing a subcommittee hearing called the Joint Commission on the Mental Health of Children, I testified before that committee. Afterward, I called my mother to give her the details. I was very proud and wanted her to have a sense of how important the occasion had been. Her first question was, "You didn't wear that red vest of yours, did you?"

• ◆ •

The differences between us and our relatives in other parts of the country may have had to do with geography, culture, regional variations, and so on. But there was more than that. Our relatives expressed the caution that so informed a great many of their actions, justifiably so. Their personal conservatism was a logical and often necessary result of the widespread, more sustained, and frequently more vicious racism they experienced in their part of the country.

But the differences also show the sense of boldness on the part of my parents and their peers. My parents had recognized an opportunity to change the lot of our family by going to L.A. They had made the move with an appropriate sense of caution themselves, given the racial atmosphere in the country at the time. But they *had* recognized the opportunity and they *had* made the move.

I sometimes wonder about the accident of birth. What if I hadn't been born into a middle-class black physician's family and instead came from a working-class family with fewer economic and educational opportunities? If all that had been different, would I have been able to come so readily to the sense I have now of this entitlement? Even today, with the Internet and instant communication and the availability of so much information, I see kids in Hunter's Point, Harlem, or South Side Chicago who have seldom been farther away than a few blocks from the place they were born. This leads me to consider whether there is a specific context within which one needs to be reared in order to expect that entitlement, to realize it simply as a given. Had my father been a warehouse worker (a position he would by no means have disparaged) without the education that he actually had, would a family vacation trip like the one we took have been possible? Would we even have considered it?

As I reflect more deeply, I answer my own questions. When I was a kid, being middle class was defined by aspirations, not the income or the education of parents. Most of the kids I grew up with were from working-class families, by whatever the definition used at that time. Many of them went on to lives of considerable achievement. Frankly, I think the context for my sense of entitlement came from the value system I was taught and the sense of struggle I inherited. A sense of righteous struggle provides a focus and a clarity of purpose. If the times in which I grew up generated rage, they also nurtured an ability, indeed a necessity, to dream and, above all, to be optimistic.

In today's world I see the fault line widening between black haves and have-nots. Certainly education, money, and middle-class status increase the odds of making something out of one's life, but there are other variables. I view certain psychological shackles as more challenging than a person's location on the pecking order. All too often I find the remnants of victimhood creeping into the discussion. The sense of struggle has been lost and there is a tacit acceptance that one is after all a victim. When being a victim becomes a fixed part of one's identity and this notion is never examined, then one feels helpless to make any changes. The most crippling aspect of accepting the identity of being a victim is that hope and optimism fall by the wayside, and a primary casualty is that a sense of struggle is lost. Feelings can be mobilized for a fight, but the battlefield invariably is misidentified, and who, what, and how to fight is lost. I sometimes talk with individuals who are struggling with core issues of who they are and what it means to be black. They express anger, but it is diffuse and undirected, and I know a sense of healthy entitlement is not there and will probably never be. When I probe them and am left to wonder if this lack is because the person has lost faith in America and its promise, or because the person has lost faith in himself, I usually find a mixture of both.

CHAPTER THREE

My parents bought a home on Trinity Street, near Forty-first Street in Los Angeles in 1933. Still very much within the Central Avenue milieu, Trinity Street was nonetheless a mostly white neighborhood at that time. We were the first black family. The homes were mostly single-family dwellings. Our white neighbors represented the remnants of what had been a predominantly German-American neighborhood.

A white family—the Prentisses—lived across the street. In those pre-freeway days, a family would live very near the workplace. The Bradley Pie Company was just a block away, and Mr. and Mrs. Prentiss worked for Bradley Pies. They were also patients of my father. Our neighbors next door were named Murillo and were Mexican-American. Both Mr. and Mrs. Murillo were from Mexico and their children, Edward and Sarah, were about the age of my brother, Prince, and my sister, Marcelyn. In addition to the Murillos, several other Mexican families lived on the block, and some were patients of my father.

A group of houses directly across the street from us was owned by a very stern white woman named Mrs. Bridewell, who was the nemesis of the neighborhood kids. We dared not play on her lawn or, worse, send a ball of any kind sailing toward her house. But she too was a patient of my father. Our house was a few blocks from Wrigley Field, the home of the Pacific Coast League Los Angeles Angels, a place we visited frequently during baseball season.

That fall, I entered the Trinity Street School, which was located a block from our new home. I doubt that there were more than ten black kids in the entire school, out of a student body totaling six hundred. As was always the case, my mother took care to instruct me in how to act at school and especially how to respond to any occasions of mistreatment.

She told me that if anyone at school—students, teachers, or administrators—were to hit me, slap me, or handle me in an inappropriate way, I was to come home immediately to tell her about it. This was the clearest of instructions, and as a young boy, I knew that my mother's word was law. And I realized she knew what she was talking about when it came to potential danger for her children. Her instructions were informed by conversations with other black mothers whose children were sometimes singled out for physical punishment.

One day, while in the third grade, during recess I was playing on the swings in a large sandbox. I got involved in an altercation with another kid. My teacher, whose name was Mrs. Shields, was on playground duty and slapped me. No questions asked. She made no attempt to find out how the fracas had begun. She did nothing to try to mediate between me and the other pupil. She simply slapped me.

I started toward home.

"Where are you going, Price?" I heard Mrs. Shields shouting as I ran away. I continued running.

I hurried across Santa Barbara Avenue (which has since had its name changed to Martin Luther King Boulevard). Even then, it was a multi-lane thoroughfare with a lot of traffic. I just plunged across it and ran up Trinity Street toward our house.

My mother knelt down before me and took me by the shoulders.

"What happened, Price?"

I blurted out the explanation, and my mother immediately grabbed her coat and hat.

My mother did not knock on Mrs. Shields's classroom door. We simply entered the room. Mrs. Shields was surprised to see us—especially to see us so *abruptly*. My mother—maintaining an attitude of polite but unmistakable resolve when she addressed the teacher in front of the entire class—got right to the point.

"Mrs. Shields, you slapped my son."

Mrs. Shields feigned innocence and surprise, but my mother remained calm and certain of herself. She fixed her gaze—or rather her now angry glare—on Mrs. Shields and in a very assertive voice said, "I know that you slapped my son Price a few minutes ago. And I want you to know, Mrs. Shields, that I do not want you ever to lay a finger on him or any of my children ever again. Do you understand that, Mrs. Shields? I am Mrs. Cobbs and this is my son. I will talk with the principal about this, and if you do touch my child again, I'll bring Price's father, Dr. Cobbs, here, and he will talk with you about it also. There could possibly be legal action as well . . ."

In those days teachers were accustomed to doing what they wished with their students, within reason. Corporal punishment, if not officially sanctioned, was permitted and sometimes encouraged. I expect that the teachers at Trinity School, who were all white, were unaccustomed to teaching black pupils, and that they may have resented it.

What got Mrs. Shields's speechless attention was my mother's very certain view that no teacher was going to hit me, ever. My mother emphasized this by making sure that Mrs. Shields understood exactly who we were, that my mother was Dr. Peter Price Cobbs's wife and that I was the son of Dr. Peter Price Cobbs. These were facts that for my mother were always extremely important, especially in situations where our integrity was for some reason in question. One could interpret her particular admonition of Mrs. Shields as being pretentious, but it would be a mistake to do so. If you have little armor with which to protect yourself, you make use of that armor to its greatest effect. My mother was individualizing us for that teacher, making sure that Mrs. Shields had a very clear image of us particularly in her mind. That we were not just some run-of-the-mill colored family, and I was not just some black kid that she could slap without danger of reprisal.

There was no retribution afterward from Mrs. Shields. I was not afraid of her. My mother had taken care of that.

This was an occasion when I saw my mother as someone fearless, with considerable personal conviction and power, despite a middle-class sensibility that emphasizes gentility and politesse toward all people, but particularly in our case toward white people. I learned on that day that when the chips are down, you drop all such pretense. Diplomacy recedes into the background. You maintain control of yourself and your emotions.

But, as with my mother, you let the adversary know that he or she must not tread on you ever again.

◆

In January 1934, Leon H. Washington, the publisher of the *Los Angeles Sentinel,* a black weekly newspaper, was arrested for picketing the Zeng Pharmacy, a white-owned establishment in the Central Avenue section of the city. His picketing was part of the newspaper's campaign in support of the idea that black people should not buy products from stores and companies that had no black employees. "Don't Buy Where You Can't Work" was the rallying cry. Zeng Pharmacy refused to hire blacks and so had come under Mr. Washington's scrutiny.

That boycott of white businesses lasted for many years and was a continuous thorn in their side, particularly those businesses operating in black neighborhoods.

As a young boy, I did not know specifically about Mr. Washington's arrest. But the "Don't Buy Where You Can't Work" campaign was well known by our family and frequently spoken about by my father. Within a few years of Mr. Washington's arrest, I was involved in a childhood picketing of my own that, while short-lived and with little actual effect on the institution picketed, marked the beginning for me of a lifelong involvement in the issue of making businesses and their products open and available to black people.

Even as a kid, I knew that discrimination against black people in Los Angeles was not only capricious but also flashed many faces. In one store you were treated kindly, greeted with open arms, like any other customer, young or old. This was after all during the Great Depression and most businesses wanted any patronage they could get. In another establishment, one might feel a definite edge from the clerk. In order to avoid actually touching you, change was dropped in an outstretched hand and minimal service was begrudgingly offered.

I believe I was about nine years old when I was refused service in a small food market at the corner of San Pedro and Forty-first streets, about two blocks from our house. It was the kind of place where a kid with a little change in his pocket after school could get a Pepsi or a candy bar, and I had gone there to buy just such a treat. The clerk had thrown me out with no explanation, although I believe he had done so because I was black. So I went home and made a picket sign that said something like UNFAIR. DON'T SHOP HERE. I returned to the market and picketed it for several minutes. There was no response from inside the store, so I continued picketing, resolute in my desire to inform the neighborhood that these owners were unfair.

Not much happened. I walked back and forth. I may have gotten a smile or two from passersby, but that was all. After a while I grew bored, threw the sign away, and went off to play with a friend of mine. To my recollection, I never returned to that market.

This little incident contained a seed of public protest that is based on the notion of entitlement. I was acting from an assumption that I had been taught by my parents, that I had the right to buy the pear or the orange or the bubble gum, or whatever it is that I had gone into that market to buy. There was no conceivable reason to refuse me in my endeavor except that, like Mr. Washington, I was black. And that was no good reason at all.

•◆•

I had begun to hear the word *nigger* with regularity, particularly when I reached the sixth grade. Although the kind of kid who would emerge as a "tough guy" in junior high school or high school was not yet evident, there were boys who were difficult, and for me these boys seemed almost always to be those who had come from the Dust Bowl. They were indigent whites whose parents had migrated from the South and particularly Oklahoma because of the drought and desperate economic conditions. We knew who they were because of their accent and language. They had a roughness in their demeanor that identified them, as well as a more marked negative racial attitude than the kids I was used to. Black kids felt the need for a higher level of vigilance when it came to these new arrivals, because the word *nigger* seemed to fall from their lips without much effort at all. It was rarely directed at anyone in particular, just said loud enough so that anyone nearby could hear it.

Ironically, some of these children and their families were quickly labeled by us as "poor white trash." We too were capable of affixing labels to certain ethnic groups. Their fathers were white, but they held jobs that were far down on the social ladder. In our world, middle-class status was a function of not just income or wealth, so that a black janitor with aspirations and a stable job was middle-class. A white man who was a janitor was just a janitor, since it was believed that, had he aspirations, he wouldn't settle for such a job. The kids of "poor white trash" were easy to see. They'd frequently be from large families who appeared to be struggling financially with many children. When they saw us, there would be an immediate impulse on their part to put us in a position that was below theirs, no matter the evidence—often plain to see—that most of the black kids and their families were doing much better than these white families.

Few of these families owned a car, while many of ours did. Most of them rented the house in which they lived, while many of us owned our houses. There was a kind of class difference which we recognized. We had better clothes than the poor white kids had. Better shoes. We often read better. We were quicker in school. Yet they were white and we were black. Being reminded of this at school by the children of those families resulted in certain overtones of anger on our part because it was clear that the difference between us that was being invoked was purely racial. It had little to do with the realities of our financial or living situations. In order to defend ourselves and to retaliate against their obvious racism, we did use that term "poor white trash" for those people. It was a term with which *we* could put *them* in their place.

With that in mind, it's ironic to consider that the first time I was actually the direct object of the term *nigger,* it came from my best friend.

I played with a boy named Frankie Prentiss, who lived across the street in one of the houses owned by Mrs. Bridewell. We were close friends, "pals" you might say, and we spent a great deal of time together. The beauty of our relationship lay in the fact that there seemed to be little difference between us. Frankie was Frankie and Price was Price. A couple of kids. I was aware that he was "white" and that I was "a Negro" or sometimes "colored." But these facts had in no way impacted our friendship. We were just two boys who lived on the same street.

Frankie went to a Catholic school about ten blocks away, and I went to school just up the street. We met after school to chase each other between houses and throw tennis balls against garage doors. We were obedient to our parents and avoided anything that would get us into trouble. They allowed us a certain freedom on that block, and we stayed within that circle. We were part of a polyglot neighborhood, with Mexican kids who spoke Spanish to their parents, and the neighbor kids next door whose grandparents spoke only German. These differences were noted by us children but didn't seem to be of any importance.

At this time, we were the only black family on the block, a fact that undoubtedly meant more to my parents than to me. Differences in skin color, the differences between boys and girls, indeed all such matters that gain much importance later are not very seriously noted by a six-year-old. The kids on the block just played with one another. The winner in our play was usually the person with the loudest voice and the greatest stamina. Little else mattered.

One day Frankie and I were playing together on the grass in front of my house. We began scuffling over a toy shovel, arguing over whose turn it was to use it. The shovel went back and forth until, with a quick jerk, I yanked it from Frankie's hands. He shouted that it was his turn to use the shovel and ended the sentence with a downturn in his voice and a pinched, angry utterance that offended me deeply.

"You nigger," he said.

I thought Frankie was a nice boy. I knew his parents were kindhearted too, because they had a pleasant relationship with my parents. They particularly worried about cars driving too quickly up and down the block. Frankie's mother and mine had had many conversations about this.

"You nigger."

The words invaded me with their dark aggressiveness. Frankie suddenly was the enemy, The Other.

I was aware of the various uses of the word and knew well whom it was intended to label. Sure, I remembered our accident in the car, but in my mind that incident was special and singular. I often overheard my brother Prince and his friends calling each other "nigger" in their talk with each other. But in that case, there were certain alleviating factors: they used the term only among themselves, and they were all black. The word was absolutely prohibited inside our house. It was equally prohibited for use within earshot of any white people or respectable black people.

"You nigger."

I was very hurt. My best friend—the boy I trusted most on the block—had used the one word that remained to him as a weapon in a childish dispute over the use of a toy shovel.

I stood up and went home. Although I could not have known it, as young and free-spirited as I was, History came into my heart that day. The difficult weight of slavery. Of bigotry. The sudden, direct presence of prejudice and hatred. And rage. White people had a weapon. When all else failed, you were a nigger. Later, I would well learn what these matters meant, in all of their complexity. In that moment, the dormant nerve that would lead me to such understanding was forever activated.

Frankie and I seldom, if ever, played together after that day.

•◆•

I sometimes accompanied my father when he visited patients who had had to enter a hospital. There were very few hospitals in L.A. at the time in which black physicians had staff privileges. I was not aware of that restriction at the time though. The hospitals in which my father could minister to his patients were either that rare white or mixed hospital that would allow such a thing, or a small private hospital that had been founded and was owned by blacks.

I knew that my father had an important job. People were bound to their physicians then in ways much more far-reaching than today. A doctor, particularly if he was black, was usually better educated than his patients and had a much wider world experience. As in my father's case, a physician could even be a counselor of sorts, a person of perceived wisdom to whom patients would go for advice far beyond anything medical. So when going with him to visit patients in a hospital, I felt that I was entering some kind of grand place, a place of much importance, and that my father was going to be one of the most important people there.

One morning when I was about twelve, he asked me to go with him to the Los Angeles County Public Hospital, to visit a friend who was ill. I was immediately excited about the prospect because that hospital was the largest in the United States and so was very prestigious, even famous. I'd never been there, and the idea of accompanying my father made the excursion very special indeed. He was just going for a visit, with no specific professional involvement. But the opportunity to go with him was not to be missed.

It was a Sunday, and we had been to church. As always on Sunday, we ate dinner early, excitedly in my case because I could not wait to get to the car and get on to the hospital. Doctors were no doubt *all* like my father: men of authority whose very profession meant that their words were listened to, that the men themselves were always respected, that they were somehow anointed and different from others. I was Dr. Cobbs's son, a young boy at his father's side, so there was a certain favor that would attend to me as well.

My mother, as always, suggested appropriate dress for me as my father put on his coat and straightened his tie—the clothing he always wore, especially when he was going to visit friends or patients.

We drove to the L.A. County Hospital, a huge facility located on the east side of the city. The activity there was immediately remarkable, even as we entered the parking lot. People were coming and going, all manner of people, in and out the entrances of this very large building. I could identify doctors by the white coats and the stethoscopes hanging from their necks. Nurses wore white in those days and the distinctive white caps that immediately identified them as well. There were patients too, and I noticed that some of them were indeed quite ill. I saw elderly people hanging on to the arms of younger relatives and the occasional wheelchair-bound person, attended outside by nurses or orderlies.

I saw parked white ambulances, the kind of vehicle one usually saw speeding up the street, red light flashing and a deafening siren pushing aside the traffic up ahead. To my eye these vehicles seemed, even while parked, to be speed-obsessed and bravehearted. I imagined the kinds of drama that had unfolded within them, and that would unfold again perhaps several times that very day, perhaps any minute.

My father and I got out of the car and set out toward the hospital. As we walked in the main entrance, I noticed that visiting hours had just begun. My father was carrying his black bag, the ever-present symbol of his profession. We walked through the lobby, up a hallway, up some stairs. No one addressed my father, and I noticed something that I had not expected. The other doctors—the men with stethoscopes—were all white, as were the nurses. The black people here were janitors and people serving meals, and there weren't many of them. My father addressed them instead of the other physicians. Indeed I noticed his silence with regard to the other physicians and the nurses. They did not appear to know him.

We quietly entered a multibed ward where a patient—a black man— lay in one of the beds.

"Hello, Dr. Cobbs," the man said. "I appreciate your coming."

My father reached into his bag and removed his stethoscope. He placed the stethoscope into his ears and began a conversation with the patient, having to do with how he felt, how the treatment was going, had the medications had the desired result? What had the hospital physicians told him about his affliction?

He was doing an examination.

My father's demeanor in that conversation was polite, professional, and even courtly, the way he always was with patients. He applied the stethoscope to the patient's chest and back, listened patiently to the heartbeat and the breathing.

"I only wish you could be here," the patient said, in the middle of his replies to my father's questions.

My father did not reply, remaining focused on his work. He seemed to want to move on, as though addressing that particular desire on the patient's part would lead to personal embarrassment.

I realized in that moment that my father was not supposed to be in that hospital as a physician. Indeed it is true that, in those years, black physicians were not allowed to treat any patient of theirs who may have been admitted to the Los Angeles County Public Hospital. My father could *get* a patient admitted. He could *visit* that patient as a friend. But he could not practice medicine there. We were officially there, I realized, as visitors.

The black bag was the one item in his possession that would identify my father as a physician, but I quickly realized that, because we were in the hospital during visiting hours, he was ministering to his patient surreptitiously, without the required staff privileges.

But my father, whose respect for the Hippocratic Oath was unquestioned and who felt about his patients that their lives were as important as his own, was not to be denied his duty to a patient. So he had had to succumb for the moment to the social strictures of the time so that he could treat this man. He had had to suppress himself, to go in undercover, to go semi-invisibly, if you will, about his sworn profession, for which he had educated and trained himself in every way equally to those white physicians who simply walked in and out of the ward without questioning their right to be there.

What I've thought most deeply about that day is that my father recognized the calling he had as a physician and yet had to subjugate himself to the racist practices of the time to realize that calling. The visit to L.A. County Public Hospital was a moment of onerous self-containment on his part against a hateful and, moreover, a medically irresponsible policy on the part of that hospital, in a society that was itself acting irresponsibly in general with regard to people of color.

When we returned to the car, my father began whistling. But I knew that for him, whistling was no carefree activity. I knew, because I knew him so well, that my father whistled *only* when he was disturbed by something. Or, to be more precise, only when he was outraged by something.

I admire him profoundly for having treated that patient, and I'm grateful that he took me with him.

CHAPTER FOUR

I was a self-conscious thirteen-year-old in 1941, attending John Adams Junior High School at Thirtieth and Broadway in Los Angeles. On December 7 of that year the Japanese attacked Pearl Harbor, and as a result my life and the entire world order would change. I believe World War II was one of the key elements in the radicalization of black people in this country that ultimately resulted in the great struggle for civil rights in the second half of the twentieth century.

But an event just before that had already had a seminal effect of a quite different sort on my personal understanding of myself, how I wished to view the world, and how I wished the world to view me.

Also in 1941 Duke Ellington composed the music for an Ellington orchestra stage show called *Jump for Joy* that was to debut that summer in Los Angeles. It was quintessential Ellington in that the music was so thoughtful, so full of swing, and had such a direct, though subtly expressed, political message.

Oddly, the idea for the show came out of Hollywood, which despite its nature (or maybe because of it) has always had its colony of radical thinkers. *Jump for Joy* was conceived as a propaganda exercise on behalf of civil rights for the blacks.

Ellington once said, "My biggest kick in music—playing or writing— is when I have a problem. Without a problem to solve how much interest do you take in anything?" I take it that he was speaking primarily of musical problems, when an arrangement isn't working or some combination or movement makes little sense. But like Louis Armstrong,

Ellington was frequently criticized for not paying enough attention to the problems of black people. My belief is that, also like Armstrong, he thought extensively about civil rights, and that the "problem" that civil rights presented brought about some of his greatest music.

It would have been impossible for a man this intelligent, this urbane, this well traveled not to have had a very well developed sensitivity to the racial problems of those times. It also would have been impossible for him not to be greatly angered by the conditions he found when his bands traveled south (or in other parts of the country as well), where they had to stay in rooming houses or rented rooms or out-of-the-way black hotels. In my opinion, part of Ellington's genius was not that he displayed so little resentment; rather it was in how he managed that anger and sustained his career—and the careers of all those stellar musicians—with such distinction.

Money and support for *Jump for Joy* came from Hollywood royalty, such as Lana Turner, Jackie Cooper, John Garfield, and Joseph Pasternak. One of the show's most enthusiastic backers was Orson Welles, who is reputed to have said that, other than himself, Duke Ellington was the only genius he had ever known. Two of the writers for the show were Langston Hughes and Mickey Rooney.

When the tickets went on sale in the late spring of 1941, there was no question that we would attend. Duke Ellington was at the peak of his career, as he had been for many years. He was a musical phenomenon, a very highly praised performer, a movie star (in the restricted way that well-known black musicians could be movie stars in those times, doing little acting but providing a lot of marvelous on-camera music as a backdrop to the plot action in the movie), and in the minds of many people he was the essence of what a black man could be. Or, more to the point, what a *man* could be.

The day of the concert, we dressed early because it was always my father's practice to arrive at a theater well before the curtain went up. This was true whether it was a concert by Marian Anderson, a touring play starring Paul Robeson, or the big bands of Erskine Hawkins or Count Basie. He wanted to see people, talk to people, and make sure that our seats were right. The Mayan Theater on Hill Street was originally a large movie palace. Built in 1927, it still stands there to this day. It had an immense stage and had been designed with extensive ersatz Mexican Mayan Indian decoration on the façade and interior that was intended to make it look like some kind of grand pre-Columbian temple.

The Mayan was one of the major Los Angeles venues for music events of every kind and was not a segregated theater. The audience that night was made up of people from almost every ethnic group in L.A., although it was predominantly black people and white people. Our seats for the concert were in the center of the main balcony section, in the front row. We watched as the audience began arriving, and to this day I remember in detail the way that audience looked and, particularly, the way the concert itself unfolded.

The empty rows began to fill. Then the bulk of the audience arrived, and we could feel, immediately, a sudden heightening of anticipation. The women were very elegantly dressed, many wearing big hats bought especially for the concert, with wide brims and astonishing decorations of flowers, feathers, face nets, and jewelry. Luckily, our balcony seats allowed a clear sight line to the stage, so that the grand elegance of the ladies' headgear did not get in our way. Like my father, my brother Prince, and me, all the men were fashionably dressed in suits and ties despite the L.A. summer heat.

Finally the lights dimmed. The crowd hushed, and the curtain went up. A tall man in a tuxedo came from the wings stage left, handsome and extremely debonair, so much so that there was a kind of collective intake of breath on the part of the audience. He walked across the stage like some sort of movie star. As he approached the piano, applause finally broke out, at first mild and then immediately greater as he acknowledged the crowd.

Duke Ellington.

He was James Edward Ellington's son, and his family lived in Washington, D.C. Mr. Ellington senior was a butler who occasionally was employed by the White House and later became a blueprint maker for the navy. Mrs. Ellington—Daisy Kennedy Ellington—was a housewife who instilled in her son a love of proper manners, elegant speech, reading (particularly the Bible, which Ellington claimed to have read in its entirety four times by his mid-twenties) and the sense that he could be whatever he wished if he worked for it. They were a middle-class family, moderately well-to-do by the standards of black families of the time.

I could see even from the balcony that Ellington had a distinctive way of looking out at the world. He pulled back the piano bench, nodded in the direction of the waiting orchestra, sat down, and twisted his body around so that he was half-facing the audience. Then, smiling, he surveyed the crowd with almost regal sophistication, a weary, worldly look on his face that I later discovered was something of a trademark for him.

It was immediately clear that Ellington had a very secure sense of himself . . . and he owned the stage! He conveyed an air of personal integrity and purpose that I had not seen before.

He nodded his head, played a few notes, and the orchestra suddenly gathered itself into an oceanic flow of sound that overcame us immediately, all at the behest of Ellington's sparse gestures and elegant, surehanded work at the keyboard. Years later, speaking about Ellington's difficulties in arriving at an appointment on time (it was well known that he would be either very early or very late), the musician and producer Irving Townsend said that, nevertheless, "I have never known him to arrive anywhere at the *wrong* moment." That is one of the essences of Ellington's music. The rhythms were so complicated, the music coming together in such astonishing ways, that the audience was dazzled into high spirits and enthusiastic applause.

The show had many acts and maintained the level of excitement throughout of which Duke's son Mercer Ellington once said, "Every night a contagion of happiness takes place out there." There was a dazzling bevy of bouncy, high-kicking, leggy dancers who were mostly . . . "high yella." During one routine early in the show, a line of dancing women slid and shimmied their way almost to the edge of the stage and then slowly leaned forward in unison to touch the floor. The farther they leaned over, the more I moved to the edge of my seat. I had never seen such women as these. Judging from the rowdy shouts of approval whenever they appeared onstage, their dancing excited not only me and my brother, but also my father and most of the men in the audience. I wondered how my mother was taking all this. She glanced at my father and my brother, then looked at me, smiled slightly and turned her gaze back at the stage. I guess she thought I was old enough to get excited.

Ellington himself had an unwrinkled face with a light brown complexion and matinee idol looks, a thin mustache and heavily pomaded, slicked-down hair. At school, we called this hairstyle either "gassed hair" or a "conk." Where either name came from I had no idea. In my young mind, the hairstyle was associated with the type of men who drove down Central Avenue in a four-door Packard in the company of women wearing a lot of lipstick, rouge, and powder. Certainly nobody we knew wore a conk. Once or twice I had seen someone in the chair when the barber, wearing rubber gloves, used what looked like a spatula to rub a lardlike substance on the hair. The man getting the conk had a bib tied high up to keep the concoction from dripping on his neck. One time I remembered the concoction dripped down a man's neck and his eyes watered, then he yelled out "aw shit" and cussed out the barber.

I had thought about getting a conk once, but I knew my mother would have promptly taken me back to the barbershop and made the barber shave my head.

Whether sitting at the piano snapping his fingers, standing in front of the band with trombones and trumpets blasting back and forth, or softly playing the piano behind a mournful saxophone solo, Ellington was definitely the man in charge, at times nodding vigorously, other times smiling, but always coaxing from the group the loud, then muted, ensemble sounds that I later came to know as his music and his music alone.

I spent endless hours in front of a mirror for years afterward trying to achieve that distinctive look and stylish presence.

•◆•

As the concert proceeded with such beautiful music and the excitement of the whirling bodies and the dance, many questions filled my mind. Most of them had to do with this bigger-than-life figure who was suddenly and indelibly dominating my consciousness. I wondered where he had grown up, what kind of family he was from, and what gave him the easy assurance to speak to the huge audience between numbers in such a way that he sounded as if he were sitting in our living room talking only to me. When he had been my age, had the girls thought he was cute? Had anybody called him nigger when he was a little boy? Had it led to a fight? Had he gotten good grades in junior high?

And with all my questions and speculation, there was one recurring thought: He must live in Harlem.

By then, I had read widely enough, particularly about the Harlem Renaissance, to know that that was the place, the one black locale where everyone wanted to go. It was where the "cool cats" lived. Whether or not it was true, I supposed that black teenagers everywhere wanted to be like those cool cats and, especially, like Duke Ellington.

Los Angeles, which on our Sunday drives had always seemed so large, now suddenly felt like a small town. I was certain there was no one in L.A. like Duke Ellington. He didn't carry himself or talk like any black man I had ever seen. At first glance, he seemed to act more like one of those white guys I had seen in Saturday matinees at the movie theater. They were always extremely sure of themselves, had smooth ways of walking and talking, dominating the other men in the picture, attracting the pretty, flirtatious women whom they presumably drove wild after they disappeared behind some closed door. What if by an act of magic I were to be in the company of such a woman? Could I drive her wild as well? The questions were there, but the answers were far beyond my adolescent comprehension.

It seemed to me then, as a boy, that Ellington had the same air of self-worth and confidence that those white men in the movies had. Now I realize that he had far more than they had. Ellington had star quality, real intelligence, and astonishing creativity. Those movie guys were not really like him at all. No one was.

Duke talked between numbers, making sly jokes while introducing various band members. He had a unique way of dragging out words, then using expressions I'd never heard, in which he would emphasize a syllable, drop his voice to a low rumble, and then smile to himself after a catchy, well-turned phrase had brought a response from both band members and the audience. He was not only a great musician and band leader but also an exceptional and talented performer on every level, and the audience responded to his clever expressions as readily as they did to his music.

The more I listened to him the more I felt some uniquely black spirit (we would have said Negro or colored back then), both in his stage personality and his music. The mellow voice, artful commentaries, and new words all sounded vaguely familiar to me, even though this was my first time hearing them and I didn't really know what many of the expressions really meant. At that early age, through my father, I had met other black men, some quite accomplished, if not already famous. But this was my first encounter with someone like Ellington: a man who set his own standards, crafted a singular style in both his music and life, and demanded acceptance on his own terms.

I doubt that I was alone that night in what I was feeling. I'm speaking more generally here, not just of Ellington and the *Jump for Joy* concert but also about other black kids in 1941 all around the country. At that time, young blacks everywhere—girls as well as boys—had their versions, even if local, of a Duke Ellington figure, somebody who could expand their world, open up the potential life they might envision for themselves. My father, Duke Ellington, and all the others elsewhere who were doing so much to bring growth and an expanded consciousness to me and my contemporaries were the precursors of those we see now who have become entitled to be simply Americans, even very formidable Americans. People like the late Supreme Court Justice Thurgood Marshall or mayor of Los Angeles Tom Bradley, or more recently the retired Secretary of State Colin Powell or the CEO of Young and Rubicam, Ann Fudge.

•◆•

And then Big Joe Turner came onstage to sing the blues. Although not a regular member of Ellington's band, Turner was one of the featured acts in *Jump for Joy,* and as such was backed by Ellington and his band for several songs.

Born in Kansas City in 1911, Turner had taken a job at the age of eighteen as a bartender at the Sunset Club at Twelfth and Highland streets in that city. He would drink while he was serving, and in the early morning hours he'd begin to sing the blues from behind the bar. The boogie-woogie piano player Pete Johnson was a house musician at the Sunset Club, and the two attracted such an enthusiastic audience that they landed their first recording contract. Johnson went on to gain the same kind of fame as the other boogie-woogie greats Albert Ammons and Meade Lux Lewis. Joe Turner built a stellar career as a blues shouter and, by 1941, he was very well known to blues aficionados everywhere in the country. But prior to this night at the *Jump for Joy* show, I had never heard of him.

When he began his first number, someone in the audience yelled out, "Sing your song, big man . . . tell your story." With the exception of during church services when a man might occasionally shout out a loud "amen" and women might scream "Lord Jesus" as they "got happy," I had not heard adults yelling in this way. Even with the competition from the noisy crowd (and their voices grew louder and more raucous with each song), Joe Turner's booming voice sounded out. Years later, he said, while speaking of his very early times as a singer, "They didn't have no microphones back then. They used them pasteboard things. Wha'cha call 'em, megaphones? I didn't have one, didn't need one. You could hear me ten blocks away."

Listening to him that night, as a very young man, I knew that the moods he was creating, the pain he was shouting about, and the images of men and women he was sketching were touching me in different places than did the music of Duke Ellington. While this was my first time seeing Duke Ellington in person, I had listened to his records, even danced to them at our well-chaperoned parties, and hummed along with some of the band's more well-known numbers. The Duke's name was a familiar presence in many of our homes. But Joe Turner was entirely different.

The powerful way he sang the blues called forth in me an entirely different set of emotions than those I had felt with Ellington. In comparison to the tuxedo-clad élan of Ellington and his band, Turner himself was something down and gritty. There was a sense of danger lurking about him and his songs. Turner's kind of music—some words shouted out loudly and defiantly, others hushed and barely heard, whole passages filled with anguished and mournful shouts and wails—had in our house been considered rowdy. The lyrics in some of his songs were suggestive, even lewd. Exciting. They were like the party records I had heard clandestinely in the homes of my friends, with rough jokes and sexual humor. Music like this was never allowed in our home.

Yet for all the danger and raw feelings pouring out of the man, there was an unmistakable presence and unfeigned dignity about Joe Turner. He was a big man, a tall man. He stood very erect with his shoulders pulled back, just like my father always told me and my brother to do. Indeed it was in this way, my father said, that real men would stand. During fast numbers, Joe's fingers snapped along with the music and his head and body rocked back and forth. Then during one mournful blues, when he arrived at a particularly dark moment, his knees bent almost to the floor, and his voice took on a deep, low moan. Then his voice wailed . . . until he sounded like he was weeping. In one of the rows below us on the first floor, I saw a woman flooded with tears. Several people began shouting out the words before Turner could sing them. Playing off this, he responded with other words. This exchange went back and forth, first a call and then a response, louder and louder, until the tension was almost unbearable and the theater was filled with a deafening noise of singing voices, slowly clapping hands, and pounding feet. Even my mother closed her eyes and began slowly swaying back and forth. When I looked at her again, much to my surprise, she was silently mouthing some of the words to the song.

Joe Turner sang about bad whiskey and fast women (neither of which I had experienced up to that time). Then he sang another song about being on his way to school and breaking his mother's rule. In all of the songs, I had little difficulty sensing a deep melancholy. It was there in his voice, of course, but also in the rapt silence and head shaking of the audience, in the accepting "yes, yes" that I had heard on other occasions when the glory of God had entered into the hearts of the parishioners at our church.

Even if the meaning of most of his songs was still alien to me, there was something culturally synchronous with me and Joe Turner that night, no matter the difference in how we may have been raised. In some way he was singing to my experience, either my actual experience or the historical experience from which I had come. Also, listening to him I sensed that sometime in my future there would come a time of unavoidable emotional scars resulting from guilty pleasures and carelessly inflicted pain. There would be primal responses protesting forced separations, the kinds of separations that Turner's voice was bemoaning, the loss of love and the shock of undeserved suffering, laced with the fierce pride of survival.

Big Joe Turner went on in subsequent years to greater importance as a blues singer and then a rhythm and blues singer. There are some who feel that without his classic "'Shake, Rattle and Roll,'" recorded in 1955, rock 'n' roll would never have become quite what it has. He said before he passed on in 1985 that "'rock 'n' roll' wasn't but a different name for the music I been singing all my life."

●◆●

That night at the Mayan Theater was a landmark for me. I saw in the personalities of Duke Ellington and Big Joe Turner elements that I wished for myself, even though the two men were so different from each other. The urbane Ellington; the blood-raw Turner. Sophistication and suavity on the one hand; raw emotion on the other. An ability to take the measure of the world and to ponder its complexities, hand in hand with a muscled insistence upon confronting the pain of this world. These were not mutually exclusive reactions. It is as possible for these apparently conflicting expressions of personality and personal history to exist within one person as it was for these two men to perform on the same stage.

●◆●

Jim Crow did not go away on December 7, 1941. Through the war, prejudice, discrimination, segregation, and injustice for black people remained the same. But the gap between fighting for freedom abroad but being denied freedom at home had been easier to stomach as long as there had been no *actual* war. Now that black people's sons, brothers, and fathers were coming home in coffins or being reported killed or missing in action, however, that gap became very quickly much less palatable. And it was by no means just my father who voiced such anger on this issue. Ministers at the black churches in L.A. were expressing doubts from the pulpit itself.

While I would not label their sermons overtly political—or the ministers themselves as by any means unpatriotic men—they were quite clearly bent on telling us the truth about what was happening. They pointed out that blacks had died in every war the United States had fought. Our men were dying or being wounded now in a war being waged by a country that continued to place severe restrictions on where we could go, where we could live, where and how we could work.

I knew, for example, that if I were riding on a public bus, there were certain neighborhoods in L.A. in which I would never pull the cord to indicate that I wanted to get off. It was just understood that, no matter how well dressed or respectable-looking a young man like myself might be, he could expect some form of harassment or possibly physical violence or being chased out if he were seen walking in those neighborhoods. If you were a black woman and had a job in service in that neighborhood, you could get off the bus. If you were a black man and could demonstrate with proof that you had a reason to be there . . . as a tradesman or a servant or some such . . . you too could get off the bus. Otherwise, you stayed on.

My understanding of this was not based on overt threats, as it would be in the South: "Boy, you stay put in that seat. They don't allow colored in this neighborhood." The South was so rigid that the lessons of where to get on and where to get off the bus would have been among the first you would learn. In Los Angeles, this knowledge was based much more on trial and error, knowledge that required a more subtle reading of the territory than was needed in the South. As I got older, I learned how to sense the situation. If I did not know for sure about a certain neighborhood through which the bus was moving—as I would have known in towns like Lynwood, Downey, and Southgate, which were predominantly white, industrial, working-class places—I carefully checked out the people walking up and down the street. I had to make assumptions about a particular place that were based on what I felt *might* be the conditions there. It was all internalized, a voice in my head which was much less blaring but no less aggressively hostile as the voice I would have heard in the South. Once having surveyed the place through the bus window and having come to a conclusion that it didn't look right, I wouldn't get off the bus because I knew, in my soul, that that was a bad idea. Given the possibilities, I chose not to do anything.

We didn't go to Glendale at all. A small, reasonably well-to-do city in the L.A. megalopolis, it was entirely off-limits to us. We knew well that if the people themselves in Glendale did not give you trouble, the police would.

The truly upscale cities in L.A.—Beverly Hills, Brentwood, and so on—were slightly different because of one very important demographic fact. Your mother or father could very well have a job in one of those places, in service. So you might be going there on the bus to meet your mother for some reason. Or if you had a car, as I and several of my friends had, you might be going there to pick her up. (You'd still have to have a reason. You didn't go to those towns, any more than you'd go to other, lesser towns, without a specific and proper purpose in mind that would have you leaving the town quickly, once that purpose was achieved.)

Of course, if you had a car, you might have to stop for gas on the way to pick up your mother. If you were passing through any of the working-class towns where black people were simply not supposed to go at all, you *could* usually stop at a Texaco station, say, to get gas. Very often you could use the toilets there, and the white guy pumping the gas might even be reasonably pleasant. But that was *all* that you did in one of those towns. After getting the gas, you kept going toward Beverly Hills or Brentwood or San Marino, wherever it was that you were to pick up your mother or father.

We also knew about the Japanese American internment camps. My father especially was incensed by the injustice of those camps and spoke to us frequently about them. He just couldn't understand how it was possible to treat loyal American citizens in such a manner—locking them up far from home, selling their property and businesses—and the understanding that we too could be treated in that way was never far from the core of his outrage. The treatment that Japanese Americans received was illustrative to us of how little the realities of life for people of color in the United States had changed. We well noted that there were no German American internment camps and no Italian American internment camps. When my father first learned of these concentration camps for Japanese Americans in 1942, he immediately got on the phone to his political friends, trying with little success to mobilize them against the government's policy of internment.

Segregation was still everywhere. For example, until I was in high school, we swam at the Inkwell, a blacks-only beach at the end of Pico Boulevard in Santa Monica. We had named it the Inkwell as an ironic designation from the internal humor for which blacks are famous. In traveling as an adult, I found out that in other places, most notably Martha's Vineyard, an Inkwell remains to this day. The Inkwell was ours, surrounded by white beaches. But of course we didn't go to any white beach itself. We did recognize the irony that, once we got into the water, we were all immersed in the same liquid sea—blacks and whites—an indelicacy that I think may not have occurred to the whites themselves. But at least the segregation on the sands upheld the illusion that they were safe from us.

•—•

It was one thing for us who were not actively participating in the war to undergo such slights, harassments, or perceived dangers. It was quite another thing for black people in uniform to have to do so, and as the war went on, the injustice of that became clearer and clearer to us.

Black soldiers, men and women, some of the men just home from the front, were being refused all manner of services. They fought in segregated units but they died like all other soldiers. They were buried though in segregated graveyards, as well.

In our community the saddest of these events were the deaths of the two sons of our presiding elder in our church, Reverend Hayes. One son had been in the Merchant Marines and another had been with the famous Tuskegee Airmen. Reverend Hayes delivered the terrible news from his pulpit. He was chagrined because there was no mention of his sons' deaths in the *Los Angeles Times,* since there were regular announcements of the deaths of white soldiers.

The ministers—and my father—would take this sad information and use it to point out that black people were fighting in this war in anticipation of "a double victory," a victory against the Axis overseas and a victory for ourselves at home, struggling against discrimination.

These were crazy times. Black Americans were separated as a group, residentially, occupationally, socially, and economically. Yet all Americans professed to be dedicated to "making the world safe for democracy." The racial dysfunction of the society as a whole remained. Black people had to make an extraordinary effort not to be cynical, not to be pessimistic, when conditions and policies cause such inequalities to be perpetuated even under conditions of extreme national duress. In my mind I had no doubt that blacks considered World War II a just war. Nowhere in local or national black newspapers did I come across any article that questioned the justness of the war. What was apparent was we didn't consider the country as "just" in the same way that white people did.

•◆•

When your nation is at war, the brevity and fragility of life become very obvious, even for those who are not actively fighting. There appears to be more willingness among people, a hurried feeling of necessity to become involved with one another, since life may not give you another opportunity. Maybe it was the war or more likely it was a restless, curious teenager heading toward manhood, but it was at this time that I began to learn about the attraction that women held for me. I was quite aware of the teenage girls in my school and in the youth groups at church. But except for the naive exchange of playful (and hopeful) conversation there was not much going on at the time: certainly fervid arousal. There was a divorced woman, however, who lived several houses from ours on Trinity Street, a woman I'll call Mrs. Perkins, who did motivate me to do more than talk.

Mrs. Perkins, a black woman in her late twenties, had been married when she had moved into the neighborhood, and my mother was friendly with her. She had a daughter who, at the time we met, was about seven. I was sixteen. Among the other errands that my mother had me do, she would ask me to deliver things to Mrs. Perkins: a cup of sugar my mother may have borrowed, articles from a sewing kit, a stick of butter, etc. When I did, Mrs. Perkins would offer me treats or little gifts . . . a piece of the apple pie she had just baked or a sandwich and a Pepsi.

While this mixed neighborhood of ours appeared on the surface to be integrated, the actual relationships between the neighbors themselves were very circumscribed. My mother would not have borrowed a stick of butter from a white neighbor, and so there would be no reason to return such a thing. But Mrs. Perkins's arrival indicated that the neighborhood was beginning to become more and more black. So while our relationships with our other neighbors tended to be "sidewalk relationships," in which we'd exchange greetings while on our way to the corner market or watering our lawns, a visit to Mrs. Perkins's home was simply a normal event. We visited her house and she visited ours.

She and my mother had a close neighborly relationship, chatted on the phone, visiting each other and so on. But they did not socialize with each other beyond that relationship. We did not go to the same church. The two women did not have acquaintances in common.

Mrs. Perkins was from Texas and had come to L.A. to work in the shipyards. She had many questions about Los Angeles. Since I had been born and raised there, I was able to supply her with a lot of information about what L.A. had to offer, where to go, and where she could sightsee. A relationship between us began to flower as we talked about this new land that she had come to. L.A. was intriguing to her, because it represented something quite unique and different. We developed a conversational intimacy.

I began to sense that Mrs. Perkins was interested in me for reasons other than the information I was sharing with her. There was the occasional unguarded glance, the touch of my shoulder as she passed me by, the flirtatious smile as I appeared at her door. I was too shy to initiate anything beyond talk. The possibility of rejection was too great.

Her marriage was breaking up, and I suspect that she was seeking some kind of physical intimacy, perhaps also of an adventuresome sort. In time and with a heightened realization that we were attracted to each other, we ended up in bed.

Such a relationship was not a common thing among my friends, or at least was not talked about. There was a sense of danger to this, I had an active social life, through school, the church, and as president of a youth club at the Y.M.C.A., with girls my own age. I would engage with my friends in stories of dalliance and conquest, but these were for the most part fantasy flirtations, and imaginary conquests. Boyish tales and lies. But my affair with Mrs. Perkins was real, and it was therefore daring and risky, even exotic. Our intimate moments together were episodic and clandestine. We saw each other every few days or so and the affair lasted for about two years.

Mrs. Perkins introduced me to the nightclub scene in Los Angeles. The Central Avenue club scene was very active. So I would dress up in a coat and tie on a particular night, tell my parents that I was going to a party of some sort, and meet Mrs. Perkins a few blocks away, where she'd pick me up in her car. We had to keep these dates secret, my parents would never have approved.

We went to a number of clubs, most especially the singer Herb Jeffries's place, the Flamingo Club. He was the same Herb Jeffries who, as Herbert Jeffrey, was the star of many black westerns in the 1930s. Two of his better-known movies were *The Bronze Buckaroo* and *Harlem Rides the Range*. For black people, these movies themselves were breakthrough events. Jeffries had approached a company in L.A. to make such films, with all-black casts and a black actor playing the lead as hero. Jeffries felt that this was important because, as he said, "I felt that dark-skinned children could identify with me." Professor Jules Rosette, of the University of California at San Diego, has written that these films had much deeper implications even than that: "These films were the first to show blacks as heroes and not servants, they allowed blacks to be themselves in a public outlet. They could be multidimensional people in the movies, while they *lived* in an outside world where they had to be subservient."

Jeffries was also, of course, a very well known singer. He had been featured by Duke Ellington in 1939 and 1940, during which time he made the recording with Ellington of "Flamingo." This was a star vehicle for Jeffries, a song that, in the several recordings he made of it, sold fourteen million copies. Jeffries said that "most people come to this world by stork. I came by flamingo, and Duke Ellington delivered me."

I felt very grown up and sophisticated. I would drink alcohol at the Flamingo, although not a great deal. I was seeing an older woman, who described me to the others that we'd meet at the clubs as her "pigmeat." I was having an affair. In other words, I was a strong, virile young man who was this woman's lover. I don't know how widespread this term was at the time, but it had to be reasonably current, since Dewey Markham, a nationally known black comedian and singer used the name Pigmeat Markham. (It was Markham who in 1968 recorded "Here Comes the

Judge," a novelty hit that was made famous on the comedy series *Rowan & Martin's Laugh-In.*)

• •

World War II was a time of political radicalization for many black people, and it was during the war that my father's views began to be more aligned with far-left progressive politics. As a result of our many—sometimes loud and sometimes quite nuanced—conversations about politics throughout the war, I began to define my own points of view as well.

In high school, I learned about the left wing and the Communist Party. I also learned about J. Edgar Hoover. I realized that certain people could become targeted for public criticism for their left-leaning views and that this criticism very often exposed them to harassment, persecution, disgrace, and even personal ruin—sometimes at the mandate of J. Edgar Hoover, who was then the director of the Federal Bureau of Investigation.

I learned of these things principally through my father. The war seemed to be driving him to the left, and I began to attend meetings with him of the various left-wing organizations in which he had become involved. He also subscribed to socialist or radical leftist publications that would be on the living room coffee table or in the kitchen that I would pick up and read. There was a steady stream of white friends in our house who visited my father to talk politics, members of organizations like the Hollywood Arts, Sciences and Professions Council, which was a Hollywood group of which my father eventually became president.

I also read the establishment daily newspapers, the *Los Angeles Times* and the afternoon *Herald-Express,* and absorbed their point of view that some of these organizations were "front" groups for the Communist Party. But I was also reading the *Pittsburgh Courier* and the *Chicago Defender,* black weekly newspapers to which my father subscribed that often gave more thoughtful analyses of these groups and their activities, based on a national, rather than a local, point of view.

I should point out that, despite the knowledge on the part of the black establishment that the war was doing little to change conditions for people of color at home, mainstream blacks and black organizations were very wary of these left-wing groups. For example, the dentist, Doctor

Somerville, who had founded the Dunbar Hotel on Central Avenue, had been a very good friend of W. E. B. DuBois. But when DuBois declared that he was a Communist and exiled himself to Ghana, Doctor Somerville distanced himself from DuBois. My father described that distancing with chagrin.

Meanwhile, the increasingly left-wing views and activities of my father worried my mother a great deal. She took the point of view that my father should not be doing anything so radical that it would appear unrespectable or potentially dangerous to him, his family, and black people in general. The ledge on which we were standing, she felt, was narrow enough. She didn't want my father to do anything that would push him nearer to the edge or, worse, get him pushed off.

One has to remember that, at least until the German-Soviet Non-Aggression Pact in 1939, even the non-Communist far left was flirting admiringly with Joseph Stalin and the Russians. The journalist Lincoln Steffens had famously remarked, with regard to the Soviet Union, "I have seen the future and it works." But even after Stalin became our ally in the war, he remained suspect to most of the American political establishment. It remained dangerous to endorse his regime too enthusiastically. On the other hand, the Communist Party was one of the few political organizations in the United States during this period that was advocating issues such as true integration, the end of discrimination, free access to housing, unsegregated education, voting rights, and social justice for all.

Part of the problem for me and my mother lay in my father's position as a professional man and a black man. Were he to be perceived as wild-eyed in any political way, he could jeopardize his career and his place in society. That had already happened to many white people. Were his views to be made public, his being black could make the punishment even worse than normal. For me, there was sheer survival to be considered before one made such a daring political leap.

So we argued.

Our arguments were different from those between most sons and their fathers. The usual scenario is that the son's adventuresome views are seen as too radical by the conservative father, who feels that the changes that the son advocates are dangerous to the comfortable status quo that the father has worked so hard to achieve. Such arguments begin usually with the father's accusing the son in a heated way of some rebelliousness that doesn't make sense to the older man. The opening question from the father might be something direct like, "What the hell are you up to, anyway?"

Our debates did start that way, although in our case there was an exceptional role reversal. He was the more liberal. I was the more conservative.

I agreed with my mother that my father was being too radical in his views. My objections were not to the sincerity of his politics or the genuineness of his feelings on political matters. Rather I felt that he was being unrealistic and somewhat romantically idealistic.

He would talk about "the workers," for example, in quite romantic terms, as though the working class embodied some sort of ethical purity. I, on the other hand, thought that his concept of "the workers" was simple dreaming and little else. My own observations of working people, particularly those who were white, had not instilled in me any particular solidarity with them, and I had seen little to indicate that they felt any for us either. I had found that, of all my fellow students at school, the sons and daughters of the white working class invariably expressed the most vehement levels of prejudice toward black kids.

From grammar school on, the kids with whom I tended to feel more solidarity were kids like me, no matter their color or ethnicity. Their parents were hard-working people, many of them holding down two jobs, who had real aspirations for advancement and self-improvement, and a broader vision of the world in which they lived. Kids who at least had some budding view of the notion of equality and that their race, religion, or ethnicity was not ipso facto superior to mine. By and large, the kids of white working-class parents didn't seem to me to represent such views. Rather than seeing them as the ideal for the improvement of race relations, I frequently found them to be the enemy.

In later years, after I'd become acquainted and saw patients from such organizations as the International Longshore Workers Union under Harry Bridges, I learned that there were indeed many working-class people who had a broader and more encompassing political consciousness than those students I'd met years ago from high schools around Los Angeles. But it still holds that I have not found any overall, all-inclusive proof that my father's idealized perception of "the workers" could represent some genuinely progressive force for better race relations.

It was through the Hollywood Arts, Sciences and Professions Council that my father met and befriended several of the people who after the war would become notorious as the Hollywood Ten: Dalton Trumbo the screenwriter, and the director Herbert Biberman among others. The Hollywood Ten were ten writers, directors, and actors who were accused by the House Un-American Activities Committee in 1947 of either being Communists or of supporting Communist causes. This was at a time when China was undergoing a civil war in which the Communist forces of Mao Tse-tung were battling the Nationalist armies of Chiang Kai-shek for control of that vast country. Joseph Stalin and the Russians had annexed Eastern Europe. There was fear in the Western democracies that Communist regimes were set to take over much of the world. Whether this was true or not remains open to conjecture, but the U.S. House of Representatives had formed the Un-American Activities Committee to "investigate," as they put, the influence of communism in the mass media, in Hollywood in particular.

The Hollywood Ten were very successful people in the film industry who may or may not have been in the party. But during the hearings in 1947 they refused to name names while under investigation and they were punished for their silence in very profound ways, either with fines and imprisonment or professionally with the loss of their careers.

My father's involvement with them came before the H.U.A.C. hearings, through his participation in the Hollywood Arts, Sciences and Professions Council.

I once went with my father to the luxury home of one of these people. This home didn't have a yard; it had grounds. A swimming pool. Servants, some of them black. It was a luxurious setting, and the people attending were very much part of the Hollywood film-industry establishment.

There was a great deal of talk during this event of "the workers" and how the "working class" somehow represented the best of what American society had to offer yet was so often deprived of its aspirations by power-hungry industrialists. The union movement was the answer, and with this movement all workers would come to achieve their aspirations. Listening to these guests talk, I wondered, What's all this about? What do *these* people know about "the workers" and their noble aims? These people were rich, favored, privileged. Their politics were suspect to me, mainly because, as the phrase is now, they talked the talk, but they didn't walk the walk. There was too broad a schism between what they professed and how they lived.

To be sure I met many very nice people at such events, who I felt were sincere and did have an honest concern for the rights of black people. But I met others who wore their politics in the same way that they'd wear a hat. They'd put on the politics or take them off, depending on the weather. And I would ask myself questions that I thought my father should ask himself: Are these people sincere? Do they really care about what happens to black folks? Are they using us?

Here again my mother was worried about my father. She felt that he was jeopardizing his position among his own people by offering himself as one of the few blacks—probably the *only* black professional that we knew—to be involved in such politics. The key thing for her, and ultimately for me, was that no one from those groups and organizations that made up our personal social milieu—The Tuskegee Club, the CME church, the various community organizations that enhanced the legitimacy of my father's profession and my parents' place in society—was involved with progressive politics at all. Just my father. So we were concerned.

My mother was highly suspicious of the Hollywood group. She thought that if these white people with money were fingered or otherwise discomfited by the government for their political activities, they would probably come out of it in reasonably good shape. My father on the other hand was more vulnerable. As a black man, he was jeopardizing everything the family had striven for, risking his reputation and position in a political jousting match that could conceivably land him in jail.

They argued about these things for years, but my father remained for the most part steadfast in his support of leftist political groups until well into the 1950s. The Senate McCarthy hearings of those years had a California counterpart in the Tenney Committee, the official name of which was the Joint Fact-Finding Committee on Un-American Activities. It was chaired by a state senator named Jack Tenney, who had himself been involved in radical left-wing politics prior to the German-Soviet Non-Aggression Pact. Tenney had been a Hollywood composer who was best known for his having penned the song *Mexicali Rose*. The Tenney Committee investigated both Communist and Nazi organizations, although it became most notorious for its pursuit of radical left-wingers and, particularly, Communist "front" groups, of which the Hollywood Arts, Sciences and Professions Council was considered a notable example. After being subpoenaed and testifying before this group, my father was named by the Tenney Committee as a left-wing fellow traveler as was his good friend, and later distinguished member of the House of Representatives, Gus Hawkins.

One thing, incidentally, about which my father and I did not disagree, was what we saw as a disproportionate number of Jews in left-wing politics. We'd discuss whether this was in fact so, and if so, why? Was it something in the tenets of the Jewish faith? Or was it a result of the treatment the Jews had received at the hands of state-sponsored pogroms in Eastern Europe, treatment that had politicized them radically? We came to no particular conclusion about this, but we did agree that the Jews and blacks were in something of the same boat together, and there seemed to be ample reason for us to support each other. Both groups were outside the American mainstream. Both groups were discriminated against. There was an affinity between us.

My father was sympathetic to the plight of Jews everywhere and wanted to help those who were being persecuted. For example, one night during the war he and my mother took me to a Hadassah dinner in L.A. at which, with a certain donation, you could be given credit for enabling a Jew of little means to be brought to Israel. The event was held at the Earl Carroll theater and was attended by many prominent Jews from Hollywood, like Jack Benny. The amount was a few hundred dollars, in those times a considerable sum. At this dinner, my father stood up and announced that he would contribute enough money to ensure the passage, not of one, but of two Jews to Israel. My mother reached up to take his sleeve, insisting that he sit down. We may not be poor, she seemed to imply, but we weren't prepared to spend *that* kind of money.

The die was cast however. The audience's applause was great for my father's generous pledge, and the money indeed did go to the cause for which he had intended it that evening.

•◆•

Despite our differences, I owe my father something very important from those years. Because he engaged me in those conversations, I had to develop political ideas of my own, if only to combat him. These were not shouting matches. I may have disagreed with him, but I knew that he respected my point of view and that he realized how much I was trying to put into it. He saw how much I was reading. He saw that I could reason, that I could debate with a certain subtlety of mind.

I argued with him in part, though, because already, at that age, I wanted my politics to flow from my heart and mind rather than from someone else's—even if that "someone else" was my own father. There may have been some innate rebelliousness in my actions, but I also sincerely disagreed with what I perceived to be his occasionally naive and reckless behavior.

•◆•

In any case, the war did ultimately have a tremendous impact on black people's struggle for equality and the civil rights movement in this country.

Those veterans coming back in 1946, their families and especially the families of those who did not come back, were not going to sit idly by while the conditions of racism and Jim Crow were simply reinstated. Too many blacks had sacrificed too much.

And it should not be forgotten that the defense industries were fueled by black workers . . . men and women, thousands of them from all over the country who built the equipment that won the war in the hands of soldiers of every race. Black people had too much to do with victory overseas to allow their subjugation in this country to be perpetuated. So, for example, in 1948, a black Los Angeles lawyer named Loren Miller pled the case of *Shelley vs. Kraemer* before the U.S. Supreme Court, which resulted in the end of the restrictive land covenants that had prevented people of color from buying homes anywhere they wanted. The plaintiffs in that case were Mr. and Mrs. J. D. Shelley, a black couple living in Saint Louis, Missouri. Mr. Shelley was a blue-collar worker originally from Mississippi who had brought his family to Saint Louis in search of work in the defense industry and had spent the war working at a small-arms bullet manufacturing company in Saint Louis. Mr. and Mrs. Shelley had attempted during the war to buy a two-unit building on Labadie Street in Saint Louis and were prevented from doing so by a restrictive covenant. With the help of Mr. Miller in 1948, they took the case to the Supreme Court and won.

•◆•

Thanks to my conversations with my father—especially those in which I opposed him—my own politics were taking shape. They received their first public airing in 1946 on a picket line that made its way back and forth across the entrance to, of all places, a minor league baseball park in L.A.

This picket line had been called by the Congress of Racial Equality in support of an idea, and there was a single man—a ballplayer whose identity we could not have known in 1946, but who would be internationally known only a year and a half later—who would come to embody the justice of that idea.

CHAPTER FIVE

Our house on Trinity Street was just a few blocks from Wrigley Field in Los Angeles, a baseball stadium that was home to the Pacific Coast League's Los Angeles Angels. Owned by the Wrigley family of Illinois, the Angels were a Triple-A farm club for the Chicago Cubs. In those days, before there was major-league ball on the West Coast, the PCL was noted for the high level of its play and was referred to by its more ardent fans as the "Third Big League." The PCL had produced numbers of major leaguers, the most notable being Joe DiMaggio, who had played for the San Francisco Seals.

In 1946, there were no black players in either the PCL or the major leagues. I thought this was a major foolishness on the part of baseball's establishment, and a major insult. Black people were well versed in the abilities of black players at every level of baseball, from the field to the front office, through the legendary achievements of the Negro National League and the Negro American League, black baseball's equivalents of the white major leagues. Players like Josh Gibson (who played in nine Negro League All-Star Games with a batting average of .483), James "Cool Papa" Bell ("the fastest man in baseball," of whom it was said that he once was hit, while sliding into second base, by the same ball that he had just batted), the extraordinary Kansas City Monarchs pitcher Satchel Paige, and many, many others were household names in the black community, and I personally felt that the major leagues were simply limiting the quality of their play by not including black players.

That year, I became involved in an effort to right that wrong, a small effort on my part that was made with no expectation of an immediate resolution to the problem in favor of black players. Little did I realize that the situation was about to change, with astonishing results.

•—•

In the spring of 1946, I was completing my senior year at Jefferson High School and graduated that June with excellent grades, having been student body vice-president there as well as a lettered athlete. I even held the Rose Bowl high school track meet record in the half-mile for a brief time.

It had been expected by my parents that all of us children would go to college. I don't think that any other alternative would have been acceptable to them. UCLA was ideal for me because it was already noted as a fine university at which I could receive the highest level of education. Also, I had had no difficulty being accepted there, because of my good grades in high school. Then as now UCLA was a state university, and so quite inexpensive. This too was a positive, since I would be depending on my parents for financial support. The burden would be much lighter going to UCLA than to a private institution elsewhere in the country. There were very few blacks at UCLA, but this posed no problem. Our aspirations far outweighed any nervousness we had in attending what was an almost all-white institution.

•—•

My brother, Prince, had joined the U.S. Marine Corps Reserve and had been called to active duty in 1944. Because he was black, he was unable to join the regular Marine Corps, which allowed no blacks at all in the regular Corps. There were no black commissioned officers in *any* marine unit, regular or reserve. Prince was assigned to an all-black unit at Camp Lejune, North Carolina, as a cook.

He was part of a marine contingent that landed in Sesabo, Japan, in September 1945, just after the surrender was signed. The white marines were issued ammunition on the possibility that they could be attacked by Japanese locals upon their arrival. The black reserve marines were told that they would be given ammunition only *if* the unit were indeed attacked. So, despite the potential danger, the black reserve marines landed in Japan basically unarmed.

Prince came home and was discharged during my first year at UCLA. I drove down by myself to Camp Pendleton on the final day of his service, to pick him up and bring him home. There was a celebration planned, and our family was very proud of him. He had served his country, putting himself literally "in harm's way" against the Japanese. I wanted to make sure that his ride home was an enjoyable one. It was a warm day, a sunny day in Southern California. I drove down the coast in my parents' 1941 Chrysler, which was, as always, polished and perfect, with little that would suggest even a speck of dust.

As I drove south along the Pacific Coast Highway, I was able to catch a glimpse now and then of the ocean on my right and the remarkable sheen of the blue water along that part of the coast. I recalled my father's love of California, how astonished he always seemed to be by its beauty and the clear-aired loveliness that it represented. He considered himself a lucky man to live in California. Driving along that road, I was heartened by the idea that my brother and I were going to drive back up the same road together, and that Prince was going to be able to enjoy the views as I was enjoying them—the golden dry hills, the blue sky with high clouds, and the emerald blue ocean so glittering in the sunlight—once more a civilian who could enjoy himself, secure in the knowledge that he had served his country well.

I entered the base and walked into a building, the sort of standard-issue military installation of the time, made of wood, painted cream-yellow. A few palm trees, indigenous to that part of California, rose up above the roof, with the ocean in the distance. When I first saw Prince, wearing a pair of slacks, a sport shirt, and dress shoes as he walked into the room where I was waiting, I was proud and overjoyed to see him. And he was just as happy to see me. We embraced, laughing, clapping each other on the back. He had made it through the war, and we simply could not have been happier.

But I recall an immediate feeling of disappointment, even a kind of rage on my part. I was silently angry about Prince's having had to serve in an all-black segregated unit as a cook, without a way to rise through the ranks. It wasn't that I wondered how *he* could accept that. Not at all. Prince had fulfilled his obligation, and he'd fulfilled it well. But I did wonder about what price he had paid to serve his country in a system that *kept* him as a cook, a man of his education, intelligence, and ability.

I also wondered where was the justice in putting a man like Prince in such danger, yet not allowing him the advantages, after that danger had passed, that white servicemen enjoyed who were returning from the war? During the drive home, I wanted to ask Prince about my feelings to see how he felt about his experience in the Corps. But I kept the questions to myself because I worried that they would put a damper on the celebratory feelings that we were otherwise enjoying. Ultimately, Prince held the memories of his experiences very close to the vest, much like other returned black veterans I had learned about. I now know that he shared his feelings that day as best as he could. Perhaps he felt that it was better to get on with his life and let that part remain in the past. I learned of his true feelings only in bits and starts as the years went by.

This silence is not an uncommon response among black people in general to the conditions with which they have had to live. Indeed, it is a response that oppressed groups throughout history have shared. You move on. You move ahead. But there is a price to the rage that you harbor within yourself, that you do not share with others. It builds. It festers. Years later, when I began to study black rage as an actual phenomenon, I recalled Prince's smoldering frustration and outrage that lay beneath the happiness on that day he left the Corps.

For myself, driving home from Camp Pendleton on a day that Prince so deserved to celebrate, and *would* celebrate, I wondered just the same, Why are we as a country engaged in this kind of stupidity?

•◆•

One day during my senior year of high school, I heard about a picket line that was going to be set up by the Congress of Racial Equality at Wrigley Field, to protest the fact that the major leagues did not accept black players, either on the major-league teams themselves or in their minor-league farm systems. It was a weekend event, planned for one of the Angels' spring games, and I decided to join the picket.

My decision was made on the spur of the moment, but it was not just something out of the blue for me. I realized that there were few avenues of political expression for black people within established party politics. Sometimes, direct action was the only game in town. So although I had many second thoughts about participating in such an event, I went ahead. I showed up at the picket line on my own and asked the people in the line if there was anything I could do to help. My second thoughts had to do with not knowing anyone on the picket line. They were all mostly in their twenties. Since I had not participated in any of the planning, I didn't know what I might be getting myself into.

My father did not know about the picket or my participation in it until afterward, but I believe that he would have joined me on the line if he had known about it. Wrigley Field was just a few blocks from our house, directly in the path of the expanding black population up the Central Avenue corridor. And, except for exhibition games with the All-Stars from the Negro Leagues, no black person could play baseball there, even though our money as fans was welcome. So the appeal of the "Don't Buy Where You Can't Work" campaign was an influence on my decision to picket. I was also simply a fan of baseball and offended by the fact that I could only root for white players every time I went to see an Angels game. How could a team like this operate within a neighborhood that was fast becoming black?

I learned only years later that there had actually been a precedent for black ballplayers in the major leagues. Fleet Walker had played for the Toledo Blue Stockings for several years, starting in 1884. But that fact was so little known that, at least among the general populace, it was believed that no black player had ever participated in the major leagues. At the time, I myself had not heard of Walker, and I didn't actually imagine— on the day of the picket line—that a true change in baseball would come any time soon.

The picket line brought little attention to itself. We had maybe a dozen people. We made up some signs, protesting segregation in the major leagues, calling for an end to prejudice in baseball, and we walked with them back and forth before the main gate of the stadium. Fans—a few blacks, mostly whites—passed us by, noted that we were there, and went ahead into the stadium, simply stepping around us. Black fans, of course, noted our presence with a more positive response than white fans. But there were not many black fans. I don't recall any vilification, any insults from anyone. Once the game got under way, the line broke up and we left.

PRICE M. COBBS, M.D.

The picket line was not momentous, it was a small effort being made by a few people of conscience. It was rather some forces being brought to bear behind the scenes, that we knew nothing about, that were making the difference. Secret negotiations in fact were going on at that very time to bring black players into the major leagues. It is obvious that the time for our ideas had come, and as small as our protest was, it was part of an enormous movement.

There was a man being prepared to open the floodgates and bring an end to racial discrimination in major-league baseball. A man that I and most of Los Angeles already knew about, Jackie Robinson. I knew of him years before he became world famous. I had read about him in the *Los Angeles Times* sports section as well as the black L.A. newspapers. They wrote especially about his prowess as an athlete (although many of the articles mentioned his academic achievements as well) in high school and junior college in Pasadena and later at UCLA. At UCLA, he was the first student in the history of the institution to play four varsity sports—football, track, baseball, and basketball—concurrently. He lettered in all four.

Robinson was the kind of person I aspired to be. Just about ten years older than I was, he seemed, at so young an age, to be a complete man who was able to balance academics and athletics in ways I had not seen before.

Later I found out that in 1942 he had been drafted into the army and sent to Fort Riley, Kansas. Robinson knew that he was qualified to be an officer. So he was mightily surprised the day he was turned down for Officer Candidate School, his university education notwithstanding, and even though he had easily passed all the qualifying examinations. The other black applicants at Fort Riley had also been turned down, and inquiries from them, asking why, had done little good. They were simply turned down . . . End of story.

No less a person than the heavyweight champion of the world, the great Joe Louis himself, intervened, and in that moment, the U.S. Army encountered the same sort of rugged, obdurately forceful character that had vanquished Max Schmeling a few years before. On duty himself at Fort Riley, Louis used his influence to get those decisions changed, and

Jackie Robinson and the others were finally admitted to OCS. Robinson received his commission shortly thereafter.

Like Duke Ellington, Robinson seemed always to know who he was. He was never easily cowed, and he did not suffer fools. When the forces that determined segregation in those days presented themselves to him, he resisted, and it seems to me that he resisted simply because he thought of himself as a full citizen who had the right to be where he was, at whatever time he decided, for whatever reason. No doubt he was badly treated, as were most blacks. Perhaps he was treated even worse from time to time because of this attitude. But he carried himself as though he were saying, "All right. So be it. I'm standing here and I'm going to remain standing here although others may want me to move."

In 1944 he was ordered by a white officer to move to the back of a bus that was filled with soldiers. Robinson refused, reassuring himself that he had every right as an officer himself to sit where he wanted as long as it was within military protocol. For his action, he was brought before a court-martial, accused of refusing to carry out an order. A vigorous defense resulted in his exoneration. His maintaining of himself in that refusal and during the resultant court-martial was a potent harbinger of the courage with which Robinson would react to the public hatred he would face, from many thousands of people day after day, after the war was over.

Robinson was discharged from the army in 1945 and immediately signed a contract to play baseball with the Kansas City Monarchs of the Negro American League. While there he was contacted by the Brooklyn Dodger organization and told that they were considering signing him to a new all-black team that would be called the Brooklyn Brown Dodgers. During the negotiations, he was asked to visit with the head of the Dodgers, a very famous longtime baseball executive and general manager named Branch Rickey. Rickey had been general manager of the Saint Louis Cardinals during the 1920s and 1930s and put together the famous Gas House Gang teams for which the brothers Dizzy and Daffy Dean pitched. Rickey was also the man who invented the minor league farm club system, in which a major-league organization will own a group of minor-league teams that were the developers and providers of players to the particular big-league team. Though this has long been a feature of major-league baseball, when Rickey first instituted such a system for the Cardinals, it was revolutionary.

It was during that now-famous meeting that Rickey told Robinson he wanted to sign him to a major-league contract to play for the Dodgers. The Brooklyn Dodgers. The *white* Brooklyn Dodgers.

The prospect of black ballplayers in major-league baseball was vigorously opposed by big-money interests and a long history of racism. During the meeting itself, Rickey said to Robinson, "Jackie, we've got no army. There's virtually nobody on our side. No owners, no umpires, very few newspapermen. And I'm afraid that many fans will be hostile. We'll be in a tough position. We can win only if we can convince the world that I'm doing this because you're a great ballplayer, a fine gentleman."

Jackie Robinson was going to The Bigs.

Rickey has been quoted as saying that he was looking for a player who could withstand heated pressure from fans and fellow players alike with quiet grace, even more than he was looking for the best black ballplayer. Robinson appeared to him to be that player, a man with character and patience, an intelligent man who could see beyond the vitriol that he could expect to receive.

I have often wondered, though, if Branch Rickey knew about Jackie Robinson's refusal to follow that order in 1944. Had he known, he may not have thought that Robinson was such a good prospect.

When I participated in the picket line at Wrigley Field, none of us were aware that these machinations were going on in the offices of the Brooklyn Dodgers, or that Robinson was at the center of those negotiations. A year later, on April 10, 1947, Robinson and Rickey signed the contract that changed everything.

By that time I was near the end of my first year at UCLA. When I read about the signing of that contract, my heart began to pound with a kind of self-assured pleasure that I had seldom experienced. That there had been no blacks in the major leagues (as we believed) was a true and huge symbol of the legacy of slavery. That symbol was now suddenly gone, and like almost every black person I knew, I felt to some degree *personally* vindicated.

There's no doubt that I identified strongly with Jackie Robinson. We both went to UCLA, but he was ten years older than me and a huge success, whereas I was still a kid coming up, ambitious but unproven. Nevertheless, I liked to think we had some traits in common: Jackie was well liked, personable, knew how to make his way in the white world, but also often smoldering and angry underneath the surface. He was a proud man, accepting no compromise when it came to his integrity as a human being, refusing to accept discrimination or prejudice. I liked to think I could have that kind of strength and integrity too.

•◆•

I had several steady girlfriends in high school, and with a few of them there was some degree of intimacy. This usually meant parking the car in some out-of-the-way place and, if you were lucky, even climbing into the backseat for some heavy kissing and groping. However, at UCLA I discovered girls in earnest and was discovered by them. The intensity of my dalliance with Mrs. Perkins was still fresh in my memory. But the relationships at UCLA were more conventional, with unattached women who were my own age. Although I hid it well, I was cautious and shy, one of only about a hundred black students in the whole university, and only about fifteen in my class. But I realized that I could flirt and be flirted with. UCLA introduced me to an entire new world, in which the caress, the kiss, and the love of women were immediate and heated goals.

Sometimes the effort to expand my social life at UCLA led unexpectedly to lessons that reminded me of my legacy as a black person. Many of the black students had participated in school government and other class activities while in high school. I had done that too and enjoyed it. At the suggestion of a close friend, Sherrill Luke, I resolved to get more involved in campus life. Sherrill took his own advice seriously and went on to become UCLA's first black student body president. In the unofficial segregation of the 1950s that was no mean feat.

So one of the first things I did was to volunteer to participate on the homecoming committee. It was the usual sort of thing to prepare for a football homecoming game, for a team that had Rose Bowl aspirations. (We did in fact make it that year, losing to University of Michigan, 49–0.) There was to be an annual big parade, with floats. I volunteered, and the day came on which I was to help decorate the floats. The event was held on UCLA's Sorority Row.

When I arrived that morning, dressed neatly and well, pants pressed, shirt ironed, a little nervous, it became immediately apparent to me that everyone else already knew one another. This was nothing unusual. I was a new student, and one could expect to have to make new acquaintances in a new place, as I had had to do on many occasions in my life. Also, for those who aren't part of a social scene, a specific purpose of volunteering for such an event is to meet people so that you can *become* part of the scene. I was there for that as well. But this occasion was different from any other similar event in which I had ever participated, because Sorority Row at UCLA was *white* Sorority Row.

I was the only black student there that day, and I felt like a guy from Mars. Within minutes of my arrival, a question began circulating over and over through my mind, and the question was, What the hell am I even *doing* here? There were all sorts of students decorating the floats, men and women. None of them paid any attention to me. I saw right away that there was a cultural milieu that these kids occupied that included an entire manner of acting, a way of speaking, a way of dressing, a very essence of being, of which I was not a part.

Everybody was talking. There were long glances and flirting. Patter. Laughter. And I was participating in none of it. Yes, it's important that I participate in school activities. But I felt foolish helping to decorate floats all by myself, since I was basically being shunned. Suddenly I realized I cared little about floats that would be a part of a parade at which my presence would not much be encouraged. I then decided I would not even go.

This was my first exposure to such a seemingly privileged white community, in which a superior, favored position in society was simply assumed. But in the short time I was there that day, I saw—in the patter, the in jokes, the sideways glances my way, and the general inconsequence of everything that was going on—how limited these people were, shielded behind their own exclusiveness, easy manner, and assumed superiority. I thought that those limitations must be as constraining to them in political and social issues as they were in the banter that went along with decorating the floats. I was sure that the deeper intellectual currents of racial issues and progressive politics that I had been discussing in such detail with my father meant little to these people. I doubted that they *ever* considered them, and that were they to know about them, they could probably be upset with them, and with me.

It was clear to me that day that I had a long way to go. I decided not to do any more decorating, and I left. I'm not that sure anyone else noticed.

• ◆ •

Many of the black students I knew had aspirations that were in keeping with traditions already established within their own families. My father was a physician, and it was expected that the three of us children would become physicians as well. It was for that reason—and, frankly, because I actively wished for a profession in medicine—that I was a premed major. This was because of our parents' aspirations for us, but it was also an acknowledgment of a collision that occurred for black people between aspirations and reality.

Life, liberty, and the pursuit of happiness was not a concept that could be easily realized by black people. Or so were the sentiments and previous experiences of most black families in 1946. There were only certain professions open to us, and medicine was one of the most important ones. As I recall now, most of the black students whom I knew at UCLA were on track to enter one of those "available" professions: medicine, law, dentistry, teaching, the ministry, or a job in "civil service."

But in 1946 something quite different was also beginning to happen. The rhetoric of the American dream was now being put on trial. The year I entered UCLA the campus population exploded with returning veterans of World War II taking advantage of the GI Bill to fund their education. Many of the hundred or so black students were recently discharged soldiers, sailors, and marines. Among this number were recent members of the famed Tuskegee Airmen. And all of them came with high expectations of new opportunities.

I knew a black student at UCLA, for example, who was majoring in industrial relations. In our small group, this made him the object of a certain measure of ridicule because it was an unusual path to follow. Who, we wanted to know, was going to hire him? With his chances so slim, what was the point?

What we didn't realize was that we were in the postwar dawn and companies like Lockheed and Hughes Aircraft were beginning to hire engineers and technicians in large numbers. The defense industries had grown remarkably in California during the war and would remain strong despite cutbacks in the defense budgets. A true peacetime economic boom was shaping up. A new phase in the corporatization of America and a remarkable period of growth in the economy were about to begin. And in small ways, by ones and twos, black people were beginning to move through the cracks in the doors into those fast-expanding industries.

At UCLA, if you were doing well and were lucky enough to come under the wing of a certain professor, he or she might suggest a course of study for you, or a campus organization or even just a single class that would be outside the realm of what, at that time, black students could expect to enter. Something that would broaden your platform a bit. So, for example, instead of following a strictly premed course, you might step into a class in which you would be *very* unlikely to find a black person at all. Like marketing statistics. Anthropology. Medieval English literature. The whole gamut of courses that were outside the norm of those professions into which blacks could expect to be welcomed.

You'd be feeling the effects of being invisible, maybe even the unrealized disgruntlement that came as a result of your legacy as a black person, and the fresh memories of what black people had just done to so effectively help the war effort, and you'd think to yourself, Well, I'm not just going to go back to the way it was. I'm going to check this out, this new idea.

So maybe you'd take that class, and like it. Maybe you'd take another, and like that. You'd get to know the lay of the land. You'd develop some expertise. You'd meet fellow students who were not black but were friendly to you and could help you. And you'd finish up with a degree in industrial relations. Advertising. Business administration. You could become an engineer. Or, if you were aspiring to be a physician, maybe you'd do something other than general practice. You'd become a surgeon, maybe. Or perhaps a psychiatrist.

Suddenly in the aftermath of World War II a small crack in the door to these industries was opening for blacks, jarred open—just a bit—by the sudden growth in the economy and the expanded need for trained professionals to fill the jobs. The results for the students who took advantage of this may not have been so publicly noticeable as what happened when the crack in the door opened for Jackie Robinson. But it was happening at exactly the same time. And surely many of us took advantage of that crack in the same way that he did and passed through it with him

By my third year of college my grades were quite poor and my parents were more and more unhappy with my performance. I was paying too much attention to my social life. I had become involved with the American Youth for Democracy, a leftist student group. I would like to say that this involvement was for purely political reasons. But the fact is that my political commitment to A.Y.D.'s agenda was secondary. I was involved with them because they threw great parties.

I had joined Kappa Alpha Psi, a black fraternity, and it was taking up a lot of my time. My father became quite angry when he learned about my pledging the fraternity. He viewed himself as a man of the people, and that his son would join a fraternity meant that I must have become some sort of elitist. The arguments that began when I was younger had not stopped just because I was now a university student; if anything, they had become more intense. I tried to sort out the contradictions. We lived a comfortable life. I accompanied my parents to parties in large mansions, yet my father hung on to this fiction that he was a man of the people. But I always thought there was something else to his arguments against the fraternity. I always wondered if my father had been blackballed when he tried to join a fraternity at Howard. In any case I was facing a moment of truth aside from my tense relationship with my father.

I was also trying to understand why I felt such a constant sense of loneliness. Few people recognized it, but I'd felt loneliness from an early age. I had loving parents and a brother and sister with whom I was very close. I was gregarious. Popular, with guys and with girls, I had joined a fraternity and moved around easily in such groups as the A.Y.D. But the outward smile, the ready phrase, and the easy social skills masked the internal conversations in which this solitary loneliness was a dominant factor.

I felt that I had something distinct to offer the world, something unique, but I couldn't yet put my finger on what it was. I only knew that my outward personality hid a contemplative center that turned itself even more inward as I grew older. Few if any people knew it at the time, but inside I was confused, unfocused, disgruntled, smoldering. I knew I was capable of doing well at the university. I could read and think, put together ideas in coherent, inventive ways, study late into the night with the best of them. But I wasn't doing that. Instead I was asking the kinds of questions—internal questions—to which I did not yet have answers. Who was I? What did I stand for? Where did I fit in? What kind of messages was I getting from outside, and what did they mean to me?

I was smoldering with a kind of coming-of-age anguish inside. I asked myself, Do I really want to be a doctor? I recall how strong the feelings of uncertainty were. I remember the constant personal questioning. Should I explore the idea of writing? Do I want to be anything? Why am I feeling this pain in my soul and how do I alleviate it? So far, I didn't share these thoughts and feelings with anyone.

There seemed to be no one available for me to share them with. I wanted discourse, inquiry, and could not find it. This kind of doubt, contemplation, and insecurity is now where I believe people find elements of an artistic consciousness. I didn't know it at the time. Maybe I always had a special interest in the workings of the mind and soul and it was that interest that led me into psychiatry. I also had a desire to write and create, and that impulse came from the same place as the contemplative questions I was asking myself back when I was in my third year at UCLA.

•◆•

I needed a fresh start. I'd been born and raised in Los Angeles. So while UCLA was a terrific place and a great university, I'd become paralyzed, too conscious of the pull of my upbringing and my parents' influence on my daily actions, and so embarrassed by my own lackadaisical attitude that I couldn't manage. I needed a change, and it had to be a radical one.

My friend Byron Barker and I talked at length, and I explained to him the doubts I was feeling and the questioning that was going on in my heart. I met Byron when we were in the sixth grade and we had gone on to junior high school together. We were running buddies and sometimes cut our afternoon classes to go downtown to the Orpheum Theater to hear one of the big bands like Count Basie. I still remember the first time I saw Jimmy Rushing stand in front of the band and sing "Going to Chicago."

I didn't know it at the time, but I guess I opened up to Byron because I didn't feel that he was going to sit in judgment of me. Byron had gone to East L.A. Junior College for two years and then transferred to Berkeley. He recommended that I also transfer to Berkeley, which he described as being very different from UCLA. I wanted to know how it was different. Well, Byron replied, for one thing you won't be living at home and driving for over an hour to get to school. I know a place where we can live that is only a couple of blocks from the campus. For another, you won't have your parents telling you what to do.

I discussed the move with my parents. My mom gave me the okay. "Yes, Price, I think maybe you'll get a chance to find yourself." It was the first time she had ever indicated that she thought I was lost. She usually asked more questions about what I was doing, who I was dating and where I went. I felt that somewhere in my answers she obviously sensed some of my confusion and uncertainty. My father gave his okay too, but it was more reluctant. I think he wanted to talk more about this important move, but our relationship was too rocky and too volatile to risk much conversation.

I called Byron, made some arrangements through him for living accommodations, and informed my parents of my decision. I left UCLA at the end of my third year and transferred to the University of California at Berkeley.

CHAPTER SIX

Berkeley at night was exactly what I had hoped for and more. A walk down Telegraph Avenue on a warm autumn evening, the laughter from the cafés, lovers whispering at tables, a student reading Keats at the next, an argument at another between two bearded men as they picked apart some obscure doctrine, the smell of coffee and European cigarettes everywhere—it was just the change I needed. More important, I was away from home for the first time in my life. On my own. Free.

Byron and I would frequently walk down to Telegraph from the Methodist Co-op on Channing Way to enjoy an evening's conversation over coffee, or a beer. I was charged by the intellectual atmosphere of Berkeley. I was also excited by the new acquaintances I had made at the co-op, an interracial place where whites and blacks lived together with no apparent outstanding problems, and by the individuality that I was now able to express so freely. As a consequence, my grades began to improve. I was still pursuing premed as a major, and my studies were indeed moving along much better.

Among the many differences in being a student at UCLA and a student at Berkeley was that I was now living two blocks from the campus. We were all students in the co-op and on our own. I didn't have to explain myself to anyone when I came and went. In L.A., the commute home would have ended at my parents' house, the same end to the day that I had been experiencing since I was six years old. At the co-op, I had my own place and could do as I wished. This both invigorated me with new possibilities for my social life and also required me to assess the nature of my own responsibility to my studies. This was very liberating to me.

Also the co-op provided my first real, close, day-to-day experience of living with white students. There were six black men in all. Four of us were from L.A. and had known one another there, including Byron and his brother Ed, an army veteran, and Vernon Dancy, a high school classmate. There were two others from El Centro—plus about fifteen white men. It was still not the norm in this country to live in an interracial house. But in freewheeling, liberal Berkeley there was no particular risk to it. Living in that co-op was an instance of "pushing the envelope" racially, as we would say later. The white men were basically accepting, openhearted fellows who did not seem to carry the chip of white superiority on their shoulders. We watched TV and listened to the radio together, studied together, talked, and so on. The only real tension would come when we would get into the territory of what I called the "liberal orthodoxy."

This was a form of political thinking that was prevalent in Berkeley at the university, that today would fall under the rubric of "political correctness." There was an entire body of political thought, basically described as progressive (that is, to the left of the Democratic Party liberal wing) that was almost a doctrinal canon from which the faithful must not stray. It was received wisdom, I thought, and seldom questioned. Some would stray, mavericklike on certain points, although they were able to maintain their credentials in the orthodoxy. It appeared to me, though, that the price of admission for a black person in Berkeley for acceptance by the supporters of this orthodoxy was that you had to adhere to it 100 percent.

Whites in a political discussion were allowed to think things through a bit more, to deviate from the canon here and there, to argue and disagree. They were cut some slack. For example, one of the tenets of liberal orthodoxy then was that to work in corporations was somehow dishonorable and constituted a sellout of liberal ideals. Corporations were conservative and thus a Republican thing. One associated Republican ideas with slavish devotion to the making of money and the use of that money to corrupt political ideals. They were depicted as having little or no interest in either the working class or the poor. Republicans also appeared to have no interest in black people, spent no time currying their favor, and appeared to vote against most programs that were intended to bring blacks into the American economic and political fold.

I had no basic disagreement about where the Republican Party stood. It appeared to me, though, that corporate life was not necessarily "Republican" and, more important, that a black person who could enter that world could very much improve the economic situation for himself and his family. It was always the case that the student arguing against corporations was white and had many friends and relations who were in business who were corporate types themselves. These same students were often supported financially by corporations in the form of investments made for them by their families or simply by dint of the fact that their fathers were employed by such companies and were paying the bills. The orthodox liberal in this setting would be civil to his family, even loving, but mostly silent about their financial support. If you were a black person, however, and interested in business or other seemingly "unliberal" activities, you'd be castigated by the orthodox, isolated by them, and cast away. You were not allowed the same ideological breathing room as a white person had. More important, if the arguments were to be believed, it meant that blacks should cut themselves off from a major source of employment and a primary American avenue of building wealth.

Conversations with my father had allowed me to develop certain prisms through which to view all manner of received orthodoxies. I had already refined my own point of view toward a lot of the liberal orthodoxy: I disagreed with some parts of it and was in agreement on others. Mostly my disagreements stemmed from viewing most political issues and indeed the world through the lens of my experience as a black American.

Yes, that may work for you, I would say to myself as a white acquaintance would rail against money and property, reminding me of my obligation to tout all the liberal doctrines, no matter their specific practicality—or lack of same—for black people. I would think, But you really don't know much about the experience of black people in this country, and you really can't say with any authority that many of your liberal ideas are pertinent to black people. In fact, you know nothing of what the world is like for people who are not like you.

•-•-•

I had made the right move in choosing to live at the Methodist Co-op. For the most part, I found that the co-op provided an atmosphere where casual conversations could turn freely from bull sessions to arguments to debates, and that I could explore all manner of political and other themes simply through the medium of conversation. My disagreements made me acutely aware of the need to continue to refine my viewpoints. However righteous their intentions might be, viewing the world solely through a white lens just did not work for me and was intellectually shallow as well. On balance, however, Berkeley was great for me, and our talk would be fueled by beer and wine plus the large amounts of reading—in history, literature, the arts, science—that we were doing in and out of class. We had constant, complicated and noisy gatherings at which we'd discuss all kinds of things.

I arrived in Berkeley at a time when the cold war between Russia and the United States was a major focus of American political life. To make things worse China, our World War II ally, had gone over to the Communist side. A conservative California senator from nearby Oakland, William Knowland, was leading the fight to find out how this had happened, and scapegoats were being sought. He introduced to the debate the notion that forces in the United States—Communists, fellow travelers, and liberal Democrats—had somehow conspired in causing our country to "lose" China. So, along with many Americans we debated whether or not China had been "lost" to the Communists and, if so, how. This was during the buildup to the Korean War, which many Americans viewed as the place where we had to take a stand against the Chinese. So we debated Korea too.

TV at that time was still a new toy, and we watched it a lot. I recall sitting one evening watching the Arthur Godfrey show, when he danced with the great singer Pearl Bailey. Today, such an event would go unnoticed. Then it was revolutionary to have a white man dancing to "Balling the Jack" with a black woman before the eyes of millions. So we talked about that.

We worried about the "Red scare," where ambitious legislators were continuing to investigate so-called left-wing organizations. Both the Hollywood Arts, Sciences and Professions Council, of which my father was a member, and the American Youth for Democracy, in which I had been involved, came under investigation to determine whether they were infiltrated by Communists. Things were heating up and I feared that perhaps my father was in danger. (He had already came under the scrutiny of the Tenney Committee in the late 1940s and been named by the committee as a fellow-traveler to the Communist Party.)

A California congresswoman named Helen Gahagan Douglas was running as a Democrat for the U.S. Senate. My father knew Mrs. Douglas through his acquaintances in the entertainment business and his political contacts in the black community. She had been a stage actress and noted opera singer and was also the wife of the actor Melvin Douglas. Mrs. Douglas was truly tireless in her advocacy of liberal programs, pushing for price stabilization and rent control; as well as for the federal control of oil drilling and for protecting the voting rights of small farmers. She was a friend of Eleanor Roosevelt and John Steinbeck and had worked closely with the Farm Security Administration, to maintain the stability of programs that were intended to help family farmers. My father admired her a great deal, and so did I.

She ran for the U.S. Senate in 1950 against a Republican congressman named Richard Nixon. Nixon ran a famously ruthless campaign characterizing Mrs. Douglas as favoring the Communist line, if not actually being a Communist herself. He relentlessly pursued Mrs. Douglas with this tactic, remarking that she was "pink right down to her underwear." Whether or not the Communists were the evil that he painted them to be was secondary. Nixon had found a theme that appealed to California voters who were angry about the "loss" of China, the ascendancy of the Soviet Union under Joseph Stalin, and the combination of the two countries lined up against the United States. The campaign was a slugfest that was entirely unfair to Mrs. Douglas, and we discussed that. Most of my co-op mates were dead-set against Nixon, specifically because of his red-baiting tactics. Even those who may have had some mild feeling in favor of Nixon's policies felt that his treatment of Mrs. Douglas was unjust. I actually did a little work for Mrs. Douglas's campaign, participating in meetings now and then, passing out leaflets.

Nixon won that election and thereby launched one of the most conflict-ridden and far-reaching political careers of any American political figure in memory, for better or worse.

We also talked sports in these bull sessions. During the 1947 major league season, Jackie Robinson had learned the full truth of what Branch Rickey had warned him about the year before. There were many confrontations on the field in which he had had to put up with relentless hostility from fans and opposing players alike, who had no interest in having a black man play ball in the major leagues.

Jackie had even had trouble with some of his fellow Dodgers. Early in the 1947 season, a number of the players had objected to Robinson's presence on the team. Some of them—most notably a player named Dixie Walker—had demanded to be traded. They had come up with the idea of a petition that they would submit to the front office, protesting Robinson's presence on the team. Manager Leo Durocher was not the kind of man who felt that liberal-minded negotiation was appropriate in a case like this. At a team meeting, he addressed the protesting players.

"Well, boys, you know what you can do with that petition. You can wipe your ass with it. I hear Dixie Walker is going to send Mr. Rickey a letter asking to be traded. Just hand him the letter, Dixie, and you're gone. Gone! I don't care what color the guy is. I am the manager, and I say he plays."

It should be pointed out that Dixie Walker was no slouch as a player, and that getting rid of him could have hurt the Dodgers significantly. He played for eighteen seasons in the major leagues, was a five-time All-Star outfielder and had a lifetime batting average of .306.

Rickey himself called the dissident players on the carpet the next day. Chastised by Durocher and Rickey, Dixie Walker and almost all the other dissident players abandoned their protest. The one player who continued, a man named Higbe, was immediately traded to the Pittsburgh Pirates, at that time occupying the National League cellar.

"He'll put money in your pocket, boys," Durocher had said of Robinson to the team. He was right, of course. Jackie Robinson was named Rookie of the Year in 1947, a year in which the Dodgers won the National League pennant only to lose the World Series in seven games to the New York Yankees. By the time I got to Berkeley, Robinson was a star, and more black players were beginning to make their way into the majors. We debated this too.

·◆·

It was at the co-op that I also had long conversations with Ed Barker, a returning veteran of World War II. Like all the veterans in general, Ed was something special to the rest of us. These vets were older, most of them in their mid-twenties, and there was a sense of real adulthood in them, of experience. I wouldn't call it a swagger, because many of them had seen terrible things and were not at all arrogant about it. But they were exotic and worldly in ways that the younger students were not.

Like most black soldiers in World War II, Ed had been in the Army Engineer Corps, stationed after basic training at March Field near Riverside, California. During his time there, he told me, there had been an occasion on which many black soldiers had attempted to enter the base recreation club, which normally was reserved for white soldiers. The blacks were denied entrance, and a dispute resulted that soon became known as the March Field Riot. Some of the black soldiers broke into an ammunition/rifle storage area and armed themselves. Many of the rioting soldiers left the base and headed for Riverside. The riot was quelled, the soldiers rounded up, with several of them being incarcerated. Ed himself did not go to the brig. But within a week, all of the black soldiers on that base were prepared for overseas duty and shipped out.

They sailed on a segregated troop ship, bound for Fiji. This meant that all the black soldiers slept together in separate bunk quarters, ate separately from the white soldiers and sailors, exercised separately at different times during the day. There was no mixing on board the ship.

In transit, the ship was attacked by a Japanese submarine and went down. There had been little time to escape, chaos everywhere, the ship sinking very quickly. The sea was covered with oil and debris, dead men floating about, others—wounded and screaming—desperately trying to save themselves, holding on to pieces of wreckage, looking for any kind of safety as, shadowed beneath the rising smoke, they watched the ship go down.

Many died that day. Ed survived, having reached a life raft intended for eight people, to which fifteen other servicemen clung, white and black. They floated on the raft for two and a half days and were subsequently picked up by another ship and taken to safety. Ed returned to duty some time later, to the same segregated army.

When we lived together at the Methodist Co-op in Berkeley, I talked with him about his experiences. We'd be sitting on couches in the living room or sharing a cup of coffee in the kitchen, having cleaned up after an evening meal. I really wanted to know what the war had been like. The stories of actual combat that I had heard from black servicemen were mesmerizing. Almost as compelling were the stories that they would tell about the treatment they had received as servicemen from their own white countrymen and officers.

I wanted to know what that kind of regimented segregation had been like. Was the training the same for blacks and whites? Was it as good for the black soldiers, or were they shorted in their training because they were black and therefore presumably more expendable? Were they punished for stepping out of line in the same way that a black man in the South could be punished for doing something that a white man would do without a second thought? Were punishments different for the same offense, when committed by a black soldier and a white soldier?

I learned from Ed that he had been hospitalized for emotional reasons in San Pedro, California, after his rescue at sea. I was interested in knowing what those reasons were. I assumed that his hospitalization had to do with what he had experienced the day the ship went down, but it was difficult to get him to talk about the specific details.

Ed was one of those veterans who had difficulty speaking about what he had seen. The moment we would enter upon a discussion of his war experiences, he would grow tense. His demeanor would become hostile, his lips tight, his shoulders bowed in a kind of slump as though he were gathering himself to explode.

Ed would talk with little emotion about the battle experience itself and the sinking of his troop ship. But he *would* voice bitterness about the way he had been treated as a black man in his segregated unit: the conditions that resulted in the March Field Riot, for example, the fact that it was almost impossible to qualify for Officer Candidate School as a black man, the different treatment of black soldiers with regard to weaponry and ammunition, and how much—or whether—they would have access to such things, the fact that the black soldiers always had to build their own latrines, while white soldiers would more often find latrines built for them. He told such stories in the context of the equal danger that all soldiers were facing, no matter their race. The troop ship experience had brought that very specifically home for him. That day he had seen the true danger he was in, and his bitterness at the second-class treatment he had received—and continued to receive after his narrow escape from death—had grown into a rage that he had found difficult to control.

Ed had a highly developed sense of what we called "racial currents." Even in casual conversation, his focus would quickly turn to race. Black people talk race in part to let off steam and in that process to gain information to develop strategies for coping emotionally and physically with the dominant society. When the Swedish sociologist Gunnar Myrdal was conducting research for his groundbreaking book *An American Dilemma,* he correctly noted that in black settings, the talk inevitably turned to things racial. It's the sort of conversation that had enabled my mother to know where we could safely go on a Sunday drive or where for the night we could stop in Texas.

Ed was great to talk with about what it was like to be *black* and a pilot, *black* and a rifleman, *black* and a sailor. Ed talked about separation, discrimination, segregation, and the prejudice that abounded. He talked about these things with a laconic, bitter reticence, all experienced in the context of saving the world for democracy.

He understood that his life had almost been sacrificed for a country that greatly undervalued him. Much had crept into his gut that was *beyond* the carnage of war itself. He had trouble talking about the mayhem and death he had witnessed, but he had less difficulty talking with me about the context of racism within which he and the other black servicepeople had had to conduct *their* war.

Ed went on to become a respected and quite successful architect. But it was obvious then to me that he had suffered during his time in the service, and that the result was a black man who was feeling a good deal of pent-up and unresolved rage. I see now how important it was for me to have had those conversations with him, those times at the co-op, because he was one of the people in my life who literally gave me the concept of black rage.

• ◆ •

I took a creative writing course from Thomas Parkinson, a professor of English who was a noted poet and the first person to encourage me to pursue writing in a serious way someday. As in a majority of my classes, I was the only black person in the room. I had been writing stories— smallish vignettes about my family and life growing up in Los Angeles. Professor Parkinson offered me many strategies on how to shape a story, how to evoke a certain emotional response from the reader, how to add color and atmosphere.

What I liked about him most was that the differences between us as a white man and a black man seemed to present no problems. He understood what I was writing about and never made me feel that I was some sort of second-class artist because I was black. He treated me like a writer. Whatever my writing lacked, in his view, could be corrected with time and practice. He perceived a certain talent in me, and he treated me as though I were fully capable of developing that talent.

• ◆ •

There was another man we talked about at the co-op, a white man of the same order of saltiness as the Dodgers' Leo Durocher. This man was Harry Truman. It was he who finally acknowledged the contributions made by black people during World War II and every other war that the United States had fought. He gave an order—on July 26, 1948—Executive Order No. 9981, which ended discrimination in the United States armed services and helped make the civil rights movement itself possible.

When President Truman signed that order, he was insisting that the apartheid within the armed forces stop then and there. General Colin Powell, soon after retiring as chairman of the Joint Chiefs of Staff, gave a speech in 1998 at the National Legal Center for Public Interest where he pointed out that the president was no orthodox liberal. Or, as the general puts it, "Harry Truman was no raving integrationist." As a young man, Truman was in the Ku Klux Klan and frequently made use of the *N* word. He pointed out that the president's home state, Missouri, is a North/South border state and that, as a politician interested in winning and keeping office, Mr. Truman would have to respect if not espouse some southern views on black civil rights.

Nevertheless, Truman was also commander in chief of the armed services. He was very familiar with the many and varied points of view held by blacks about the important roles that could be played by black people in the military, even including the view of A. Philip Randolph, the respected head of the Brotherhood of Sleeping Car Porters. Randolph had said, "I personally will advise Negroes to refuse to serve, to fight, as slaves for a democracy they cannot possess and cannot enjoy." Mr. Truman seemed affected by the sentiment voiced by Mr. Randolph and by the many other people, black and white, who for many years, and to no avail, had decried segregation in the armed forces.

When we first read about Truman's order in the papers the day after he had signed it, my family and I were jubilant.

• ◆ •

During my time at UCLA and these first years at Berkeley, three enormous changes had been made that would have profound implications for all Americans. Jackie Robinson's entry into the big leagues in 1947, the *Shelley vs. Kraemer* Supreme Court decision on restrictive land covenants in 1948, and the signing of Executive Order No. 9981, also in 1948. I noted each event with a sense of deeply felt vindication, and I discussed all of them at length with my father and friends.

My father was pleased by the decisions, although they had come too slowly for his taste. There was still a large body of thought in the United States (even among many of the black civil rights organizations, like the NAACP) that true integration in American life would take some time and had to be carefully organized and prepared for. My father disagreed. "Freedom Now!" was the phrase he used. I thought that my father was being impractical, but not because immediate freedom was an unacceptable idea. Rather it seemed to me that he had not given enough thought to *how* freedom could be achieved now. There was a legal framework that had to be constructed, as well as bureaucracies that could manage such changes and agencies that would enforce the new laws and make sure that they were perpetuated.

But we agreed, at least, that these decisions were emblematic of profound changes taking place in the United States, and that, with them, there was more opportunity for black people to become fully vested citizens. The truth is that I thought these decisions were nowhere near *enough*. My personal, internal sense of unease and distress was, if anything, made more pointed by the decisions. Why *had* it taken so long for these things to happen? And really, why *should* we have to wait for the rest, beyond the time necessary to implement whatever laws were necessary as soon as possible? The rage that black people had felt, one of the more trenchant legacies of slavery, was fanned by these events.

The unrest, which had remained veiled behind the quite justifiable mask of caution that black people had been wearing for so long, was beginning to come out in the open. I would not have guessed the day I graduated from high school that any of these three events were at all near realization. Once they did come to fruition, I began to feel that there was much more to be gained, but I also remained filled with my own rage that so much resistance still remained.

But now there had been great changes. Suddenly it looked to me as though a door of opportunity was open before me, and I think that somehow I was not sure how to deal with this. That uncertainty was part of the self-questioning that I had been undergoing in school. I think that many of my contemporaries were having similar difficulties. Ironically, it could be said that the sudden release from so many restrictions left us dazzled by the possibilities and unsure of what to do next.

A few years after President Truman's signing of the executive order, I was called to the army draft. I had been living in Berkeley for two years, and although I could have gotten a student deferment, I decided instead to accept my draft notice and go into the army. There were various reasons. I was still receiving financial assistance from my father, and this was becoming a bone of contention between us. Although my grades had improved, he was impatient with the pace of my education. By this time I had been in the university system for four years, taking premed courses.

But I'd also been taking other courses not specifically included in the premed curriculum, and so was still a year, perhaps a year and a half, away from a bachelor's degree. We had been arguing about this. I thought that the armed services would enable me to support myself through the G.I. Bill, and I felt that that would alleviate some of the pressure that I was getting from my father.

There were also reasons of patriotism for my decision. I agreed that the second half of the "Double Victory" fought for by my brother, Prince, by Ed, and by all the other black veterans had not yet been won. Even though the president's executive order regarding segregation in the armed forces had been signed, and the recommendations were being implemented, the process was moving very slowly. It might take years for the changes to be implemented entirely. Nonetheless I *was* a citizen of the United States and felt a duty to fulfill my military obligation.

I was like almost every black person in that respect. The United States was fighting in Korea. Even though I did not relish the idea of going there, I felt the time had come for me to fulfill my obligation to my country, no matter the state of desegregation and no matter where they would send me.

So in late 1950 I informed my parents and the University of California that I was going to submit to the draft, and I found myself—just after New Year's Day 1951—on a bus to Fort Ord, California.

CHAPTER SEVEN

‑ⵔⵔ‑

Outside of a few moments of religious fervor during church services, I had never seen my mother cry. But standing on our front porch on Trinity Street, the day I left for the army, she did, and it made me realize that a turning point of a kind had been reached in my life, for me and for my parents. I was so excited by the prospect of going into the army—by the good-byes to friends, the last-minute round of visits and parties, and wondering what the army would bring—that I hadn't noticed how my leave-taking was affecting my mother. I was the baby of the family and there was a war going on in Korea. She had worried terribly when my brother, Prince, had gone off to the marines. Only seven years later, she was sending a second son off to another war.

When I saw her standing on the porch next to my proud and just as concerned father . . . when I saw her tears, I realized that this was an important juncture for me, a step into real manhood in which the consequences could be very significant, in which there could possibly be real dangers.

But I was still excited. For one, I felt that this was an opportunity to express my patriotism for my country. It was not just the wish to show my personal feelings for the United States. There was also my wish to disprove a bothersome suspicion that black people often have, that their commitment to their country is viewed by the white majority as insincere.

I felt that this country offered me and other blacks a broader canvas on which to sketch out our lives than was available to us in other countries. We're part of this country, and have been so since its inception. Anyone who would question the value of this country, and the broad opportunities it offered even to blacks, would be foolish. But I also saw that there was ignorance about us, resistance to us from the larger white majority, ambivalence about us, and hatred of us . . . all of it quite real, demonstrated, and palpable.

As a result, our unalloyed patriotism carried with it an undercurrent of anger. As if to say, "Damn it! Don't people see this? Why are people oblivious to this?"

•—•

After a short time at Fort Ord for induction, I was sent to basic training at Camp Roberts, near Paso Robles, California.

Basic training was completely integrated, the three main ethnic groups being white, black, and Hispanic. There is an irony in a situation like this. When the society "outside" is still segregated, the integration of the "inside" organization is a kind of "spot" integration, mix and match, that is more for bureaucratic appearance. Within the "integrated" barracks, we would still tend to congregate with our own: whites with whites; blacks with blacks; Hispanics with Hispanics. So, ironically, there was a kind of de facto segregation that we imposed upon ourselves.

The training itself was arduous. A lot of marching, running, calisthenics. Shooting guns. Classes. Digging holes. Teamwork. Yelling. Simply the learning of what to do in a combat situation. It was emotionally exciting and enervating in the same breath. You imagined engaging an enemy and, like a romantic hero, vanquishing him. But because you saw what modern weapons could do, you also worried about what would happen to you if he were to do the vanquishing.

It was here and later, at Fort Lewis in Washington, that I had my first real encounters on a day-to-day basis with the kind of white southern mentality that my father had told me about so often. To this day, I often associate the word *nigger* with hillbilly music, because it was during basic training that I heard a great deal of both being expressed or appreciated by the same working-class white southern recruits with whom I was sharing bunk space. Throughout basic training there were occasional scuffles between several of these white men and me as well as other blacks. The scuffles wouldn't last long. We'd be separated and a tense peace would be reinstated.

But the black recruits had no intention of putting up with any disrespect from our white counterparts. This was a new world. The services had been desegregated. We were the latest in a large number of blacks who for centuries had offered themselves for service, and there were no plans to let these white guys diminish our right to be there.

Having said this, I should also say that I don't think the level of aggressive institutional racism or mistreatment of blacks was all that high during my basic training. The whole experience was such a whirlwind of strenuous physical and mental activity, with one's emotions coming fast, high, and low, all at once, that most of us didn't have the time or energy to treat one another truly badly. To some degree in basic training there was a "we're-all-in-this-together" kind of understanding, in which our best chance of survival was to help one another.

The first real shock that I did encounter came after basic training when I arrived at Fort Lewis and was assigned to the Thirtieth Engineers Battalion. The shock was that I was to be part of an all-black unit. I had assumed that any unit to which I'd report would be integrated, as basic training had been. It was, after all, a full three years since President Truman's signing of the executive order desegregating the armed forces. So to find that whole battalions were still segregated came as a great surprise to me.

Reason dictates that such a monumental change as President Truman had authorized takes time. At the moment of its signing, the symbolic value of the executive order had created a euphoria that had masked the knowledge that there would be a process through which we would have to go before the thing was fully implemented. I'm sure that a good deal of my disappointment was a result of that initial euphoria. But I was not alone.

Many of the officers of this group were veterans of World War II who were Reserves and National Guardsmen called back to active duty because of the war in Korea. A number of them voiced opinions similar to that reported by Prince and my friend Ed, resentful of the fact that they had been called up to an "integrated" army that was not in fact integrated, asked to put themselves in harm's way once more under the same conditions that had prevailed before the president's order.

"Is this worth dying for?" was a question I heard on many occasions. "I can get killed for this?"

So the atmosphere in the unit was charged with a kind of smoldering rage that I had not expected. I understood it, though, because my own expectations were not being met. There was no question that I would still serve and still fight. But I had expected an integrated army too. The anger I felt was as palpable as those of the reserve officers, even though it did not come with the same full slate of previous military experiences that they had.

I couldn't figure this out. In basic training, I had heard many racist slurs from the white recruits, but no one had taken these people aside to set them straight. And now, on active duty, I was stuck in an all-black unit. Hadn't the United States Army gotten the word? I wondered. Or was the president's executive order being honored in the same spirit as that of the Emancipation Proclamation? Acknowledged with lip service, the rearrangement of a few laws to put a good face on things, but not much else? Coming from more-or-less liberal L.A., with a good portion of a major university education already completed, and feeling that I was quite capable of making my way in any circumstance, I was not prepared for this and not happy about it.

•◆•

But to be honest, the conditions were not all bad. For one, a good friend of mine from L.A., Frank Qualls, was in the same unit, and we spent a lot of time together. There was ample nightlife in Tacoma, Washington, and we took advantage of it as well as we could. We set about our training with the Thirtieth Engineers and tried to make the best of it.

It was at this time that I learned that my organizational skills and abilities with speech and writing could help me improve my own situation. I was at the bottom, a private in the army. But I'd been to code school at Camp Roberts and had found that I had an aptitude for Morse code. The fact was that listening to it reminded me of listening to music, so that it was easy for me to learn and master. So I applied for a company clerk's position, realizing that such a position could afford me a bit of breathing room—which a raw infantryman may not have—to pick and choose other situations for myself in the service as I went along.

I was accepted for that training, and went back to Fort Ord for a couple of months. When I returned to Fort Lewis, I learned that we were to ship out soon, not to Korea, but to Germany.

In 1951, Germany was still basically an occupied country. Forces from the United States, France, the United Kingdom, and the Soviet Union held an uneasy sway over the lives of the Germans. That "unease" had found its most vivid expression in the Berlin airlift of June 1948 to May 1949, when Allied planes had supplied food and fuel to West Berlin's populace after land access to Berlin had been cut off by the Soviet Union. We were happy not to be going to Korea, of course. But any notion that Germany was to be some sort of easy assignment was dispelled by the very real hostility that existed between our forces and those of the Soviets.

When we arrived in Germany, at a base near Stuttgart, I found that there was only one black officer in my new unit, and he was a warrant officer. The rest of the officers were all white. Also I discovered that because the enlisted men were all black, we were viewed by our officers as less qualified than other soldiers to perform the duties that *any* soldier would be asked to do. So we were treated with indifference, even with hostility. The training regimen, which should be ongoing and thorough for any military unit, was spotty for us. We were not given the respect that should accompany the responsibilities that a good soldier has to shoulder. Discipline was slack. The officers gave us the impression that they felt that black soldiers were the bottom of the military barrel, and that they—the white officers—would therefore serve their time and get out as soon as possible.

As a company clerk, you sit in an office and have quite a bit of contact with officers. I heard repeated language between our officers that suggested that the black soldiers were subhuman, somewhere between humans and monkeys. "These black boys just don't know what they're doing, do they?" There was the *coon* word, used liberally. The *nigger* word, used even more. Laughter at the comic idea of black soldiers actually being asked to perform tasks of any complexity. Evocations of *Amos 'n' Andy* and the stock blackface figures that caused such hilarity among whites. Imitations of those figures in conversation among white officers. These men seemed to feel that, because their troops were black, they (the officers) were somehow being punished for something. These stated opinions went back and forth among them as though I were not there. It was my first experience of something I had read about: the experience of a servant who is almost invisible to his master. I was a faceless clerk of no importance and no sensibility.

A large number of these officers had been enlisted men during World War II. Many of them had joined the reserves in order to get a second income. Also, many of them had been policemen in "civilian" life. The captain to whom I reported directly was a cop from Long Beach, California, with slightly more than a high school education.

Others were R.O.T.C. officers fresh from school, college boys with little experience of life who nonetheless treated us with unconscionable arrogance. All of them appeared to resent having been called to active duty and took their resentment out on us, as though we were some sort of bad hand of cards that the military had dealt to them.

I tried in innumerable small ways to fight back, although this was probably an ill-advised thing to do. An officer fresh from R.O.T.C., one day ordered me to pick up some cigarette butts, something I did, although with a demonstrated lack of enthusiasm. Another time I failed to salute one of these newly minted officers, and he called me on it. I did salute him then, but it was not a true salute and had little of the respectful snap that such a gesture should have. The fact is, it was disdainful.

Later, I thought to myself, That sort of thing will get you in trouble, Price. Don't fuck up like that. Don't do that again. But I *did* do it again, out of anger and frustration, many times. I avoided serious trouble because I became so adept at walking the thin line that disgruntled black people have always walked in the United States. Their civil disobedience has frequently been shown through the slowing of task work, by performing tasks with just enough verve to get the thing done eventually, but not necessarily completely to the white person's specifications. They have understood just how far you can push a white person before angering him and thus getting yourself in real trouble. These are time-honored

talents on the part of black people, deceptions and illusions that have allowed black people to fool the oppressor for hundreds of years. They're a
real and valued form of protest.

So with all this, I had to bide my time and bite my tongue. I filed,
typed, sorted, and shuffled papers, unable to stand up for myself or my
fellow black soldiers because of my dutiful respect for the army's line of
command and the knowledge that I was simply an enlisted man. I took
all these white men's ill-considered remarks, slights, and insults in silence.

But all day long, most days, I was pissed off. What the hell did they
think I was doing there if not to serve my country? I was once more in a
situation, as I had been in elementary school in L.A., when the poor, un-
educated white southern kids, newly arrived in L.A., had used the last
weapon at their disposal to underscore their "superiority" to me and my
black friends: they were white and we were black. However, in the U.S.
Army, unlike in school, if I didn't like the treatment, there was nothing I
could do about it.

Each of those remarks from the white officers entered into my consciousness like a salvo, but a salvo that did not explode. I absorbed them,
along with the knowledge that the "desegregated" armed forces appeared, at least to my eyes, to be a sham. I kept a tight lid on the anger
growing within me.

Stifled anger comes to flame slowly because it is kept in the dark, away
from the air and the flash point that clear air provides. So it heats in the
darkness. It grows. And the trouble is that, once it does flash, it can be
quick and quite violent. The rage that each of these comments caused
and festered in me was to remain silent for many more years until I saw
it come out in others, in people like me on college campuses and in Viet-
nam and on the streets of major U.S. cities. For the moment, though, I
put a damper on the rage, attempted to reason it away, and kept it quiet.

I should reiterate that in 1951, West Germany and West Berlin were at
the front line of the resistance to the Soviet Union. So our units were in
a conceivably dangerous place where a war could break out at any time.
A very big war. I knew that I was a good soldier, potentially a fine soldier,
and that the same was true for all the others in my unit. However, given

the level of hostility that my unit was getting from its white officers, and the lax discipline and practices that resulted from their lack of interest and leadership, I concluded that, if this were an indication of the true quality of the "integrated" army's commitment to its own personnel, we were going to be in a lot of trouble if any war occurred.

•‑•‑•

My friend Frank Qualls had an accounting background and was in charge of keeping track of battalion finances. This was an important position for an enlisted man, and one of his duties was to take financial reports to battalion headquarters every day. So he had a fair amount of mobility. As a company clerk, I had access to jeeps, and anyone who has been there knows that one of the most important commodities available to any soldier was transportation. So ... . Frank and I got to see a lot of Germany.

This was a mixed blessing.

Even with the level of devastation it had suffered, Germany remained a very beautiful country. We traveled to many towns, spending a good deal of time in beer halls, cafés and clubs, doing quite a bit of sightseeing. The experience was very special for both Frank and me because neither of us had ever traveled outside the United States before. For that matter, we had not traveled a great deal within the United States either. So the fun of seeing old-world châteaus and palaces, of hearing a language so different from our own, learning to understand it and trying to be understood in our own language, led to a kind of bracing exhilaration in our hearts. Also, at least in the beginning, we felt free of the fetters that so often proved such a pain in the neck in our own country ... its racism, the suspicious looks of white people almost everywhere you would go, the need to scout things up ahead with meticulous care. We *were* notable for being black, and would be pointed out by Germans from time to time, more as a novelty, it seemed to us at first, than as a threat. European culture—German culture—was a thrilling novelty to us. It was riveting to discover that the way we led our lives was not the *only* way to lead them.

We also saw the devastation that had come to Germany as a result of World War II. There were still ruins, and large sections of cities were still being rebuilt. I had not known how to think of war until then, not having seen what it does to a society, a landscape, a city. But now I was coming to realize that war was indeed a very serious matter from which extreme devastation would be the result.

Seeing those ruins gave me a much deeper understanding of what I was there in Germany to do, ultimately, if war were to come. There would be ghastly battles. Refugees. Vast fields of dead civilians and, I well understood, dead soldiers. Even more devastation. And I would be on the front line of this fighting war, not just a witness to it. I would be a full participant in the full fury of it. So the excitement of travel was tempered by the realization that Germany was very far from being a safe place.

After a while, however, Frank and I began to encounter some of the elements of our own world. During our sojourns through the cities and countryside, we began to hear the muttered phrase that became so familiar to us: *"schwarze soldaten."* It's an innocent appearing couple of words: "black soldiers." But the manner in which they would be uttered would give them all the weight that we'd grown used to in the United States when a white person would use the word *nigger.*

Many of the Germans were quite civil to us, but just as many voiced the same anger that we had encountered on a daily basis in the United States, hostility to us that was caused only by the fact that we were black. Most of the black soldiers turned a blind eye to the insulting ways that Germans had of noting our presence. But there were occasional confrontations—in a café, on a market street, in a bar or club—in which a fight would break out. I was involved in a few of these minor scuffles, aggravated shoving matches and so on. When I would complain about them to my commanding officer—the same white captain from Long Beach—he would advise me to forget about the insult, to let that alone, as he put it. Race as a reason for complaint was exempted, and my captain colluded with the Germans—a people whom we had defeated—in making sure that that was so.

I was reminded of a story we had heard from one of the returning black veterans from World War II, a man who had had a hand in guarding German prisoners being held in the United States during the war. On occasion, some of those prisoners would be allowed to attend movies in a public theater in the town nearby the prison compound. Descending from the army bus in which they would be transported from the camp, the prisoners would be allowed to enter the theater and sit down in seats on the main floor. Black American servicemen serving at the same camp would not be permitted on the main floor of the theater but instead would have to sit in the balcony, segregated from the white soldiers and the German prisoners. It was simply an outrage to us to learn that German prisoners could receive preferential treatment not available to blacks in the armed services.

In Germany, when my commanding officer would tell me to "let that alone," he made it clear that he did not believe we as black American troops deserved the respect of the Germans whose safety we were helping protect. I felt, in effect, we were being shunted into the balcony again. I could end up dying for these people, but I couldn't expect to be treated with respect by them, and could not expect to be backed up by my own officers.

I absorbed this frustration in the same way that I had absorbed the disparaging remarks made about black troops by our own officers. The rage within me continued to grow. The worst of it was that, as company clerk only a couple of semesters short of college graduation, I would often be approached by other enlisted black soldiers who had had similar experiences, and asked what to do about them. Should they appeal to the army inspector general? Should they complain that they weren't being supported by their officers, that they were Americans and were getting treatment from their officers and from German nationals that white Americans would simply not stand for?

I counseled these men to just suck it up and leave that alone, realizing that their complaints would get them nowhere just as such complaints would get me nowhere. Despite the legitimate gripe that we had as black soldiers, saying something about these conditions would probably just get us into trouble, label us as malcontents or, we feared, as "Communists."

At the time the label of "Communist" was truly an ugly one. The Army-McCarthy hearings were soon to come, in which a U.S. Senate committee chaired by Senator Joseph McCarthy of Wisconsin was to accuse the armed services of harboring Communist spies that were giving military secrets to the Soviets and the Red Chinese. The charge was never proved, and McCarthy was eventually disgraced. But there was an atmosphere in the United States during the time I was in the army in which "red-baiting" was an acceptable practice when dealing with left-wing organizations or individuals. It was also an acceptable practice when trying to stifle all forms of racial protest. So for a soldier in the U.S. Army to be called a "Communist" would be a very serious accusation indeed.

The irony for me personally—an irony that I understood at the time, yet stuffed into my gut with all the other resentments that I was beginning now very much to feel—was that I was parroting my own commanding officer, a man for whom I had no respect at all.

In Europe I came in contact with a blues singer in a most unexpected way. I had some time off, and among the places I traveled several times to was Zurich and Lucerne, Switzerland. Lucerne was a medieval city and unlike anything I had ever seen, with its board-and-batten houses hundreds of years old, the famous Chapel Bridge, and of course the Alps in the clear-aired distance. The Swiss seemed more tolerant than the Germans, and Lucerne was certainly a different kind of place than Stuttgart. The sights were so unique to me and—the ambiance of the place so old-European and unspoiled—that I liked it from the start.

I went out one evening to the Club Metropole in Zurich, a jazz nightclub that I had heard about from a taxi driver. To my astonishment, an advertisement announced that the blues singer Joe Turner was to appear that evening. I was very excited because I figured this would be an opportunity to see the great Turner once again, to revisit the excitement I'd seen at the *Jump for Joy* concert in L.A. more than ten years before.

I was disappointed, however, to find that this Joe Turner was not the same Joe Turner I had seen in Los Angeles. An American black man, this Joe Turner had been living in Zurich since the end of World War II and was married to a Hungarian woman. I didn't have to listen to him for too long, though, before I realized that he too was a fine musician and could also sing the blues. I was so enthused about hearing this great music again that I approached the bandstand at the end of Joe's first set.

He turned out to be a very friendly man, and we talked a lot during that break. He asked me if I could sing, and I told him that I did not, at least professionally.

"Yeah, but *can* you sing?"

"Well, I think I can," I replied.

To my astonishment, he asked me to sing a blues for the patrons of the club. So I stepped up to the microphone and, accompanied by Joe on piano, sang "Goin' to Chicago." There was reasonable applause, although I was under little illusion that I had anything close to Joe's own talent. But he encouraged me. He invited me to come back to the club and told me that he'd teach me how to sing the blues.

Over the next few days and several other visits to Zurich, I studied with him and found that I did have ability as a singer. Joe continued encouraging me and suggested that we could actually work together. There was money in this, Joe said. "You've got real talent," he said. I became so enthusiastic that I quickly found myself entering a career crisis of a sort. Joe was telling me that I had a future as a professional jazz singer. The prospects for this were so attractive that I began to make the kind of emotional accommodation that allows one to enter upon such a change even when there are many elements, strong elements, standing against it.

In my case, there were my father and my mother, to whom I had written about my newfound career goal. They wrote back quickly, explaining that they expected me to return to Berkeley after my time in the service and to go on to medical school. This was an expectation that had never been questioned. The life of a jazz singer stood more or less in opposition to such a goal, and my parents added that singing jazz was not a "respectable" profession for someone with my talents, or for someone who was a son of theirs.

Meanwhile, Joe continued telling me that I had a future, and I truly wrestled with the conflict for some weeks. But in the end I knew my parents were right. On my next visit to Zurich, I had to inform Joe that my previous goal, to be a physician, was the one to which I felt truly closest. As much as I loved the music, I sensed that I would love medicine and what I could do with that profession even more.

• ◆ •

My experience of the army brought to a fine point my understanding that, despite being raised in L.A., despite my parents' professional upbringing and demeanor, despite my own university background, I was still a black man.

I realized that white soldiers suffered from rank and arbitrary treatment as well. But it was clear to me that the mistreatment they suffered was part and parcel of the military experience. It had to do with the discipline and order that is necessary to maintain a military organization. What we blacks were getting was different. It had little to do with military preparedness and a great deal to do with racism against black Americans. Having such an understanding, I felt my gut beginning to churn with real outrage.

The invisibility I experienced when I was a company clerk accentuated the kind of loneliness that I had felt as a student. This was not a melodramatic, precious, self-pitying loneliness, but rather it was a sense of trying to figure out where I fit into this larger group, this army, and this society.

It was a question of trying to a find a niche, a place from which I could conduct my life most profitably. But as I searched for this among my travels in Germany and Switzerland, the experiences I had with my good friend Frank Qualls, and the thoughtless racist brickbats being thrown around my office by the white officers, I found myself more often than not keeping my own counsel. I engaged in a lot of internal dialogue, asking myself whether I should attempt to complain about the lack of integration in this "integrated" army; whether I should confront the officers who called the men in their units "niggers" and "coons"; whether I should or should not pick up cigarette butts when ordered to do so. Should I endanger my standing in the army by performing such a protest? Would anything of value really be served by doing so? Should I start a protest movement? In these dialogues, I would play my own devil's advocate. I think really that they were part of an attempt to get closer to my own identity: as a soldier, as an American, as a man, as a black man.

Ironically, because of court decisions in the United States that were beginning to put aside Jim Crow laws, and because the experience of World War II had reoriented so much of black people's thinking, I felt that avenues for real complaint were slowly beginning to open. It would be dangerous to stride down these avenues while a private in an all-black unit in Germany during the "red scare" years. But at least I felt that those avenues were there. Simply *because* they were there, the rage I felt was beginning to be more acute. I sensed that the possibility for expression would someday cause the rage to be expressed.

I now feel that I was fortunate to go through the army experience, serve without getting into trouble, and receive my honorable discharge in December of 1952 without being court-martialed. There are many ways to rebel in military situations without getting caught at it and punished for it. I did serve honorably, but I probably exercised all these rebellious options in some way or another, enough to satisfy my own wish for self-expression, but not enough to get myself thrown out of the service altogether. Basically, I used my intelligence to thwart the system while at the same moment taking advantage of it.

I was discharged from the army a different man from the one who entered. As a black private, later promoted to corporal, I had been on the lowest rungs of the ladder. The treatment I had received from the white officers had galvanized in me the notion that I was never going to be on the bottom of the ladder again. When I arrived back in California, I was more than ready to return to Berkeley and to get very serious about my studies. I was going to medical school, and there was to be no question about it.

CHAPTER EIGHT

I could tell immediately how proud of me my father was when I told him I'd been accepted to medical school. He glanced at my mother, whose own face was taking on a very affectionate smile, extended his hand across the dinner table and took mine, shaking it with real enthusiasm and a glow in his eyes for both of us that was very unusual. This serious man, with whom, yes, I had argued over politics many, many times, was still the one man I respected more than any other. I very much wanted to go to medical school, and to know that I had the emotional backing of such a respected physician who also happened to be my father meant a great deal to me. His only disappointment, if it could even be said to be a disappointment, was that I had been accepted in Meharry Medical College in Nashville, Tennessee, rather than Howard University Medical School, his alma mater. I had applied to other medical schools: Howard University and the University of British Columbia in Canada. I heard from Meharry first and immediately accepted.

Meharry had been founded to train former slaves and the children of former slaves in the medical sciences. It remains today a highly respected center of learning and research, the oldest private institution in the United States for the education of black health professionals. Founded in 1876, the college's initial individual contribution came from Samuel Meharry, a white man who had been befriended by a black family as a boy. Meharry had promised that one day he would assist institutions that would enable black people to further their higher education in the sciences.

Meharry was also one of the most prestigious medical schools in the country, and a degree from this school carried significant weight. Forty percent of all black physicians in the United States had gotten their degrees from Meharry at that time. Only Howard graduated more black physicians every year.

When I arrived on the campus in Nashville in the fall of 1954, Meharry was an elite black enclave in Nashville. The students and staff were all well educated, and there was a sense of being favored simply by virtue of having been accepted there. I understood the opportunity that presented itself. Like all the students I was now meeting, I felt that acceptance to Meharry was a key to success, and that the opportunity should under no circumstances be wasted. There was an air of intensity among the students, as well as the sense that we were something special, that we had some kind of mission to fulfill. We were the elite, the medical students.

Not everyone in Nashville felt the same.

Los Angeles, with its relatively benign treatment of black people, was a long way off; Nashville, as my father would have put it, was the "old country." Discovering the South was always to be a revealing experience for me, often disconcerting, sometimes scary, and frequently quite angering. But it was another part of the same country, so I understood the basic rules of the game. And right from the beginning, I uncovered substrata of experiences in Nashville that were completely new to me.

You had to remain aware of where you could sit on the bus. But, the rules were not as rigid as in other parts of the South such as Montgomery, Alabama. Nashville had a softer attitude toward its black population than did other cities in the Deep South. There was a more nuanced treatment of black people there, although one had to keep in mind at all times that it *was* nonetheless a southern city.

When you got onto the bus at Meharry, you were in a black neighborhood. As you got closer to downtown, more and more white people would get on the bus, and they'd have first choice of certain banks of seats. So if there were many blacks on the bus at first and no whites, available "white" seats would remain empty, while many of the black passengers would remain standing. I did not like this arrangement, but I acquiesced to the advice I got from my fellow students. "You're in the South now, Price. We do things differently down here."

Arriving downtown, I'd walk around with my fellow students and no-tice other basic differences. Eye contact, for example. There wasn't quite the same directness of eye contact across racial lines as there would have been in L.A. Rather, I would be expected to look at white people in a more circumspect, a more "respectful" way. Also, people talked with me differently in the South. There seemed to be an unspoken requirement of deference that I was to pay to white people when I spoke with them. Of course, I had been raised in L.A. to speak politely with everyone. Here, though, I would have to think much more strategically before replying to anyone.

We were all young, so there was nothing unusual for me in being ad-dressed by new acquaintances with my first name. But there was a certain *way* in which I'd be addressed by white people in Nashville, which car-ried the suggestion of a patronizing status, a dismissiveness in the tone of it. A downturn at the end of the word, maybe. Something subtle in that first-name usage that would nonetheless convey to me the certainty that "Goddamn it, I'm never going to call you *Mister* Cobbs, much less *Doctor* Cobbs."

One day early in the semester I joined several of my classmates on a trip downtown to do some shopping. I needed several shirts and a desk lamp. One should recall that in those days you had to do a bit of scout-ing ahead when you went shopping in the South. You had to make sure who would take your business and, as important, how you should act in each of those stores. In Nashville, I was told, if clerks could determine whether you were a student at Meharry, they'd usually be more solicitous of your business, because your presence at that institution meant you had money. So we could shop in those stores, where they'd gladly let us spend our cash.

In those days, men's shirts were mostly sold loose, not in packages. So men could try on a shirt before they bought it. Some men, that is. We'd seldom be allowed to try anything on before the purchase, even though we may have noted that there were customers who were being allowed to do so. Those were, of course, white customers. If I had inadvertently tried on a shirt in a store that would sell it to me, but would not allow me to check it out first, I could be forcibly removed from the premises. There could be a lot of insults, maybe even shouting and recrimination. And the sullied shirts would have to be thrown away.

I got this kind of orientation to the local customs from my classmates. My personal attitude, honed in California, was that if a store didn't want me to try on their goddamned shirts, they could keep them, and I'd shop somewhere else.

Nevertheless, we arrived downtown, got off the bus, and started walking down the main shopping street one day. The other students were like me, young men joking around, making fun of one another with a lot of humorous talk as we walked along. They were medical students, intelligent and quick-witted. I was already reveling in the sophisticated verve being shown by my fellow first-year students, happy to be a part of the group. We were all dressed well, making sure that others seeing us on the street would understand that we had a certain favored status.

Suddenly I heard a shout from across the street. I looked around at two white policemen who were sitting in a squad car on the premises of a gas station, looking at us.

"Hey, you!" one of the policemen yelled, beckoning toward us. No names. No politesse. Just "Hey, you!" His voice had a kind of clanging authority in it. He wanted our attention and he wanted it now. But he clearly did not think much of us.

"Hey, hey!" he yelled again, beckoning toward us. "Yeah! You!" We immediately crossed the street toward the policemen, and I felt a change in attitude in all of us as we trudged toward him.

To be sure, I would not have reacted in L.A. to such a challenge in any way that would get me in trouble. The police were the police, no matter where. But in this case, there was a radical shift in body language, speech, and demeanor in all of us. I knew immediately that in L.A. I would be "one-down" in a confrontation like this. But right away it seemed to me that, here in Nashville, I was "two-and-a-half-down." In Mississippi I'd probably be "four-and-a-half-down." Or "five." Nonetheless I thought, Well, who the hell are you, to be yelling at us like that? But I too crossed the street, stifling the urge to show my anger at the cop's rudeness.

As it happens, we were not really the object of the policeman's ire. He simply wished to ask us whether we had seen some character who had been involved in a street altercation a few minutes before. But as he asked the questions, I noted how guarded the tone of voice in my companions had become. The cool, blasé demeanor that they'd demonstrated just a moment earlier, the almost elegant arrogance, had suddenly disappeared. I looked around and saw obsequious and even frightened young men standing around me. The previous masks had been shed and this new one adopted, magically, instantly, and to me, shockingly. I'd never seen anything quite like this change before. Their shoulders were sloped. They were having trouble looking the cop in the eye. In L.A. I would have been able to converse with a cop in such a situation, to look at him and to expect that he would acknowledge me, although I would have to exercise a certain caution, to be sure. But I would not have reacted with the body language of servility that the southern students were exhibiting in this moment.

We were suddenly put in a very specific role to which I was not accustomed, that of blacks in the South. I could feel the restriction that was as much acceded to by us as it was placed upon us. There was a long history of relationships between black people and white people in the South that was being played out here. I had experienced similar confrontations in my life, but seldom with the overt, aboveboard acknowledgment of those relationships as on this occasion.

One thing that was common to all of us on that day, though, no matter where we were from, was the sense of shared anger that we felt at being summoned so summarily by that cop, questioned in a way that showed so little respect for us, and dismissed without another word. We talked about it afterward, and stored the memory of it away.

In my case, it got stored in the same emotional chamber that was harboring my memories of being called a "nigger" by the kid across the street when I was six, of not ever being permitted to enter certain parts of L.A. without a demonstrable reason for being there, the dismissal of my presence by the other students while decorating the floats at U.C.L.A., my treatment by the white officers in the army, and innumerable other such incidents throughout my life and the lives of my family and all my acquaintances.

I later bought the shirts I needed and did *not* try them on before doing so. That purchase, the conversation with the policeman, and the shock I felt at the sudden change in my friends' behavior would augment the other memories, that I was to discover some years later were even then fueling a simmering rage.

•-•-•

As that first year in Nashville unfolded, I made more observations about the South. There was a *very* distinct boundary between black people and white people. That was without question. The way in which that boundary was negotiated was of great interest to me. I saw both cruel hostility and remarkable friendliness between blacks and whites, and the subtleties of the treatment of one group by the other, and vice versa, had an almost endless variety.

There was always a tension, however masked. But there was also a kind of intimacy between the whites and the blacks, although that connection seemed most understandable to me as one between "masters" and "servants." I assumed that this almost familial intimacy was based on centuries of familiarity with each other and the roles that had been established during the time of slavery, then modified to acknowledge what had happened during the Civil War and afterward. Perhaps the connection was based as well in a secretive and quite emotional way—on the clandestine intermingling of races that had taken place throughout this long period. The shared sexual experience. The recognition on the part of both groups that the separation between them was by no means genetically total. I wasn't the only one, I'm sure, to realize that a lot of the white people in Nashville had features that were similar to those of black people. And of course there were ample numbers of light-skinned African Americans who were "black people" but whose ancestors had quite obviously included a white person or two.

The separation was by no means emotionally total, either. I witnessed numerous instances of kindness and regard between whites and blacks. The simple occurrence of being at the Nashville airport one day, for example, and witnessing the leave-taking of a black nanny, going to visit members of her own family somewhere, and the quite genuine affection for her being shown by the white man and woman and their family who had driven her to the airport. There was the exchange of hugs and kisses, the very real wish that she travel safely, and the genuine anticipation of her safe return.

I found, early on, that I was quite different from a good many of my southern classmates. The episode with the cop during my first days in Nashville had rather suddenly pointed this out to me. For one, I seemed always to be identified, with good humor, as "the guy from California." I was always too much wanting to raise the issues in some encounter or other, to discuss the situation, while many of my classmates would take a more conservative point of view.

"What's wrong with you, man?" a fellow student would say. "That's just the way it is down here, don't you get it?"

This was a view that I personally felt was dictated by resignation or denial. I recall now Henry David Thoreau's famous remark, "The mass of men lead lives of quiet desperation. What is called resignation is confirmed desperation." I'm not so sure that we're talking about confirmed desperation here. But I felt that many of my classmates restricted themselves to a simple acceptance of the status quo that had existed for so many years in the South. Perhaps my more eclectic upbringing, with much more day-to-day involvement with white people, made such resignation an impossibility for me.

• ◆ •

There was also conflict among the black people at Meharry, although it had little to do with the racial climate itself in Nashville. Rather it came from a kind of class expectation and jealousy.

In the first two nonclinical years, there were many instructors on the staff who were not M.D.'s . . . teachers with degrees in various kinds of science: biologists, biochemists, physiologists, and so on. Many of these people had themselves applied to medical school and not been accepted. I sensed from the beginning a resentment that I felt was based on our probable future. We were going to be M.D.'s and therefore, these instructors assumed, going to make a lot more money and would be able to advance ourselves much further than they had. So I felt discriminated against by them, and from time to time punished for my presumably favored status, as though they were saying, "All right, I'm going to take you down a peg or two, my friend."

The curriculum was one thing, and it presented us with significant difficulties. But those were acceptable problems, simply a matter of the rigor of study and the sheer amount of information we needed to absorb in order to become physicians. But the offhand and often hostile attitude of some of the instructors made me feel resentful. Again, I was less accepting of this than the others and occasionally rose up to argue, thus reconfirming that I *was* some kind of "California guy." It was known, moreover, that I was from freewheeling Los Angeles, and there was also the assumption on the part of some of these people that I personally needed to be taken down a further peg for that as well.

I want to emphasize the importance of the stakes for me the day I entered Meharry. In 1954, something like 90 percent of black physicians in this country had gotten their medical degrees from either Meharry Medical College or Howard University. Being in one of those medical schools, you were indeed considered the crème de la crème. In those days, big business was not open to blacks. As I've mentioned there were only a few professions open to us. So once having gotten into medical school, actually becoming a physician was a very high-pressure economic and social endeavor. Those instructors jealous of our money-making potential were actually right, to a degree. If I can get through this, I'd say to myself, I may still have to be on the segregated bus, but I sure as hell won't have to sit on the backseat!

This pressure could further exacerbate the difficulties between the students and the staff, particularly from the student's point of view. Indeed, and most shockingly, at Meharry over the years there had been a couple of professors killed by disgruntled students who had failed a course or a curriculum. You can imagine the mind-set of a person who thinks to himself, All of my dreams were wound up in the idea that I was going to get through medical school and I was going to be a big guy in Athens, Georgia, or Chicago or L.A. And you're flunking me out? There's no way you're going to flunk me out! I knew a physician in L.A., a contemporary of my father, whose own father had been a professor of medicine at Meharry and had been killed by just such a disgruntled, failing student.

I have an acquaintance who did flunk out of medical school forty years ago and has worked ever since as a medical technician in a hospital system in L.A. There's nothing wrong with that job on the face of it. But I can imagine the crushing emotional defeat that he must have felt the day they asked him to leave school. I and my family would have regarded it as a profound failure.

In any case I developed the strategy that I should keep my nose to the ground and my ass covered at all times. I was never certain how my instructors would react to me, the guy from California. Their reaction could often be capricious with regard to who flunked and who passed, what kind of grades you got, how much advancement you could make. My solution was to work unobtrusively and hard, and to get through it as quickly as possible.

• ◆ •

There was less conflict now between me and my father. My angry, noble-sounding remarks of accepting no money had been conveniently set aside. I was still receiving money from him, although the amount was somewhat less because I was also on the G.I. Bill. The relief of the financial strain allowed him to relax a bit. I knew that he was happy. This was one of the goals he had had for his children, and I was the one to follow in his footsteps as a physician.

My father wanted me to be a surgeon. But I had been thinking, since my first years at Berkeley, about the possibility of psychiatry. I had read the work of Sigmund Freud, and what I admired most was his ability to put words and imagery around human feelings. He opened my curiosity and made it possible for me to better understand how people truly functioned.

There were other writers as well, some whose work may not have been specific to the study of psychiatry, but whose insights into human emotions and, sometimes, emotional dysfunction, influenced me as well. W. E. B. DuBois was one. In *The Souls of Black Folk,* he wrote, "Herein lie buried many things which if read with patience may show the strange meaning of being black here in the dawning of the Twentieth Century. This meaning is not without interest to you, Gentle Reader; for the problem of the Twentieth Century is the problem of the color-line." I had thought about this a great deal and had wondered how this central question would affect the individual soul of individual black patients. As a teenager, one day my father kept me out of school so I could meet Dr. DuBois. At that time he was the most famous person I had ever met, and I tingled with anticipation. Yet the most impressive thing about him was that he was interested in me. He wanted to know what I was reading, what my thoughts were about various issues, and even whether I was interested in girls.

I was also influenced by the crazy uncle in Laurence Sterne's *Tristram Shandy;* Booker T. Washington's *Up from Slavery;* James Baldwin and his explorations of the alienation of contemporary young blacks in urban situations; Ralph Ellison's *Invisible Man,* in which the unnamed main character's sense of his own invisibility fans his ultimate rage into flames of self-expression; Richard Wright's *Native Son,* in which Bigger Thomas is backed into a corner by the racism that has determined much of his life and the personal responsibility for what his own explosive rage has led him to do. These writers had further fueled my efforts at self-discovery that had surfaced at U.C.L.A. and Berkeley, the questions I had been asking myself about where I fit in and how I fit in. They helped me think about questions of the soul and its meaning; questions that I felt the study of psychiatry would open up even further to me.

While at Meharry, I began to wonder what differences race and ethnicity made in the treatment of patients. Could you really effectively treat a black schoolteacher from L.A., a white Anglo-Saxon protestant patient from rural North Carolina, a Chinese-American patient from San Francisco, or an Eastern European Jewish-American patient the same and have good results? There were baseline understandings of human behavior, human motivation, issues and challenges that I knew to be common to all patients. But it didn't appear to me that there could be one psychotherapeutic model that fit all.

I thought that as a psychiatrist it only made sense to exercise a certain artfulness and consider the unique cultural context of each one of them, be it religious, racial, gender oriented, economic, or whatever. All of that would help me understand the patient. But I'd really have to listen to them. To keep my judgments open, and listen, listen, listen.

One day during the summer of my second year at Meharry, I was back in California on vacation. I was driving with my sister, Marcelyn, up the San Joaquin Valley to San Francisco, to inquire about a possible internship at San Francisco General Hospital. As we were driving, Marcelyn suddenly began acting in a way that I had never seen before. She was hearing voices, responding to them out loud, as though suddenly she were in some place other than the car in which we were riding. I drove on, glancing at her, trying not to be panicked by her behavior as she appeared to be having a complete psychotic episode. She acted as if I was not there. Even when I spoke. When I spoke to her, she did not respond. The voices in her mind were stronger than mine, and she lost herself to them.

We came up on a drive-in hamburger joint off the highway where I was able to stop the car. We were near the town of Modesto on Highway 99. But fundamentally we were isolated in the middle of nowhere. The San Joaquin Valley was entirely agricultural then, and I did not know what to do. I sat quietly and watched my own emotions become a riot of fear and waited for Marcelyn to come back to herself. It was one of the most terrifying moments of my life.

Once she settled down, we set out again. But the shock of the event, and the worry that another would follow, continued to frighten me as we drove on toward San Francisco.

Marcelyn was about thirty years old and then a teacher in Los Angeles. I had not been with her much since high school, having visited with her only a few times. After one semester at UCLA, she transferred to Howard and graduated there. She had been married and divorced during that period and living in Washington, D.C. We had not discussed a great deal about any of those experiences. Really, we hadn't shared much of our emotional lives with each other at all. When we arrived in San Francisco, I phoned my mother and father, to tell them what had happened. They were of course alarmed and instructed me to get Marcelyn back to L.A. immediately.

For the next thirty years or so Marcelyn was in and out of the hospital. This initial episode, and others that followed, set up all kinds of preoccupations and challenges for me. Why was this happening? Where had her troubles come from? In those early years of her affliction, there were many theories that schizophrenia followed family lines, and there was much speculation about the influence of parents, particularly mothers, on schizophrenic children.

This was over fifty years ago, when such events were much less well understood than now. At the time a prevailing theory held that the disorder was caused by significant family malfunction or might even be genetic. I worried about this as, I am sure, my parents did. Such a thing could be a very ominous cloud hanging over you and your family.

Mental illness, you thought to yourself. My God, we can't let anyone know about this. Not our neighbors. Not our friends. We've got to keep this under wraps. Shut the door.

From that moment on Highway 99 on, I pondered the ways that society deals with mental illness. I thought about how families dealt with it, especially black families. So much of what drove us—my own family, the small group of people that I grew up with—was the importance of being considered respectable. No matter how we rationalized it, problems like my sister's implied that there was a taint on the family.

So we felt we had to deny what was happening to Marcelyn. We tried to ignore and explain it away as some temporary malady that would soon disappear. Denial and more denial. We were to keep a clamp on this information, and no one was ever to know about it. We were not to talk about it, even with each other, unless—as subsequently occurred on more than a few occasions—an emergency were to come up that required us to come together to help Marcelyn during a particularly difficult episode. At those times, we would talk *only* about the process of caring for her: how to get her to the hospital, who'd be responsible for going to the pharmacy, and other crucial supportive details. The deeper implications of my sister's case—where this affliction had come from; what it meant in the larger picture of our own family; and what *we* had done to possibly affect Marcelyn's condition—remained undiscussed.

I was also more than a little worried about such a possibility within myself. Was there a family taint on me? Had there been behavior on either of my parents' part that would indicate some level of passed-along irrationality or instability in me? Was there a family curse? Could I too be subject to delusional madness? Was some event to befall me and render me a chronic schizophrenic?

In those days, prior to any training in psychiatry, I did not know what to think. It's difficult to understand much about these things, and it is quite normal to be very frightened, as I was. The irony for me was that I had always thought of Marcelyn as the best adjusted of the three of us children. She had always had friends. She had a steadiness of judgment and personality that I admired.

Many years later, medical discoveries were to show us that such afflictions can have a biochemical source that no patient—no matter his or her nascent intelligence, basic decency, and good-heartedness—can easily withstand. But I didn't understand that then. No one did.

•◆•

Marcelyn's difficulties motivated me further to pursue psychiatry. Her troubles took me beyond the world of ideas, or of some academic pursuit that would be challenging and engaging to my mind. Marcelyn made my choice personal and emotional. Her troubles preoccupied me throughout my time at Meharry. I read all kinds of papers and books about her affliction that helped me understand the issues of treatment. And later, when I was beginning my studies in psychiatry, Marcelyn's difficulty gave me a level of comfort with chronic patients that I may not have had without her.

As I read and pondered her condition, I continued looking into myself for answers. I wondered, Where do I fit in to Marcelyn's troubles? What sort of figure have I been in her life? Are there elements in *my* personality that, because we are brother and sister, could shed light on *her* illness? How were we raised? Where does being black fit into it? I wanted to be helpful, sympathetic, a good brother. But I must say as well that I continued being worried about myself. Is this going to happen to me? And if so, how can I avoid it?

Nonetheless, I saw that I could do something real and important to help people who were suffering as she was. A specialty in psychiatry was no longer just a medical preference for me or an academic goal. I began to pursue it with a kind of heart-driven intensity, during which I always kept Marcelyn clearly in view.

CHAPTER NINE

Evadne Priester was a southern girl, born in Savannah, Georgia. I met her my first year at Meharry. She was an instructor in physical education at Tennessee State in Nashville. She was introduced to me by Clarence Beverly, a classmate from D.C. with whom I had become good friends. He had met Evadne when he was a pharmacist at Florida A and M. She had been teaching where my father had briefly considered working many years before.

Evadne was the younger of two girls, whose father was a postman. Their mother had graduated from Saint Augustine College in North Carolina, and the Priesters were now pillars of the black social establishment in Savannah. Keep in mind that a job as a postman for a black man in a southern city, or for that matter any American city, was a very good one, an indication of this man's, and his family's, position as solid members of the black middle class. Evadne herself had graduated from Tennessee State and received an M.A. in physical education from the University of Michigan.

One of the things that interested me most about her was that although she was a physical education instructor, she was by no means just a jock. Though not a tall woman, she had played basketball. She was also a gifted dancer, a very coordinated woman with a sense of true grace when she moved, especially on the dance floor. Although I enjoyed dancing, I always felt that I just paled in comparison to what Evadne could do. She could see a step once, then do it well.

She had wanted to be a professional dancer and once considered auditioning for a company that Carmen DeLavallade was forming. DeLavallade was a friend and fellow dancer with Alvin Ailey, and both were from

Los Angeles and worked with the legendary Lester Horton. They also had attended Jefferson High School, the same school I attended. However, Evadne put aside the idea of pursuing a dance career and instead pursued her advanced degree in education. Black dancers were then so few and far between in the theatrical dance world, and the few that did carve out a career made a pittance.

I was taken with Evadne the moment we were introduced. She was extremely attractive and had a kind of liveliness in her eyes that I found demanded my attention. She was living in an apartment in Nashville with a roommate, and I quickly found myself spending what little spare time I had with her. She offered kindness, a quick smile, and a sharp sense of humor. I could see right away that Evadne was going to be something special in my life.

• ◆ •

Medical school required that I keep my nose in the books and work extremely hard. Any physician will corroborate this view, that there is little time for anything in medical school other than your studies. But the sense of inquiry that had been so important to me at UCLA and Berkeley had in no way diminished. So I still questioned much of what was happening around me, especially so since I was now living in the South and the conditions for black people were so different from what I was used to in California.

The conversations that I had enjoyed with my friends in Berkeley, though, were not to be had at Meharry. Not that my fellow students weren't interested in politics, the issues of race, the arts, music, and the whole matter of where they fit in to the society around us. We just didn't have time for those kinds of sessions.

But Evadne engaged me in that kind of conversation. Like my father, Evadne had an edge, and it was most finely honed when it came to the subject of racial prejudice and the way black people were treated. She had lived most of her life in the South and had never traveled to the western United States. So she had not grown up in the more moderate racial atmosphere that I had known in Los Angeles. As a result, her rage was closer to the surface than mine.

She was an extremely thoughtful and inquiring young woman, and I learned early in our relationship that a conversation with Evadne was not going to be some one-sided affair in which I was going to be doing all the talking.

Among other things, Evadne helped me articulate and clarify my own rage. Because she would not allow herself to be pushed around or gainsaid in any way, she put me on my best behavior to act in similar ways. That meant recalling why we had to stand for ourselves, and what it was that had been done to black people. I understood all that quite well, of course, but Evadne helped me maintain that understanding through her own constant insistence on her right to be who she was, to know where she was, and to understand why she was there.

For example, at that time in Nashville, in most restaurants you would be refused service if you were black. One of the few places where you would be served was at the airport. Racism was displayed there but it was more subtle. You would arrive at the restaurant, be welcomed in a kind of halfhearted way, and shown to an inferior table in a less attractive part of the restaurant . . . say a smaller table near the door to the kitchen in a noisy corner.

Most black men at that time would accept such treatment. Few would protest, because protesting could get you summarily thrown out of the place. Just being accepted into a restaurant whose clientele was mostly white people was considered a kind of breakthrough, and if you were with a date, you didn't want to ruin the evening by causing a big scene over such treatment. So, you took it!

Evadne wouldn't take it. If we were shown to such a table, Evadne would look around, note the other empty tables in the restaurant, tables that were much more pleasingly located, and indicate one of them.

"Well, thank you," she'd say to the white maître d', "this is a nice table. But we'd prefer sitting over there."

If there was a protest on the part of the management, she would insist. If the protest persisted, we would leave.

Evadne did not care about the feelings of those people or the niceties of the social milieu in which a black person had to operate in white Nashville. I—as her date and escort—would observe this kind of behavior and realize that I couldn't just accept the status quo either. If I didn't insist in the way Evadne did, I'd be lessened in her eyes and maybe dismissed by her.

I cared for her. So there was no way that I was going to acquiesce in such situations. Evadne showed me how to insist and kept me vigilant in that insistence.

This was so in many of our conversations. Indeed, I was able to enjoy a similar complexity of ideas to those I'd found in my father and my friends at Berkeley simply because of Evadne's sharp dissections of politics and the cultural differences between whites and blacks. She had a lot to say, and in her behavior she was a fine example of how to act in situations in which a lesser person would simply give in.

The talk continued. We were dating. It was obvious to me that Evadne enjoyed my company, and I soon fell in love with her.

•◆•

Evadne was a feminist before that term had gained currency. For example one day a man came to her house to repair a television set. He was a fellow faculty member at Tennessee State and was doing this to make some extra money. He set about repairing it, and soon after Evadne had paid him, the television broke down once more with the same problem. Evadne complained to no avail, and complained again. The fellow always found a reason not to come back, and eventually he stopped responding in any way to Evadne's insistent calls.

She knew that this man loved his car. It was always as cared for as could be, and he had added many extras to it, to make it even flashier than it had been when it was new. Evadne staked the car out and one day took the wire-wheel hubcaps that he had put on it. They were remarkably, decadently showy. She took the hubcaps back to her apartment and then called the television man. Remember, he too was member of the faculty at Tennessee State.

"I have your hubcaps," she said. "When you fix my television set, as I have paid you to do, you will get your hubcaps back."

The television got fixed, quickly. And it stayed fixed.

Although Evadne had no medical training, she was able to help me significantly with my own schooling at Meharry. In first-year pathology courses, it was required that the students make original colored drawings of organs or parts of the body. The drawings were intended to help you recognize various diseased conditions. To do a good job on a colored pencil drawing of a kidney, for example, you had to have a sure sense of color, of modulation of tone, and of artistic concepts and perspective. I have always had a way of describing things visually with words, but I was a lousy graphic artist. So Evadne did my drawings for me, with my standing at her shoulder coaching her about what to emphasize and what not to emphasize. Because of her I had wonderful drawings!

•◆•

Our romance blossomed quickly, and I accompanied Evadne to Savannah for Christmas of 1954 to meet her family. I had never visited Savannah but had heard a great deal about the beauty of its antebellum homes and especially about the islands near the city—particularly Hilton Head—off the coast of the Carolinas. So I was looking forward to this trip very much.

We went by train and had to change in Atlanta. There were still signs in the Atlanta station that delineated the white waiting room from the colored waiting room, the white restrooms from the colored restrooms. But in 1954, legislation had been passed at the federal level that made such discriminatory practices illegal in interstate transportation facilities, since they came under the aegis of federal, rather than state, law. This new federal regulation had just come into being as we were traveling together to Savannah.

The law had tried to put aside many decades of Jim Crow practice. But its passage was so fresh an occurrence at the time that it wasn't quite clear yet whether black people could sit in the white waiting room or not. Given the consequences that someone who had crossed that threshold in the past would face, it was understandable that one would pause at such an opportunity to join the white folks.

Evadne didn't pause. During our time in Atlanta between trains, we sat in the white waiting room. The white people in that room did look us over, some aggressively, some more surreptitiously. But all looked at us in ways intended to convey the question "What the fuck are *you* doing here?" We sat there anyway, Evadne and I.

•◆•

A taxi brought us to Evadne's home in Savannah. Her parents lived in a two-story house in a black neighborhood that was headed for somewhat run-down gentility. Although the immediate neighborhood was black middle class, being in the black middle class in a decaying southern city did not mean that you could necessarily keep your home in completely pristine condition. The houses on this street were a bit ragged. They could use some work. And the street itself was a major one-way thoroughfare for traffic going from downtown Savannah into white middle-class neighborhoods and suburbs. Evadne told me many times how concerned her mother and other mothers in the neighborhood had been for their children's welfare, given the way cars just flew by on this street.

We took our bags from the trunk of the taxi and ascended the steps of the house to its porch. When the front door opened, Evadne's mother greeted us with kisses for Evadne and a big hug for me, her daughter's new boyfriend. Mr. Priester had retired from the postal service, a heart condition making it difficult for him to continue working. When I met him, he had already had a few heart attacks and was a frail man.

I was very much welcomed into the Priester home. If I had had any worries about how I would be accepted by Evadne's family, they quickly evaporated in the hospitality that was shown to me. I think Mr. and Mrs. Priester were pleased that their daughter had found a very presentable young man who was training to be a physician, whose own father was a physician as well. Also I was from Los Angeles, which was viewed as a progressive community—maybe a little too progressive—but nonetheless a place with a forward-thinking pedigree. It was obvious early on that I was quite suitable to Evadne's parents, and as I was shown to my room (separate, of course, from Evadne's room) Mrs. Priester told me how happy she was to meet me at last.

Because it was during the Christmas season, there was a kind of celebratory atmosphere everywhere we went during that first visit. School chums of Evadne's, whether they still lived in Savannah or had, like her, gone elsewhere, were all in town during this time. And they all came over to Evadne's house to see her and to get a look at me. We in turn went to the homes of several of these friends, and there evolved a kind of moving party, with drinks, food, and a very festive atmosphere that went on the whole time we were there.

Most entertaining by black people in a southern city at that time would have been done at home. There were clubs, of course, and the occasional formal dance or reception held at a hall somewhere in town. But, in their social life, southern black people mostly had to keep to themselves, and so the parties we attended that Christmas were mostly held in private homes. It was very enjoyable, and very much exemplified what is known as "southern hospitality." Had it not been for the fact that the prevailing racism *required* us to stay at home, it would have been altogether enjoyable.

Walking around during that week, I noticed that there were a number of white families mixed in to the neighborhood. It was extremely unusual for whites and blacks to live in a mixed neighborhood anywhere in the South, so this was a pretty unique situation. During that visit Evadne told me about a racial incident that gave me a further idea of her very secure respect for herself.

One day when she had been a young girl, a white boy who had lived in a house near Evadne's family's home called her a "nigger." Evadne was about seven at the time, and she chased right after that other kid, who took off running. He ran into his own house, and through it, Evadne pursuing him the whole way. In the front door, through the living room, kitchen, and whatever other room, and right out the back door. I don't recall if she caught him or not. But he didn't call her a "nigger" ever again. The thought of chasing the white boy through his own home still amuses me. It shows in a very graphic way the strength of her feelings and the value she held for herself even as a child. It's one of the things that I loved about her most.

◆

During our visit in Savannah, Evadne suggested that we go to Hilton Head, where she had often spent summer days as a little girl with her family. In those days, the island was not the major world-class resort that it is today. Its original history is far richer and more colorful than that. It was a predominantly black island in 1954, as it had been since the days of slavery. There now lived a community made up of the descendants of slaves, who owned the land and were active speakers of a language called

Gullah, a kind of patois that combines sixteenth-century Elizabethan English with the Geechee language of West Africa. The language is now studied and documented and is still spoken by a few hundred people on these offshore islands. Julie Dash's 1991 dramatic film *Daughters of the Dust* made knowledge of the Gullah culture and language known to audiences across the country and in other parts of the world.

In 1954, Hilton Head was accessible only by barges on which you could transport your car. The island was dotted with little communities. It was like visiting a foreign country. Many of its people had never been to the mainland, which was separated from the island by a narrow channel of water. The upscale part of Hilton Head, an area called Bradley Beach, was dotted with summer homes owned by black physicians, dentists, undertakers, lawyers, or schoolteachers who had saved their money. These were not mansions but were nice modest homes. It was a lovely place and we had a great time there.

Returning from Hilton Head to Savannah, Evadne and I spent a few more days with her parents. Mr. and Mrs. Priester made it clear to me that I was the right man for their daughter, and we returned to Nashville surely anointed with their blessing.

•—•

At the age of seven, a girl named Linda Brown in Topeka, Kansas, had to attend a segregated black school that was twenty-one city blocks from her home. The white school in her neighborhood was seven blocks from her home. To get to the black school, Linda caught a school bus every morning on the other side of the railroad tracks from her home, and rode it along a circuitous route—picking up other students on the way—for one hour before arriving at the school herself.

Linda's father, Oliver Brown, sued the board of education in Topeka, stating that he wanted nothing more for his daughter than the same conditions for getting to school that pertained to all the other children in their particular neighborhood, that is, to the white children. Linda should be able to walk to the nearest school with her neighborhood friends.

When this case first came before the Supreme Court, whose new chief justice, Earl Warren, had formerly been the governor of California, my father was very chagrined. We both remembered how Mr. Warren had been attorney general of the state of California in 1941, and how he had argued strenuously for the internment of West Coast Japanese, whom he felt must be disloyal to the United States.

We felt that Warren was the wrong man to be leading the Supreme Court in a case like *Brown vs. Board of Education*. Chief Justice Warren had shown his stripes with regard to minority groups during the war. We didn't expect much from him in this decision.

Earl Warren appeared to shift his point of view, to our astonishment. On May 17, 1954, the decision came down from the Supreme Court to overthrow the "separate but equal" doctrine that had been imposed by *Plessy vs. Ferguson* in 1896. In the *Brown* opinion, which was unanimous (also to our astonishment) and actually written by Warren himself, he stated that education is "perhaps the most important function of state and local governments. . . . The very foundation of good citizenship." He asked the rhetorical question "Does segregation of children in the public schools solely on the basis of race . . . deprive the children of the minority group of equal educational opportunity?" His response to his own question was: "We believe that it does."

Warren wrote, with direct and unequivocal clarity, "In the field of education the doctrine of 'separate but equal' has no place. Separate educational facilities are inherently unequal."

I was elated with the decision, as were my father and mother. We could not have known at the time that Warren himself had undergone a kind of transformation in his feelings with regard to people born outside the mainstream. He later wrote in his autobiography about his role in the establishment of internment camps for Japanese Americans. "I have since deeply regretted the removal order and my own testimony advocating it, because it was not in keeping with our American concept of freedom and the rights of citizens. Whenever I thought of the innocent little children who were torn from home, school friends and congenial surroundings, I was conscience-stricken."

Mr. Warren's conscience must have led to his change of position. But, the unanimous vote—nine to zero—by the Supreme Court also spoke to Warren's political acumen. No matter how he personally felt about this decision, he surely understood what a huge decision it was. So he wanted to make sure that the decision be truly heard. Apparently, he mightily lobbied the other Supreme Court justices to join with him. A unanimous decision by the court would assure that it be taken seriously by every element of American society.

My father and I talked about this over the kitchen table as well. That it had been Earl Warren who had done this amazed us. My father felt that Mr. Warren had been chosen by President Eisenhower thinking that he would be getting a more or less conservative chief justice. Governor Warren had been considered a moderate Republican, although not nearly as "moderate" as, say, the young Nelson Rockefeller. Mr. Warren was a man who could be trusted to keep the Supreme Court in line and not allow it to become a policy-making body by handing down decisions more properly left to the executive and legislative branches of government. My father thought that the *Brown* decision must surely have come as a surprise to President Eisenhower, and we chuckled over the consternation that the Republican Party must have been feeling.

It was as though we had entered into a new era. I felt that *Brown vs. Board of Education* was a very big step toward the entitlement of black people as full citizens of the United States. Although guaranteed by the Fourteenth Amendment, this entitlement had been more honored in the breach, it seemed to me and my father, than in the observance. That "separate but equal" had been struck down meant that many of the Jim Crow laws that had been established after Reconstruction to keep blacks separate from whites—and "inferior" to them—would surely fall as well.

The only thing that gave us pause in our conversations about this decision was whether the government, and the people of the United States, would have the gumption to implement it.

•◆•

Adlai Stevenson, the Democratic nominee who ran twice against Eisenhower, once famously remarked, "We live in an era of revolution—the revolution of rising expectations." Evadne and I talked a good deal about this too.

"It's coming, Price," she said. "And we're going to be a part of it."

Evadne and I knew how big a decision the Supreme Court had made in *Brown vs. Board of Education.* A revolution of some kind was beginning to take place, and it was gathering steam as the expectations of black people everywhere in the United States began to be realized. I was beginning to think that I *should* be part of it, now!

I mentioned this to Evadne from time to time, and she reminded me that medical school was important too, and that I was on one kind of mission already, to become a physician. The groundswell that was beginning to occur in the civil rights movement would still be taking place in a few years, after I'd gotten my medical degree. It was important that I put myself in a position in which I could do the most good in these coming events.

Evadne said, "There's a voice in you, Price, that's telling you that you're training yourself for a role in this. We don't know what the role is. But it's coming." I followed her advice and kept my shoulder to the wheel at Meharry Medical College.

◆

In my third year at Meharry, we began thinking about another goal. Evadne and I had been together for two years, and our relationship had gone through some significant ups and downs. We were both given to our own opinions, and both of us were passionate people. So we had argued, broken up, come back together, argued and broken up again, many times. But we both realized that we were in love with each other. So in the first of what was to become many such conversations over the years, we sat down and laid all our cards on the table. What was right with our relationship? What wasn't so right? We talked about everything. And in the end, we discovered how much we really did care for each other. With our hearts so laid open, we decided to get married.

We arranged for it quickly and were married in Nashville at the home of a classmate of mine and his wife, Tom and Edith Gates, in May 1957. It was a small ceremony, attended by friends from Nashville and Meharry.

Evadne's sister Marion came to the wedding, although her parents did not. Mr. Priester's heart condition was quite serious, and neither he nor Mrs. Priester wished to risk his health with a trip to Nashville. Evadne herself had no problems with this. She worried about her father, and she felt that her mother's caretaking of Mr. Priester was most appropriate.

My own family did not attend the wedding either, only because Evadne and I had made the arrangements so quickly and it would have been too costly an undertaking to get them all there. At the time Evadne and I felt that we just wanted to get married. We made the plans. We wanted to take control of our lives. We knew that people very important to us would not be able to attend. But with their blessing, we simply went ahead with it.

We decided to go to California right after the wedding. I wanted to introduce Evadne to my family, of course, and my parents wanted to have some kind of gathering to celebrate our marriage. I was also beginning to think quite seriously about internships and residencies, and I wanted to visit a few of the hospitals in California to which I was thinking of applying.

Fortunately, a woman who had been Evadne's roommate in Nashville was moving to Los Angeles, and we were able to drive cross-country in her car. Evadne had never been west, and I had a lot of fun being a tour guide for her as we went back along the route I had taken with my mother, Prince, and Marcelyn when I was a boy. Evadne's enjoyment of that trip, the adventure of passing through so much exotic countryside, so new to her, was probably even greater than mine had been when I had first seen those things.

This was 1957 and the network of lodgings that had existed when I'd made my first trip to the South with my family in 1934 still existed. One had to take the same care that my mother had taken, to ensure that there were places to stop along the way that would take us in. So Evadne and I stayed with friends or in church-related private homes as we drove to California.

As we approached L.A., I worried a bit. I realized that I was coming home with my new wife, and that my parents knew nothing of her except what I had conveyed to them in letters home. Would they accept Evadne? Would there be any suspicion on their part that I had acted too willfully, that Evadne had been a wrong choice? I loved her and knew that she would always remain my choice. Nonetheless, the prospect of this first meeting between my wife and my family loomed large. A dutiful son is always anxious about whether his choice of a bride will meet with his parents' approval.

I had no reason to worry though. Evadne fit right in from the start. I think both my mother and father saw the quality that pervaded her personality and her heart, and they were glad that I'd had the good fortune to find her.

•◆•

Evadne and I had talked a good deal about children. We both wanted them, and Evadne herself very much wanted to become pregnant right away. One year later, our son Price was born in Nashville.

It's interesting to me to have learned over the years how many decisions made on whim or from desire result in profound change. In some cases, these changes can be detrimental to your life. In other cases, they can change everything for the good. The exchange of affection and love, so fine a moment in its own right, can have lifelong consequences that shape your entire existence. The birth of our son Price was one such—a wonderful change for the good.

A year earlier, I had been a single man, a medical student, a youth. Now I was a married father of a small child who needed love, protection, and nurture. I knew Evadne would provide those things to Price Junior from the very moment he was born because I had observed how much she enjoyed her pregnancy. The caresses of her ever-growing tummy, the whispers of encouragement to the baby inside, and the sense of settled calm that she exhibited throughout her pregnancy had thrilled me.

But there was a transition in me too. I had had a kind of easy time as a kid and as a young man. I was smart. School had never been particularly difficult, as long as I hung in there. Yes, I could have done better at UCLA and Berkeley in terms of my grades. But I had had a lot of fun.

But Price's arrival moved me into fatherhood, into responsibility, into my manhood. I suddenly understood my own father's regard for me because I felt a similar regard for little Price as he lay in Evadne's arms. My father's watching of me. His arguing with me. The steady intensity of his attitude toward me.

I'm not sure to this day that I've necessarily duplicated those things, or would want to in every way. But I could see then how serious my father had been about me, my brother, and my sister. I determined that, in my love for Price and what he meant to me—and means to me—I would try in my own way to exhibit a similarly serious respect for our new life and its new responsibilities.

Price Priester Cobbs was born toward the very end of my time in medical school, and I knew by then that we'd be moving to California. I had accepted an internship at San Francisco General Hospital, having done so in part to maintain a sense of independence from my father. We would be relatively close to home, but not too close. I was worried that if I went back to Los Angeles, I would become known as "Little" Doctor Cobbs or something of the sort, and I wanted very much to be treated as my own man. So when the opportunity to go to San Francisco came, I took it. I was soon to be a doctor, and I was a man with a family. There were to be four more years of preparation for going out into the professional world (the one-year internship in San Francisco and three years of psychiatric residency). Much was changing in our lives, and Evadne and I began preparing for this very significant move.

•◆•

One day toward the very end of that fourth year in medical school, I went to downtown Nashville with a group of my classmates, on a kind of field trip to test out the sense of privilege that we, as soon-to-be physicians, were all beginning to feel. We'd made it. We had nearly finished medical school. We were going to be doctors. And so, as a gesture to acknowledge that, we were going into town to check out the latest model automobiles. A couple of my classmates were even bent on buying new cars. A few had the money to do such a thing then and there, and all of us had the future potential to do so. Yes, we were black, and you wouldn't see a black man riding around very often in a new Chrysler convertible. But we all felt the heady confidence in those moments of having finally come into some kind of favor. So we embarked upon this shopping trip with a lot of spirited laughter and a sense of being newly minted with our new degrees.

At the dealership, we strolled about the showroom floor, talking about the automobiles, comparing the convertibles to the sedans to the sports models. The possibility that we could own such cars made us almost giddy. We were no longer just kids with a dream of possessing such a car. We were going to be able to do it.

A white salesman approached us, asking, "Can I help you boys?" He introduced himself and shook several of our hands, asking us for our names, and then began addressing us by our first names. There was a very clear tone of condescension in his voice as he asked us why we were there at the dealership. Some of the fellows asked him about the showroom models, and he started his sales spiel, continuing to address them by their first names. The spiel came out in a flat, matter-of-fact way, as though it were just memorized language. He would repeat it from rote because he was expected to repeat it.

It was clear that, to him, we weren't serious. None of us, he assumed, could possibly have the wherewithal to buy one of these cars.

We were soon going to be doctors. I knew that I would then expect to be called "Doctor Cobbs," in the same way that my father was. I also realized that we weren't doctors yet, and that this salesman wouldn't have known, necessarily, that a degree in medicine was in the offing for all of us. But I did know that we were potential customers of his, intent upon purchasing a very big-ticket item. So I felt that he could at least call me Mr. Cobbs, and refer to the others there that day as Mister as well.

But he continued with his use of our first names, and I quickly got the sense from him that he had no notion of us as actual potential customers. We were simply a bunch of black boys having some fun, though judging from our appearance, our clothing, and our talk, we weren't just your average black boy.

I interrupted the fellow with a question. "We're here to look at these cars of yours. Some of these gentlemen are interested in *buying* a car from you. So I'm wondering, how dare you call us by our first names? Would you do that with a white customer?"

The salesman looked at me with sudden and glaring disbelief. There was a moment's silence. Quite loud-seeming silence. My companions appeared embarrassed, as though, with the lightning bolt of my question, I had stepped right out of line. A few even appeared to protest, with the looks they gave me, the very question itself. Their looks conveyed a kind of fearfulness, that I had just gotten all of us into some kind of trouble. Even in the heat of that moment, I realized that, try as they might, these fellows had not yet understood that they could move on from the sense of "victimhood" with which they had grown up. This despite the fact that they were soon to be doctors, full members of one of the most important professions in our country.

The salesman responded with immediate hostile language, about how, if I didn't like the way he was addressing me, goddamn it, I could damned well leave the showroom. Which, of course, I did, but in the company of all my friends. As we walked up the street, I looked back and saw him, still standing in the showroom, still steaming with anger, surrounded by those wonderful cars, alone as he watched us go, and happy to have gotten rid of that dumb-ass black kid and all his friends. I imagine to this day that, if the salesman is still alive, he has not yet figured out how many sales he probably lost that day.

When I got home, Evadne was feeding little Price. She sat quietly, nursing as I told her what had just happened. As I recounted the tale, a smile began to come to her lips. When I finished it, she laughed out loud and took my hand. I leaned over her, Price secure in her arms, and she kissed me.

•◆•

It was late spring 1958. I was twenty-nine years old. The boxes were packed and sent off to California. The car was waiting at the curb. Evadne was getting Price ready for the first leg of the trip, and I stood in our empty apartment in Nashville. I was well aware of how much life had expanded for me during these four years at Meharry Medical College. I felt I had achieved a great deal by becoming a physician, and that Evadne and I had achieved even more by becoming husband and wife and parents. I knew, though, that much more was *going* to happen as I ventured into the medical profession, especially into psychiatry. I was so excited, standing in that empty apartment, that I could barely wait to get started.

Our last day in Nashville was far more complicated (and hectic) than planned and I was anxious to get moving. The original plan was for all of us to return to Los Angeles in my father's Chrysler, but that had suddenly and drastically changed. Always full of delightful surprises, mother waited until graduation day to inform me she was not driving back to Los Angeles with us and instead was traveling by train to visit relatives in Ohio and Kansas City. Since I had vivid memories of how precisely she would plan and lay out her clothes prior to short trips, I knew this post-graduation jaunt was months, if not years, in the making. Then, at the last minute my father surprised us with an airline ticket for Evadne and Price. I was almost trembling in anticipation knowing that after putting my wife and infant son on a plane to California, then coming back and taking mother to the train station, I would pick up my father and we would begin a long drive back to Los Angeles.

"Shall we go?" I asked Evadne.

She looked up at me and smiled, her baby asleep against her shoulder. She was to be leaving the South and her own home, maybe for good, to establish a home in exotic San Francisco. I sensed what she was feeling and her sadness at being even farther away from Savannah and her parents and sister. Yet her smile gave me the assurance I needed.

"Let's go," she said.

CHAPTER TEN

❦

When I arrived at San Francisco General Hospital in 1958 for my medical internship, it was a teaching facility for the University of California and the Stanford University Medical schools. The great brick behemoth of a complex on Potrero Street was also a public hospital for the citizenry of San Francisco, and remains so to this day. On any given day in the enormous public waiting room of S.F. General, you can see a microcosm of the world's population, people from countries everywhere speaking all manner of languages, from all walks of life. The hospital is an invigorating place, filled with remarkable drama and medical discovery. And as such it is one of the great teaching institutions in the world.

An intern in such a place faces a grueling year of daylong shifts, patient after patient, grand rounds in the company of physician/professors and a seemingly endless array of afflictions, diseases, births, and, one must firmly add, mortality. One spends time in each of the possible specialties, making rotations in surgery, pediatrics, internal medicine. I had already known for some time that my own specialty would be psychiatry, and I opted for two rotations in that area.

"Get into something where you cut," my father had said to me. I believe he felt that surgery was the finest expression of the medical art, and he wanted me to pursue that area of study. I myself, though, wanted to spend my life in the mind and the soul, probing in my patients for an understanding of the emotions and, most particularly, emotional dysfunction. I wanted to understand such dysfunction and to help my patients understand it as well, so that they could do something about it.

I already knew that, as a black physician, I would be leading a kind of dual role. I'd be expected to adhere to the classic model for treating patients no matter the affliction: the presenting problem, the diagnosis, and the treatment. That was well and good. But I was interested in far more than that. I had other ideas that were fairly unconventional at the time. Especially with regard to mental illness, I wanted to understand the broadest context in which the patient lived. What was his life like played out against the background of his society? Where did he fit or not fit in? What about her race, her culture? Was race for her, as it had been for me, a determinant of most of the events in her life? What about religion? Did she have conflict, always seeing pictures of a white Jesus? What forces ran his family life? How much money did he make? What was the social environment in which he lived? How did this patient get to this point with this affliction? Was she poor? Was she rich? Was he ambivalent about his identity? Was he confused by his sexuality? Was she hiding her true sexuality and suffering from the lie?

Early in my internship I began reading psychiatric textbooks where mentions of race were confusing to me or just plain muddled. The most puzzling book was the widely acclaimed *Mark of Oppression: A Psychosocial Study of the American Negro,* by Abram Kardiner and Lionel Ovesy. This book described the deep wounds on the personality of black people. They wrote as if the scars of race were immutable and permanent, and they offered little hope for treatment or change. In my view the book viewed the black experience itself as a pathological condition. Yet however insightful other authors might be about the human condition, there was little that was specific (or helpful) in terms of treating black patients. In terms of the psychiatric model for treatment, they were not considered in any way differently from whites or anyone else. They were to be treated in the same manner as all patients—meaning white—had been treated by Freud, Horney, Jung, Sullivan, and the others. On the one hand, race was viewed as a nonissue. On the other hand it was seen as an issue that could not be resolved and therefore did not matter. It was not discussed. And in my opinion, this was simple racism.

I realized that black patients spend more energy than others wrestling with the notions of inferiority and superiority. Consider the issues of body image alone. Black people for example have been assaulted over and over again with stereotyped images such as thick-lipped and flat-nosed buffoons, despite the fact that they are as diverse-looking as they are diverse thinking, and are intellectually aware of this. For black women the prevailing images of beauty at that time were that one had to be blond and blue eyed. Growing up black and female and developing a healthy self-image was no mean feat. There were so many ubiquitous false notions that an individual's ability to transcend the assault and the consequential feelings of one-downness and inferiority could be a major barometer of good mental health and successful functioning.

Heavily influenced by psychoanalysis, the traditional view of psychotherapists at that time was that behavior was determined from the inside out. To understand a patient, you looked at his birth experience, his toilet training, his suckling of the breast or the lack of it, the attitude toward him of his older brother or sister when he had been an infant. Mom. Dad. Then you looked at other relationships with people. And while all these experiences and relationships were important, I knew there was more.

I knew that a patient's emotional state was also heavily influenced by external factors. He was black. So how had white people treated him? What in his life let him know that he could attain success and be powerful? What messages told him the opposite? How much of his father's hostile attitude toward him had been determined by white people's treatment of his father? How much of his mad ravings in the hospital had to do with the fact that he hated his own black skin? Did he hate it because he had agreed as a child that he was subhuman, in the way that his great-grandfather slave had been told by white society that he was subhuman?

In the end the question is: What has been the quality of your interaction with the world if you've been an outsider rejected by that world's dominant power-holding group? The chances are, it's been pretty low.

These are issues that I identified from simple observation against the background of my own experiences. There was nothing revolutionary about them, as far as I was concerned. I didn't believe that these were ideas in any way unique to me. The fact is, they weren't unique to me. But I do know that I was, simply, a black man graced with the education and the powers of observation to notice that these were supremely important questions.

There were many, many people whose suffering—and anger—had been exacerbated by their being born outside the American cultural mainstream. Just looking around me at San Francisco General, I could feel my perspective broadening and developing a true multicultural complexity. Only some of the people in that waiting room at San Francisco General were of western European origins. If the mixture of ethnicities simply in that one place were an indication of what was awaiting me as a psychiatrist, I realized that I would have to do a great deal more to understand the life tracks of these diverse patients. What I might understand of the problems of a white man of English origins named Smith would probably be far different from those of a Mexican named Gonzales or a Filipino named Ramil. I already knew that was the case for any black man named Smith. So why not for these others?

So despite my father's wishes, the treatment of physical affliction did not interest me nearly as much as the study of emotional suffering. I felt I could do far more in that field, particularly given my unique background, since at that time I would be one of the few black men available to black psychiatric patients.

•─•

In the meantime, Evadne and I were struggling to make ends meet. In 1958, an intern made so little money that supporting a family was impossible. Evadne was struggling professionally as well, finding it very difficult to find a full-time teaching position. I had lulled both of us into thinking that San Francisco was a more liberal-minded town than it really was where black employment was concerned. To our surprise, she was unable to secure a position in either the San Francisco or Oakland public school systems. Black teachers were a rarity in both cities, and it seemed to Evadne that there was not much interest in the head offices of either system in changing that situation.

After several months, she was finally offered a full-time position at Mills College in Oakland, a private women's liberal arts college. Though she would like to have accepted the offer, the pay was very low and the commute (necessarily involving a car) would be expensive and time-consuming. Most important, she would have to leave little Price in the care of a babysitter, something she was loath to do. So Evadne decided against Mills. In time, she was able to fashion a schedule of sorts as a substitute teacher in San Francisco. It was not what she wanted, but it certainly helped our financial situation.

•◆•

Despite our economic difficulties and a relative lack of free time, we did have a social life in San Francisco. Centered around the hospital, it was largely a white social life, in which Evadne and I mixed with other professionals—physicians, teachers, and so on—and their families. It was fun, and we were enjoying making new friends. But we found that the friendships were often superficial when it came to one subject that was of profound significance to us.

We were beginning to realize that discussions about the emerging civil rights movement and the politics of race made our new white friends very uncomfortable. I was learning that being an educated man, a professional, and a physician meant somehow that I was no longer to be perceived by my white colleagues as being black. If you were middle- or upper-middle-class and black, many people assumed that you were so different and above the norm that what was going on in the lives of most black people was alien to you. A term frequently used was that you were "exceptional." The compliment was a backhanded one that implied not so much about any individual accomplishments, but more about the view that black people in general were unexceptional at best. Being "black" meant that you were surely deprived, that you were being buffeted, and that you were being kicked around. Being "black" was not a description but a status that was reserved for those colored people who were unemployed or on welfare or who held such jobs as laborers, railroad porters, bellhops, and hospital orderlies. My having become a physician seemed to infer to our white acquaintances that not only had I left the ranks of average black people far behind, but also that discrimination, prejudice, and racism was limited by social class.

My wife and I were expected to nod approvingly when a white acquaintance began a sentence with "One of my best friends is. . . ." We were not expected to discuss issues like the difficulty in finding jobs or apartments, since that would be discomforting to our friends, who did not wish to be reminded unnecessarily of the less happy aspects of being black in tolerant San Francisco. After all, Evadne and I were perceived as examples of why the legacy of slavery was no longer relevant. We'd lifted ourselves from our low beginnings. Why couldn't all the other colored people do the same?

So at a cocktail party, there might be mention of something like *Brown vs. Board of Education*. But the mention would always be a nod of the head, a clap on the shoulder, an agreement on the part of the white physician with whom I was talking that this decision had been too long coming, Price, and that we're glad to see a wrong that was done to your people being put right.

Sipping from my glass of white wine, enjoying a cracker with cheese on it, I would reply gently that, yes, this decision *was* too long in coming, and what it really does is open the door a bit farther to all the subsequent decisions that will have to be made to set the world right in its entirety. I seldom, if ever, went much further in my reply, because I had realized that the price of white friendship for a black person then was that I never disagree with that white person when it came to being black. There was no room in this fragile, new relationship between me and my white acquaintance for disgruntled or idiosyncratic opinions on my part.

Were I to reply with the truth, that the *Brown* decision was just the first step, and that much, much more had to be done to dismantle the racial inequalities that were part of the very fabric of American life, my new friendship would suddenly evaporate into a professional relationship only. And even that relationship could be jeopardized, especially if the white physician with whom I was speaking were someone powerful in the medical community who could derail my career in some way.

But nevertheless, at the same time Evadne and I were making our way so gingerly into the white professional community, a very big step for black people was being taken. After the breakthroughs enabled by the experience of World War II and the many court cases that were changing so much of the legal status, we were seeing the beginnings of outright black refusal to recognize Jim Crow laws. On December 1, 1955, Rosa Parks in

Montgomery, Alabama, had refused to relinquish her seat on a bus to a white person. That seemingly small event—by a respected member of the local chapter of the NAACP, it should be remembered—sparked a huge bus boycott in Memphis. The resultant civil rights movement was now truly beginning to gather steam under one of its remarkable new leaders, Martin Luther King Jr.

Evadne and I had watched on television as Governor Orville Faubus brought in his Arkansas National Guard troops in 1957 to keep 270 black students out of Little Rock High School. We watched with admiration as those students persisted in their efforts to attend that school over the following weeks and succeeded in doing so. When President Eisenhower sent in federal troops, white mobs having gathered at the high school to throw the black students out, we saw the troops' arrival as a good thing, although it was obvious to us that Mr. Eisenhower was sending them in "to maintain order" rather than specifically to protect the black students. No matter the reason, the country had seen on television the abuse that those students had taken coming and going to school, and black people watching felt their rage beginning to boil.

Although few of our new white friends spoke with us about these events, Evadne and I talked about them quite a bit. It was odd to us to have our professional friends be so unknowing of such critical events. We were black, had been black, and would continue to be black, and we both felt frustrated that the truth was of so little interest to these people. They didn't really want to know about us, and few wanted us to bring up any of these recent developments. Perhaps the true meaning of the developments—that a sea change was in motion that would very profoundly alter the relations between black and white people—was becoming evident to them. And I believe they were fearful of it.

•◆•

What I remember most about that year of internship was my incessant need to study and work. I had thought medical school was difficult, and it was. But for those who do it, being a medical intern requires a kind of steadfast, dogged devotion that few people have to undergo in their lives.

There were many things about the job that made it stressful. The hours were long, fourteen to sixteen hours a day. Staying alert was tremendously stressful. Physicians, particularly teaching physicians, question you all day long about patients' afflictions, and you're expected to have the right answer. The level of your involvement in the patients is very high and extremely intense. You want to make sure that you know all you need to know about them and what they need to heal.

Stress also stemmed from the fact that I was a curiosity to those around me. I was a black man and I knew people would say "That fellow Cobbs . . . you can't expect him to have what it takes."

Working with patients effectively requires research. Not the kind of relaxed classroom, lab, or quiet library time that you may once have enjoyed in medical school, as feverish as that was. No, this is research done on the fly. I'm still amazed at how much reading I did when I was an intern. A lot of it was done while I was standing up in a hallway, in the middle of the night, a book in one hand and a sandwich in the other, gulping down a quick coffee in a cafeteria; or sitting on a stairway trying to keep focused on the page while fighting off the need to sleep.

San Francisco General is a community hospital, and it treats many of the poor. In spite of their best efforts, many poor people have difficulty taking care of themselves. Just finding a sitter or obtaining transportation can be a major difficulty and limit the kind of regular medical care that others who are better off or who have insurance can afford. So they often arrive at the hospital when their condition has often already become quite grave. It was at San Francisco General, for example, that I learned the truth of the phrase common among medical people at the time that "pneumonia is the old folks' friend." Even though the revolution of antibiotic medications had begun, pneumonia would quietly end the desperate pain, the breathlessness, the fear of the elderly who had finally brought themselves, or were unwillingly brought by ambulance, in for treatment. More often than not it was too late for any medicine to save them and in that time-honored but seldom discussed practice, they would be left alone to make their final transition in peace.

The experience for any intern who could do no more than stand by their bed and hold their hand was a true test of that intern's physical and emotional mettle.

•◆•

At the end of that, though, comes the residency, a period of three years of continued work and study. With the residency, you begin to feel like a real physician, because you're working in your chosen specialty and you're able to step back a bit and assess what it is that you're doing.

In my case, I went to the Mendocino State Hospital in Talmage, California, about a hundred miles north of San Francisco, for a residency in psychiatry.

I chose this institution in part because it was housed in a number of Spanish-style stucco buildings in a vernal setting with large grassy grounds and many large oak trees. I share with my father a love of the outdoors. When I was a child and we would go on our Sunday family excursions around Southern California, my father would frequently remark about his love for the countryside. We would drive south to Laguna Beach and stop for a view of the Pacific Ocean with the island of Catalina like a dark sail silhouetted in the distance. Sometimes we would drive past the extraordinary canyons of Pasadena on our way to San Bernardino, past the seemingly endless orange groves of Orange County (now, sadly, almost entirely disappeared), as their spring blossoms unfolded in white clouds into the distance. The mountains that rose up into the then pristine clear air to the east of the Los Angeles basin were like upright granite castles that were far away yet appeared to be just a short distance from your own front yard.

The countryside north of San Francisco has its own glories, maybe a bit more subdued, not nearly so large scale as its Southern California counterpart. But there is little on earth that provides the same pleasure as the hills to the east, west, and north of Santa Rosa that rise up and roll so softly, covered with such fine oaks and low shrubbery.

Talmage was like that. It's cold there in the winter and very warm in the summer. But there is a kind of softness in the air, no matter the temperature. When we moved into the small house that had been assigned to us on the hospital grounds, Evadne and I felt that the next few years were going to be very nice indeed. There were a few grand oak trees sheltering our own house. In the distance, the soft hills, new yellow in midsummer, held the promise of turning green in the winter and spring. Our son,

Price, now almost two years old, was with us. We were a family. We were happy.

•—•

In my new residency program I was able to discover and, with time, to confirm an approach to psychiatric work that focused not only on individual pathology but also on the larger issues of a patient's life such as: family, community, ethnicity, and financial and political situation. I didn't realize at the time what a breakthrough this was going to be, because the discoveries I was making seemed rather obvious to me. They came to me, nonetheless, with some significant help from others.

For example, there was a patient at Mendocino whom I found particularly interesting, an older black woman whom I'll call Mrs. Thomas. Emily Thomas. Mrs. Thomas had had severe difficulties for a good deal of her adult life, having suffered several periods of psychotic outburst in which she had been barely controllable. When I first saw her, she was walking up a hallway of the hospital dressed in a nightgown, a bathrobe, and slippers. She appeared barely approachable, as though she were angry, disoriented, and threatened. She had spent years in and out of the acute treatment ward. There were many such patients at the Mendocino State Hospital, so I didn't spend a great deal of time at first dealing with her specifically.

But early in my acquaintance with Mrs. Thomas, I noticed an error in the treatment she was receiving that made her anger seem more understandable to me than it may have been to the other physicians on the staff.

She was like many other matronly black women I had known in my life. Gray-haired, a bit lined, having lived through a great deal in her life, she reminded me a lot of the women I had seen in church when I was a child.

But the psychiatrists on staff could not reach Mrs. Thomas. They would sit down to speak with her, and she'd recede into a cocoon that seemed to be made of rigid disgruntlement and anger. She wouldn't answer. She'd look away. She'd treat the staff with a combination of fear and cold rage.

"Hello, Emily," the psychiatrist would say. "How are you today?"

There would be no reply.

"Could we go over what we discussed yesterday, Emily?" he would ask. Once more, Mrs. Thomas would grimace and look away. She was so angry that the only reply of which she was capable was no reply at all. And that was given with a strong dose of offended bile.

Mrs. Thomas was severely ill. Everyone could see that. She needed the highly professional treatment she was receiving from the staff at Mendocino. But I could see that, at least in the areas of politesse and basic human regard, Mrs. Thomas was not being well served.

It was the same problem we had in Nashville with the car salesman who used only first names. Here was a woman who, despite the many difficulties she had had in her life, expected by now to be addressed as "Mrs. Thomas" not as "Emily." Maybe the use of the first name would be appropriate to white people or others, depending upon their upbringing. But in the black, middle-class, church-reared upbringing that Mrs. Thomas had experienced in her life, she was now in a position in which she felt she deserved to be addressed properly, that is as "Mrs. Thomas." Calling her "Emily" was an insult. Unintended, maybe, since the white staff would have no sense of such a social nuance. But an insult to Mrs. Thomas nonetheless.

During a staff meeting early in my time at Mendocino, I brought this up with the others. I explained how it was that Mrs. Thomas may be as distant as she was, as angry as she was, because she was not being paid the proper respect that a black woman of her stage in life expected. This was the time of the "Therapeutic Community" pioneered in England, and people were thought to be yearning to be addressed more informally. Therefore the notion was dismissed, basically, by the other staff people, and the conversation went on to other things. But I knew I was right because, to me, this was simply a matter of etiquette. Any well-brought-up black person would understand this. While there were several other black professionals at Mendocino Hospital, I was the only black physician on *this* ward. And I was well brought up.

"No, you've got to understand this," I insisted. "She may be psychotic. She may be very sick. But she has the right to be addressed appropriately, and I'll bet that if you do that you'll have better luck with Mrs. Thomas."

After several attempts to influence my colleagues were ignored, my suggestion was finally taken. Mrs. Thomas was not cured by my suggested approach, but she was more approachable. She would not automatically recede into silent rage. She would reply and sometimes even civilly. Occasionally I would observe her walking around the ward, then venturing outside. Once, when I said, "Good morning, Mrs. Thomas," she smiled at me and replied, "Good morning, Dr. Cobbs."

She did affirm my idea of how important my knowledge of her upbringing and culture was to our treatment of her affliction. That observation was acknowledged by some of my colleagues, and I began to think about it in true earnest as I continued my studies of mental illness. Mrs. Thomas gave me a gift, by showing me a key to unlock the door to what would become Ethnotherapy.

• ◆ •

Fritz Perls, considered the father of Gestalt therapy, visited Mendocino State Hospital during the first year of my residency. Gestalt was a technique based on the immediacy of feeling. It was a here-and-now approach. The operative word was "present centered." In working with patients the therapist's focus was always on the actual; what is happening now, not the future or the past. Gestalt therapy could be summed up in the famous phrase of the Danish philosopher Søren Kierkegaard, "Life is not a problem to be solved, but a reality to be experienced." The German-born Perls had fled Western Europe in the early 1930s, lived in South Africa during World War II, and then migrated to the United States. He had a reputation as a flamboyant personality, and as a result of many books and personal appearances, by the time he visited Mendocino, Doctor Perls was a famous man.

I felt that this kind of therapy might have value in my work, given that my own ideas about ethnicity and therapy were experimental as well. I thought the two theories could work well together, and I wanted to speak with Perls about that. So his arrival at Mendocino State Hospital was an important event to me.

While he was speaking to a gathering of physicians, staff, and residents in the hospital auditorium, a patient—one of those who had relative free rein to move around the hospital—walked into the room. He was a man who had a number of problems and had spent significant time in the back wards of the hospital. I remembered him from visiting his ward. He had a diagnosis of chronic schizophrenia. When he wandered into the room, he was immediately greeted by Perls in a jocular manner and was asked by Perls to explain why he was at Mendocino and if there was anything he wished to talk about with the group.

The patient was immediately baffled and really did not know how to react. This man was after all psychotic. He turned to leave, but Perls would not excuse him. Instead he continued asking this man questions, about the nature of his difficulties, about the level of care at the hospital. The man would sputter out some sort of an answer, and Perls would counter him on the answer, embarrass him, make him appear foolish.

We who were in the audience were shocked. This was the great Perls, the father of Gestalt therapy, a man whose work and writings celebrated the breaking down of the barriers between doctor and patient. But this patient was being made into some kind of comic victim by the celebrated psychiatrist.

I walked out of the room at the end of the session saying to myself, He may be famous. He may think of himself as some kind of role model to us. But I do not want to be that kind of psychiatrist.

I was offended by the treatment Perls meted out to this poor man and have looked upon his work with considerable suspicion ever since, because of the professional insincerity and personal insensitivity that he showed that day.

◆

Virginia Satir arrived at Mendocino State Hospital one day to conduct a seminar with our staff on the subject of family therapy. Although not a physician, Ms. Satir had become well known through the work she had done with families and the need to understand how a family's interactions can affect a patient's emotional stability. Conversely, in the case of patients whose emotional situation is very unstable, the family and its input can be quite important in the treatment of that patient. It was Ms. Satir's view that the whole family had to be involved in treatment because improved relationships and communication among family members could help resolve the specific problems from which a patient was suffering. Shared family knowledge was the key to understanding a patient. Family communication was the key to healing.

Once we began working together, she was far more instrumental in my studies and my residency than Perls. She helped me translate the kinds of observations I was making in the case of someone like Mrs. Thomas into the basis for a new kind of thinking.

Ms. Satir was a tall woman, very intelligent, straightforward, and funny. Her ideas seemed right from the outset. I had never understood how a patient could be viewed as some solitary entity anyway, in isolation from the family—the basic unit of society.

Virginia Satir was respectful of patients. She treated them with humor, good sense, and dignity. Her greatest professional challenge was being a woman and a social worker, rather than a male psychiatrist. Several of my colleagues on the Mendocino staff therefore dismissed a good deal of what she had to say on the basis that, to them, she was "unqualified." She did not have a medical degree. She was a mere social worker who wouldn't have the wherewithal to understand how things really worked.

She and I connected in part because we were both outsiders. She, as a woman and a social worker, and me as a black man. In any case, Virginia Satir was a genius when it came to working with families.

And I saw something else in her work that I felt few others had considered. It was something that fed upon what I had learned from the patient, Mrs. Thomas. There is a link between studying a patient's family and a patient's social patterns and culture as keys to his or her difficulties.

Mr. Jones, a white patient, for example, has a wife and three grown children, all of whom are healthy, middle-class, and respectable. His family members would describe Jones's particular troubles of course based on their history together. Another white patient, Mrs. Poindexter, lost a first husband to war, married a second husband who became an alcoholic, and had an autistic child and another child who has led a successful life in business but had an unsuccessful family life. Her family could also provide much information to explain her emotional afflictions. It makes sense that the emotional difficulties of these two people will be different, and the difference may well come from the dynamics of their two families.

Having watched Ms. Satir, I saw how her ideas could be important in a consideration of black patients in the larger socioeconomic, cultural, and political milieu in which they lived. I came to understand subtle differences in how a history was given, how people talked about their families, their communities, and their assessment of where they stood in the eyes of the surrounding world. Once all these factors sunk in, I was even more convinced there was a difference in the treatment we should give to a black Mr. Jones as opposed to a white Mr. Jones, a black Mrs. Poindexter as opposed to a Scots-descended Mrs. Poindexter, based on the different dynamics of their cultures and their position in society.

• — •

Evadne and my father had immediately found soul mates of a kind in each other. He congratulated me often on having found her, and there was a close bond between them from the very beginning of their acquaintance. My mother cared a great deal for Evadne too, but the feelings that existed between my father and Evadne were instantaneous and deeply shared.

Something new was taking place in my own relationship with my father as well. After Meharry, he had softened his attitude toward me. Until that time, we had argued over many things, throughout my life. Politics and the progressive movement. Money and the financial difficulties presented by my continuing education and my father's financial support of that. My up-and-down grades at UCLA and Berkeley. Many things.

But once having received my medical degree, I felt my father's acceptance of me in ways that had never before come to the surface of our relationship. I had proven myself to him. I had found the key that would open the door between me and my father. This meant so much to me. My father was a new and great companion in life. A role model, to be sure. A mentor, yes. But now, he was a friend. We were establishing true, recognized, and shared love between father and son.

He began to tell me about himself, things that I had never heard. He let drop the façade that he had always maintained, of formal rectitude and patriarchal distance. My father wore a suit and tie, the outfit that seemed most to define who he was as a man, a physician, and a father, nearly every day. Until now, he had, as it were, worn that suit in all his relations with me. So while we had love, we also had competition and conflict. Now, as he was loosening his tie and removing his jacket, he was also comfortable as he sat at the table with me.

•◆•

The most telling example of this was in the drive that he made with me across the country to California after I had graduated from Meharry. We had sent Evadne on ahead with baby Price on an airplane, so that they would not have to suffer from the heat and travail of the long drive. My father had arranged all of this, worried for the well-being of his daughter-in-law and his infant grandson. But upon reflection, I think that my father also arranged for all that so that he could spend time alone with me.

So we set out on the drive, the very route my father took across the country to Los Angeles with his new wife, Rosa, my mother, in 1925. We stayed again in some of the same homes that my father and mother had stayed in during their trip. It was as though my father wanted the various people whom he had known to understand that his son Price was with him now. Not so much a passing of the torch as the lighting of one.

My father had told me about one town in which there had been a black-owned corner pharmacy. The owner used to spend all his time out on the sidewalk talking on the corner rather than paying attention to his business. When we entered that same town thirty-three years later, the same pharmacist, now gray-haired and slightly stooped, was out on the same corner talking to passersby. His business appeared to be running itself! Nothing had changed. Before my father could point him out I remembered his story and I knew who the man was. We laughed together out loud.

I felt during this trip that I was finally being accepted by my father as an equal. It meant that I was finally going to have a long-term friendship with him, after thirty years and more of trying to be a proper son to this man and feeling—sometimes—that I somehow didn't really measure up.

We drove on, visited with his acquaintances, enjoyed the scenery the entire route, and became close, close friends.

•◆•

My father was involved in an automobile accident in January 1960. I was surprised by this, because he was such a "good driver." He drove around L.A. in the same late-model Chrysler Imperial in which we'd made the trip cross-country. He lost control of the car and passed into oncoming traffic. He suffered some injuries in the accident but fortunately they were not life-threatening. The bad news came with the medical examination he got as a result of the accident. Doctors discovered that he had a malignant cancerous tumor in his brain. The tumor was probably the cause of the accident.

He lost weight. His hair grayed even more. He went into violent mood swings, in which one moment he might seem almost healthy, making jokes, glad to see you. The next, he would pass into a profound depression, into silence. We prayed for him. The members of his church prayed. Numerous physician colleagues came to visit and commiserate. The attending physicians did what they could, taking extraordinary measures to save him. But he never left that hospital, and in the first week of February 1960, my father Doctor Peter Price Cobbs died.

I arrived at the hospital shortly after his passing. I sat with my father's body for an hour, alone in the hospital room gathering myself and mourning. I called mother and told her, "Daddy is dead," and there was no reason for her to come to the hospital. She called Marcelyn and Prince and told them the sad news.

The hour I spent with my father that day was one of the most emotionally intimate hours I ever had with him. I treasure it. I reflected on the formal way in which he had lived his life. I thought about the grit he had showed taking himself—a young black man—from his small-town southern beginnings and making himself into a first-rate, highly respected physician. I thought of our arguments. I recalled his love of singing in the teas after church on Sunday. I looked back on the visit I had made with him to the hospital when I'd been a boy, when he had had to pretend that he was not a physician. I thought of our trip across the country, of the laughter in Nashville, this or that anecdote in Texas, the Pepsis we had enjoyed in Phoenix on a hot afternoon, the knowing smiles he had given me when I had told him about my experiences in an anatomy class or the long late hours at the library at Meharry.

But mostly I just sat there in that room and tried to comfort him in his journey to a new life in another world.

•◆•

My mother went into a period of formal mourning. She took to her bed for several weeks, from which she held a kind of court in memory of her deceased husband. I assisted her for several days before returning to Northern California, ushering people into her bedroom, serving coffee and tea, receiving condolences, and joining in with the conversation. Many people came to visit her. Women from the church that she had attended with my father sat on the side of the bed or in chairs gathered beside it and spoke with her for hours about him, about the loss of loved ones, sometimes about their own loss of a husband or of close relatives.

Her pastor and pastors from other churches also came, ministers who had known my parents from interchurch gatherings and projects. These were almost always very formal men who felt that Mrs. Cobbs deserved to be visited, to be helped in prayer and mourning, to be assisted in the emotional trial she was going through with the loss of her husband. Dr. Cobbs had been an important man, and these churchmen wished to acknowledge that importance by bringing kind condolences to his widow and family.

Other physicians and their families came to visit my mother also. The black physicians particularly had a shared membership with my father in "the community of firsts," that brotherhood made up of the first black physicians in Los Angeles. So there were many stories—of patients black and white, Asian and Latino, of difficulties with white hospitals, of black physicians founding their own hospitals—that my mother enjoyed hearing, particularly if they included some anecdote of help or advice that my father may have given.

Left-wing political figures also came to visit, most of them white people. My mother had been of two minds about these people. On the one hand she had enjoyed knowing some important movie figures in Hollywood, like Dalton Trumbo and Helen Gahagan Douglas. But on the other hand, as she had felt years before when my father had been so closely associated with them, they represented a political precariousness that my mother felt as black people we could scarcely withstand.

She was magnanimous to all. She lay in bed in regal repose, sharing her mourning, her thoughts on death and those left living, on the love and affection of her departed husband. She would be beautifully dressed in black, surrounded by pillows and covered by the most decorous of bedspreads, a small tray at her side with a cup of tea, a few cookies, her watch, some note cards she was writing, some notes she had received that day in the mail.

She missed her husband, and she would mourn in this way publicly for weeks. She had loved my father, and I loved her. She deserved this period of mourning. I admired her for it.

•◆•

The third year of my residency was to be spent in San Francisco at the Langley Porter Psychiatric Institute at the University of California. Price was now three years old and growing fast. Evadne told me in the spring of my first year of residency that she was pregnant once more, and our daughter Renata was born on December 1, 1959, in Ukiah, California.

The move was of great importance because our family was growing, I was feeling pressure to get out into the world to start making a living for them, and we were going back to a city for which both Evadne and I cared a great deal. We left Mendocino with some regrets because our life there had been in many ways bucolic. But San Francisco awaited us and our two little children, and I personally was very excited by the prospect.

CHAPTER ELEVEN

Our life in Talmage was pleasant and very challenging. We worked hard. We enjoyed ourselves. And we prepared for the third year of my residency, when we would move back to San Francisco. When we got to San Francisco, something happened that neither Evadne nor I expected, but that we soon learned was part of a racist pattern that was still being drawn out in one of the most liberal cities in the world.

Price enjoyed riding around in his stroller waving his arms, making a mess of his food in the high chair, jumping up and down on our bed in the morning, and generally he kept life funny and lively. Renata was very pretty in her crib as she slept or cradled in her mother's arms. Evadne often pointed out that she was "a lot like you, Price." I've always enjoyed my children. But maybe I enjoyed them most during this time because they were so obviously needful of our love and protection during a period of real change in our lives.

Evadne secured a position with the San Francisco Unified School District as a "permanent" substitute teacher in the spring of 1961, so she went to San Francisco and found a house for us to rent, in the Westlake District. The kids stayed with me in Talmage, and we eventually moved to San Francisco in the early summer.

We saw the small house we were renting as a momentary stopping place until I completed the third year of my residency. It was in the neighborhood later made famous by Malvina Reynolds's song "Little Boxes," with its identical dwellings one after another into the foggy distance. After that, we planned to move to something better, maybe to buy a place, since I presumably would be making quite a bit more money.

Our neighbors were all white, and to either side of our house, there was a working-class family, whose members looked at us as though we were pariahs. We felt their hostility as soon as we arrived. I later found out that one of these neighbors had moved out of his old San Francisco neighborhood because blacks had been moving into it. Panicked by the expected plunge in the value of his property, he had sold out quickly and bought this place in Westlake, where I suppose he felt safe from the black invasion. To his chagrin, we were the very next people to arrive on his block after he and his family had made their move.

This man and his family reminded me of the Dust Bowl whites I had known as a child in Los Angeles. The *N* word floated from their conversation with free dispatch, and Evadne and I had the feeling that we had perhaps been mistaken, that this San Francisco was not really the San Francisco we had thought existed. Maybe, we mused, we'd unknowingly ended up down south.

Our neighbors were rough, crude, and distinctly unneighborly. As during my childhood in Los Angeles, I noted how different we were from these people in terms of our education and upbringing. We spoke well. They talked like bumpkins. We spoke with our children. They yelled at theirs. We kept to ourselves. They made a point of imposing their displeasure on us, through innuendo, threatening looks, and obvious anger.

We did nothing about it. We had as much right to be on that block as anyone else, and we simply went about our business. One Saturday night though when we went to a dinner party in Berkeley a frightened babysitter called to report that the living room window had been smashed. We rushed home to find that someone had indeed shattered a large window on the side of our house. Shards of glass had been flung all over the floor. There was no brick or rock, no kids' ball or other plaything. The window was just smashed.

Walking gingerly around the room, taking care that the children, who were quite frightened, wouldn't injure themselves, Evadne and I inspected the damage. I then went back out to the street, but it was silent and devoid of activity. I walked up and down the sidewalk.

Outside the house there was no indication this had happened. There was just the broken window. That area south of San Francisco is quiet and, on the surface, neighborly looking, but the silence on the street in that moment was chilling to me. The neighbors seemed oblivious to what had just happened. Maybe they waited—from behind closed curtains—to see what was *going* to happen. You would have thought, judging from the quiet up and down the street, that nothing had happened at all.

I went next door to ask the man who had fled his previous rapidly integrating neighborhood. He said, "Yeah, the kids play between the houses. Maybe one of them did break the window." He surveyed me with a sinister smile.

I answered, "Did you see anybody? Is that all you can tell me?" I got the distinct sense from his body language that he'd like to inflict more damage on me and my family than just the broken window.

This wasn't the work of a couple kids playing in the evening. We had surely been singled out for attack.

•◆•

Over the next few days, I thought about something that had happened to my parents when they decided to move from the Trinity Street home in which Prince, Marcelyn, and I had been raised, to a much roomier house, a much more beautiful house on Nadeau Drive in the Victoria Park section of L.A. This was in 1953.

At the beginning of her search, my mother had engaged a real estate agent, a woman, to help her look for a suitable house. They'd driven around many different neighborhoods together, all-black neighborhoods, mixed ones, all-white ones. Then she saw this beautiful two-story home in white stucco, of a Spanish design at the top of a rise of grass on a beautiful residential street lined with palm trees. Other houses along the way were just as beautiful, with fine gardens that were well kept up and flowering, but her heart simply settled on this one. It was the home she wanted.

The neighborhood was almost entirely white though. My mother imagined that there could be resistance from the outset if the immediate white neighbors were to see her walking up to the house in the company of the agent looking like she was ready to buy. Houses frequently went off the market—with mysterious speed—when a black family arrived for a walk-through, and my mother was well aware of that.

So she dressed up as a maid. She put on a white maid's dress with a proper black apron and some sort of maid's headgear. So disguised, she went with one of her white woman friends, the wife of one of my father's progressive Hollywood connections, to do a walk-through of the Nadeau Drive house.

She told me later that if someone is standing in front of you, keeping you from what you want, you figure a way to get past them. And that is what she did.

If some other real estate agent than the one she was using had been there as well that day, or maybe by chance the actual owner of the house, or if some white neighbor had happened to be glancing over the fence as she toured the backyard, my mother would have had to keep her responses to herself. As it was, she could at least survey the beautiful hardwood floors, the light streaming into the bedrooms, as she imagined which rooms would be occupied by which of her children when they came to visit, the idea that her friends from church would be able to come to this beautiful place on a Sunday for tea, the recitation of Langston Hughes's or James Weldon Johnson's poems and the singing of fine music around the piano. The backyard, its trees turning to leaf with the spring, the flowers blooming in her very hands as she brought them to color every summer.

And my mother did accomplish her goal. She and my father did buy that house on Nadeau Drive and lived in it happily for many years, without racial incident.

Disguise has often been a feature of the actions of black people in this country. There are the numerous well-documented examples of black slaves singing songs of protest and anger in happy voices intended to fool the master. The ingratiating shuffle so familiar in characters like Lightnin' in the *Amos 'n' Andy* shows or by the famous comic Stepin Fetchit—as the happy-go-lucky, shambling black boy—were constructs that made the actors a great deal of money while lulling the white audiences into agreeable, misled laughter. In my mind, I'm certain that those play-act characters masked feelings of rage, feelings that must have existed in the hearts of those actors for having to play such parts. In my opinion, the money they got for playing the parts was well deserved and, no matter the amount, far too little. The same could be said for Hattie McDaniel and Butterfly McQueen in *Gone With the Wind* and the other numerous maids' roles they played. McDaniel and McQueen took appropriate advantage of the system as it existed, and they certainly deserved the money and recognition they received. But they were playing limited roles as demeaning clichés, far below their true talent.

Also, anyone who has seen films or tapes of Louis Armstrong singing "What Did I Do, To Be So Black and Blue?" would be foolish not to realize that Armstrong was disguising his true feelings and intentions. It is one of the bitterest of songs about the condition of being a black person, but the smile on Armstrong's face as he sung it did much to disarm any white viewer's discomfort at being confronted with the vitriol of the song's lyrics. Armstrong's rendition of this song is a remarkable performance phenomenon about which Ralph Ellison wrote eloquently in his great novel *Invisible Man*.

The story of my mother's maid disguise illustrates how black people find ways of pursuing their desires. If you wanted to step out of the rigidly defined territory that was left to you as a black person, you had to do it carefully, with an eye mindful of the watchdog laws and agents that were intended to keep you in your place. The smile and easy and agreeable personality that has been portrayed by white society as the black ideal . . . the black maid! . . . all of that was at least partially a disguise you have to use to advance your interests.

Evadne and I had not done that when we moved into our Westlake house. But we were facing some old-fashioned retribution that would have been quite familiar to someone of my parents' generation. I began looking for ways to secure *my* wishes, especially a way that would both protect us and put our neighbors on notice that we were not going to accept the shattered window with a limp shrug of the shoulders. So I called the *San Francisco Chronicle*.

•◆•

The paper sent a reporter out to our house, a white man who interviewed me about the attack. Evadne served him coffee, and I told him what had happened. I was actually surprised by their interest in the story. The

Chronicle was a white-owned newspaper, and I had not expected that they'd be at all interested in a single black family's efforts to break the color barrier in some neighborhood out in the fog belt, well beyond Golden Gate Park.

The reporter seemed interested in the fact that I was a physician. This made me unusual to him, and he did find it a little odd that a well-educated physician would be discriminated against in what was clearly a working-class neighborhood. We talked about that a little, he shook his head some, wrote down the story, asked me more questions. He left, and I had the impression that not a lot was going to come of the story that this man was going to write.

We were not the first black family to whom such a thing had happened in San Francisco. The family of baseball legend Willie Mays had a similar experience just four years earlier.

•◆•

While Jackie Robinson gave to many black people a sense of entitlement in 1947, there was another ballplayer—Willie Howard Mays—who followed him.

One seldom sees an athlete of such transcendent ability as Willie Mays. In 1957, when the New York Giants were preparing to move to San Francisco, Mays was twenty-six years old and had already made one of the most famous plays in baseball history. In one of the games of the 1954 World Series at the Polo Grounds in New York, the Cleveland Indians' first baseman Vic Wertz had come to the plate and had lofted a monumental blast to deep center field. Mays ran a very long way to catch that ball and made the catch over his shoulder in a flat-out sprint with his back to home plate, an impossible play that he made as though there were nothing to it. He whirled immediately and threw the ball back into the infield, thus stopping the base runners from advancing, and thereby saving the game for the Giants. When you see films of this play, you realize why there is no equal to it in the annals of baseball.

But in 1957, the man who had made that play and who already was being thought of as one of the greatest ever to play the game, encountered racism in the neighborhood. Knowing that the team was coming to San Francisco, he and his wife, Marghuerite, were looking for a house to buy, and they found one in the Sherwood Forest section of the city. This is a much more well-to-do neighborhood than Westlake, although it is also in the fog belt toward the ocean in the southern part of San Francisco. Mays and his wife made an offer on the house, which was accepted by its white owner.

Many of the neighbors, all of whom were white, objected mightily because of the damage that they perceived would be done to their property values by the presence of a black family. That it was the great Willie Mays's family made no difference. So there was a concerted effort to keep Mays out, an effort that got publicity in the local newspapers. On November 14, 1957, the *Chronicle* ran a headline: "Willie Mays Is Refused S.F. House—Negro."

As a consequence, the mayor of San Francisco, George Christopher, a man of Greek heritage who had made his fortune by founding a milk company, invited Mays and his wife to live with him and his family in their home in Pacific Heights. The Mays's were touched by the offer but did not accept.

The very next day, the deal to buy the home went through over the objections of the neighbors, and Willie and Marghuerite Mays moved in. A year and a half later, a bottle containing a note with a vicious racial slur was hurled through the main front window of the house. Outraged, Mays and his wife moved their residence back to New York City, although four years after that, he did buy another house in the Forest Hill section of San Francisco and moved in more or less without incident.

Marghuerite Mays later said, "Down in Alabama where we come from, you know your place, and that's something at least. But up here it's a lot of camouflage. They grin in your face and then deceive you."

• ◆ •

On August 7, 1961, an article appeared in the *Chronicle* telling about the attack on our house. The neighbor next door was interviewed and was described as making no secret of his "steamed" feelings. He was quoted as saying, "They can live anyplace they want—except next door to me. I don't think I'm any better but I just don't feel comfortable with them around." He went further. "They even had white kids over who kissed their boy on the cheek. I don't want my children to see that."

This was vindication. An ugly, hateful incident had seen the light of day. I had expected nothing to come of the interview but had told the truth about what had happened, and the incident was respectfully treated by the paper.

•—•

The day after the article appeared, our doorbell rang. I opened the front door to see three black men standing on our porch.

"Doctor Cobbs?" one of the men asked.

I acknowledged their greeting.

"We're bus drivers. We drive for the Muni . . ."

The Municipal Railway is San Francisco's public transport system.

"We read about you in the papers, and we're here to tell you that, if you need any help protecting your home, we'd like to volunteer."

I stood for a moment in silence.

"We're here to guard your house, Doctor Cobbs, twenty-four hours a day for as long as it takes."

"That might be a while," I said, grinning.

"For as long as it takes," the man said.

I thanked these men profusely. But I did not accept their offer. I felt that the notoriety that the newspaper report had given the event would actually protect us. The perpetrators of the attack, and those that would support it, were cowards, as shown by their disappearance the day of the attack itself. With the sudden fame we had received, we didn't think they'd be back.

I was nevertheless grateful to these three men. They were strangers to us and had no obligation to put themselves in harm's way for us. But I recognized in them something that was becoming more obvious to me as these events unfolded.

Black people had for centuries remained mostly silent when attacked, and this made sense. They were surrounded by an enormous hostile presence determined to keep them bottled up. The history of what had happened to those who stood up to such monolithic disapproval was well known to black people everywhere in this country. You needed only recall a newspaper photo of some lynching somewhere. So these men who had volunteered to help us, and had just shown up on our front porch, were evidence of a commitment on their part to a new form of response.

These men saw that I and my family were being attacked, and an attack on us was as good as an attack on them. Now silence was not an option. Now caution made little sense. We were black. These men were black and their response to the events was not silence but clear unmistakable rage.

•◆•

Some time later I received a call from a man I had never met. His name was George Leonard, and he was an editor at *Look* magazine, which was then one of the premier national magazines devoted to news and American culture. George's accent was that of a southern blueblood aristocrat. (It remains so to this day.) I realized right away that he was a white man, just by the sound of his voice. But he told me that he had read the *Chronicle* story, and he asked me if I and my family would mind if he sent a writer, a man named Chandler Broussard, to my house for some interviews.

We want to do a story on this, Dr. Cobbs," he said.

I agreed, and a few days later Chandler Broussard arrived at our front door. In addition to writing for *Look,* Chandler was a published novelist and was accompanied by John Vachon, a renowned photographer. They stayed for about a week and followed me everywhere I went. I was on a neurology rotation at the University of California at San Francisco Medical Center, and the *Look* team accompanied me there. Chandler interviewed everyone in sight, but John was not allowed to take any pictures. So they could get a flavor of our lives, we threw a party for friends, and Chandler talked with everybody and John shot pictures. When they were not with me, they followed Evadne and the kids to their activities.

An article did appear in *Look* later that year, but it was much shorter than George had wished. He explained to me that the article had to take a lesser position in that issue because of the historic flight of the Russian cosmonaut Yury Gagarin, which was everywhere in the news at that time. That was O.K. by me. That the article appeared at all on the pages of this magazine struck me as a major breakthrough because it was a very public acknowledgment of a very real problem for black people on the pages of a magazine that we previously would not have expected to be concerned.

George Leonard and I were to have many collaborations after that. We became quite close friends and colleagues, and worked in the late 1960s on joint projects which were significant in the development of my theory and the clinical application of Ethnotherapy.

•◆•

I couldn't shake from my mind what had happened to us. You want to get on with your life. I've long felt that people who don't want me or my family around are bound in the long run to be satisfied because I'll be damned if I want to be around them. It was gratifying to have people recognize what had happened. I was glad to have found some support in a part of the white world that had not usually been so supportive of black people. All that was fine.

But not every white person was in favor of this. There were colleagues of mine who felt that it was rash, opportunistic, and even unprofessional to have such publicity come my way. They didn't want a member of the medical profession bringing such events down upon himself, and then going out of his way to publicize them. It did not fit into their view of medicine as being a well-mannered club filled with wise, untroubled, suitable men. I kept quiet about that attitude. But it was clear to me that this was racism talking, not some professional priesthood's quiet, well-meaning advice.

After an uncomfortable talk with a colleague about the *Look* article, I recalled my discussions in Berkeley when the slightest deviation from orthodox liberalism threatened banishment from the club. This was another side of the same coin. The price of a grudging acceptance into the medical club meant that I was supposed to be silent. After all, Evadne and I had been invited to their parties. How could someone who had gained social acceptance by whites go out and protest about something? Going public about being discriminated against reminded my white friends of certain truths they didn't want to accept about themselves.

The truth was, I was pissed. When was this going to end? When was white society going to understand that black people were there and had every right to be there? I felt the rise of rage. I was a doctor. I had passed all the tests for acceptance into professional recognition. We had a fine family. I was making my way. And I felt the edge that I had so often noticed in my father, in my friend Ed at Berkeley, in Rosa Parks when she had refused to give up her seat, the edge that Evadne had . . . I felt it being sharpened in me. And one day, while watching a speech by Martin Luther King Jr., I felt that rage clearly and distinctly.

I had gotten a position as a consultant with the California State Division of Corrections at the Duell Vocational Institute in Tracy, California. Originally a part of the juvenile justice system, it was now also a prison for adults who were considered too dangerous to be housed elsewhere. My job was to be a psychiatrist to individual prisoners and also to make assessments of their emotional states for the court and penal systems.

I had been shocked when I had first arrived at Duell by the state of absolute segregation that existed there among the prisoners. The blacks were always all together. The whites remained together, and separate from the blacks. And the Latinos were separate from the other two groups. I would have only expected such rigid separation in the South.

Most of the prisoners were emotionally isolated. It was in the interest of the prison authorities that they remain so. Control of such a group is made easier by each prisoner's innate sense of aloneness. They can be manipulated, pushed around, kept in their place, when they have very little notion of community with their fellow prisoners. The Black Muslims were the one group in that facility that seemed to have organized themselves thoughtfully and well. They were men who may not have been readers or politically sophisticated on the outside, but here at Duell, they had learned to be so.

While their religion had no appeal for me personally, it was apparent to me that in prison a rigid moral compass helped bring order and stability to usually chaotic lives. The very naming of the "blue-eyed devil" allowed them to clearly define an enemy, plot their course, and discipline themselves to contain their rage. And they scared the hell out of the guards.

I admired the empowerment that the Black Muslim program gave individuals. They had an organization that supported their claim that they were human beings, and a political agenda in prison to which they adhered. They were able to meet and share ideas on equal ground with one another, and it was very difficult for the authorities to break them up. They had a point of view.

Many of these men had committed awful crimes and really did deserve to be in prison. But they had found a way, with their faith and with each other, to protect themselves emotionally and, one could hope, under the shelter of that protection, to rehabilitate themselves.

Some of the prisoners had actually seen the *Look* article, and they treated me with considerable respect. For them I was a kind of media star. I learned though, with time, that this respect was only sometimes genuine, and more often a sham. The thing I came to understand best about prisoners was that, as far as they were concerned, they were not responsible for being in that prison. There was always some other person who was the cause of their incarceration, some political agenda that had put them there, some personal vendetta over which they had no control. My media importance gave them an opportunity to tell an observer from the national stage that the murders they had committed, the armed robberies, the rapes and mayhem for which they were responsible, really had been foisted on them by somebody else.

Some of the guards had seen the *Look* article as well, and their response was in a way similar to that of the prisoners. I was a celebrity because my picture had been in the pages of a national magazine. But in the case of the prison guards, this celebrity made me into someone they couldn't trust. The prisoners had been interested in how I'd gotten into the pages of *Look* and had had all sorts of questions. I was kidded by them, made fun of because of my celebrity. The guards, on the other hand, seemed to feel that the pages featuring me would be better torn out of that magazine, crumpled up, and tossed away.

When I would come to work in the morning and pass through the gatehouse, I would feel their anger at what I had done. I was an uppity black doctor. I was making the grand sum of one hundred dollars a day for sitting around talking about nothing with murderers, they thought, and as such I was pulling the wool over people's eyes. That article had been written because I had been living in a neighborhood in which I really should not have been living. I was a troublemaker.

When I arrived at work on August 23, 1963, as I passed through the guardhouse, I saw the image of Martin Luther King Jr. on the television set. He was speaking at the march on Washington. I'd been listening to the speech on my car radio. When I saw Dr. King on television, I noticed a white trooper of some sort standing in profile to Dr. King's right. He was wearing a trooper's hat, he was stony-faced and impassive, and I assumed he was on the podium as a kind of bodyguard to Dr. King. But there was a phalanx of black men standing behind Dr. King, and it seemed to me that this trooper wasn't really needed. Maybe he was just there for display. I knew that wasn't so, but the idea amused me. I've studied the tape since them. I believe that that man is the only white man in the scene. But he had a lot in common with many people watching the speech around the country. Like many Americans, he was an impassive bystander, probably filled with a confusing mixture of feelings—bewilderment, anger, and fear. On that day, the guards at the front gate of Duell—all white men, as was that trooper—were watching the television with intent resentment.

I stopped behind them.

Dr. King arrived at the final peroration. "When we let freedom ring, when we let it ring from every village and every hamlet, from every state and every city, we will be able to speed up that day when all of God's children, black men and white men, Jews and Gentiles, Protestants and Catholics . . ."

"And the fuckin' niggers," one of the guards injected. The others laughed.

". . . will be able to join hands and sing in the words of the old Negro spiritual . . . ," Dr. King intoned, his voice rising at the end of the phrase with obvious emotion and excitement. "Free at last, free at last!"

"Who does that fuckin' nigger think he is?"

"Thank God almighty, we are free at last!"

I stood at the back of the room, transfixed. Doctor King stepped away from the podium, to the roar of the crowd. One of the guards looked around at me, and the group of them dispersed, going about their business once again. I showed my ID and went on to work, stunned to speechlessness by Dr. King's words and outraged by the response of the guards. As I passed from the guardhouse, I felt their eyes glaring through the back of my head. I went my way, intent on getting to my job, the usual. But I was in a black rage.

"Free at last!"

I wondered, What would it really take for me to be free at last of the attitude of those white guards?

CHAPTER TWELVE

I finished my residency in June 1962 and followed that with a series of positions as a staff psychiatrist at various institutions. I spent six months at the Napa State Hospital, a large state-run institution sixty miles north of San Francisco and then worked for a couple of years at San Francisco General Hospital. Following this, I put in a stint as a curriculum development officer for the Continuing Education Department of the University of California at San Francisco, where I developed classes to be taught by physicians of many specialties as well as other psychiatrists. It was a time of testing the waters. Not yet having found a compelling avenue of study to which I could devote my professional life, I was working where I could and still learning.

My time at the Duell Vocational Institute was just such a job, and it was a place where I saw very real black rage. Duell showed me the consequences for people who had allowed their rage to come to the surface and recklessly explode. This was a major point of learning for me. It taught me that the rage of black people had to be acknowledged and understood, opened up and dealt with. Without that candor and appreciation, our collective feelings would lead to the dead end these prisoners represented.

Because many of the prisoners were Black Muslims, I found myself talking and learning a lot about Malcolm X. Some of the prisoners knew a few of the specifics of his life, but the details were not to become common knowledge until a few years later, with the publication of *The Autobiography of Malcolm X,* written with the help of the writer Alex Haley.

As the best-selling book recounts, Malcolm had suffered greatly as a child. His family's house had been burnt down in 1929, and it is believed that the event took place at the behest of the Black Legion of the Ku Klux Klan. Malcolm's father, Reverend Earl Little, was outspoken on the subject of discrimination and was an avid supporter of the Black Nationalist Marcus Garvey. But as if burning Reverend Little's house wasn't enough, two years later, he was murdered. His body was found mutilated and cast aside on some trolley tracks.

Subsequently, local authorities took the opportunity to place Malcolm in foster care, isolating him from his family. His mother was under extraordinary pressure, and her health and the family's well-being were in jeopardy. Malcolm had real ability as a student, but in school the environment was hostile and his home life was difficult, and Malcolm descended into a life of petty crime.

Malcolm's conversion to the Nation of Islam while he was in prison and his rise as a national spokesman after his release totally captured my interest. For one, he was the first black figure to articulate the rage of black people so forcefully and so well. Many blacks, including myself, who totally rejected the doctrine of the Black Muslims, were drawn to his words. Second, he was able to connect the legacy of slavery to the inner lives of blacks at that time. He knew that a people with a victim's mentality would never obtain the psychological freedom of entitlement. Both of these facts intrigued me. His boldness made me question my own cautiousness. I was aware that many black professionals of my generation gave lip service to "the struggle" but sat on their hands while the civil rights movement was written about on the front pages of most newspapers and seen daily on TV.

By the time Dr. King made his speech at the march on Washington in August 1963, Malcolm had articulated a different message. Malcolm said that white society did not want black people to empower themselves in any way that would lead to economic independence, social entitlement, or political power. He believed it was futile to believe that white America would ever accept or allow its former slaves to have real equality, justice, or power. That being so, a separate Black Muslim state was the only logical alternative.

By 1963, Malcolm had become a major leader of the Black Muslim movement. In 1952, there had been five hundred Black Muslims, brought to the movement by its leader, Elijah Muhammad. In 1963, there were thirty thousand Black Muslims, and that growth was largely attributed to the organizational acumen, the powers of articulation, and the public-speaking ability of Malcolm X.

The governing word among the prisoners when they spoke of Malcolm was *truth*. "These other guys, they talk about integration and stuff, getting along with the white man. But Malcolm, he tells the truth!" For most of these men, getting along with the white man was not possible. The white man was untrustworthy, hateful, and imprisoning. It was the white man who had imposed slavery on us, the white man who had made up the Jim Crow laws. White men lied. White men lynched. You couldn't trust the motherfuckers.

One should remember that Martin Luther King Jr. was not the benign, fatherly figure that he is now sometimes portrayed as having been. He was at the forefront of a nationwide expression of black dissatisfaction and made use of quite powerful and uncompromising language and tactics in expressing that dissatisfaction. In January 1965, for example, while speaking on the subject of voting rights from the pulpit of the Brown Chapel African Methodist Episcopal Church in Selma, Alabama, King said, "We must be willing to go to jail by the thousands. . . . We are not on our knees begging for the ballot. We are demanding the ballot."

Doctor King occupied the moral high ground, the soul of black people in the civil rights struggle, while Malcolm presented a clear view of the pent-up feelings that fueled that message. That's why he is crucial to understanding why black people were demanding their civil rights so forcefully. Malcolm X represented the point of the lance of black rage.

•◆•

By 1965, black and white civil rights workers—particularly those connected to the Southern Christian Leadership Conference (SCLC) and the Student Non-violent Coordinating Committee (SNCC)—had been working in the South for some years in the effort to gain the right to vote for black people. Despite the Constitution's guarantee of the vote to all people at the age of twenty-one, in 1964 half the voting-age population in Dallas County, Alabama (where Selma is located), was black, while only 2 percent of those were registered to vote.

Voter registration was a risky business, though, and violence was often perpetrated against the people working for it. One of them, a black man named Jimmy Lee Jackson, was killed on February 18, 1965, during a voting rights demonstration in Marion, Alabama. Jackson, trying to protect his mother and grandfather from being attacked by Alabama state police during the demonstration, was himself beaten to death by the troopers.

Black people in Marion gathered together and decided to mount a march to protest this killing and the brutality of the state police authorities against black people in general. Dr. King agreed to walk at the head of the march. It would go from Selma, Alabama, to the capital Montgomery, where the marchers would petition Governor George Wallace to respect the rights of blacks to vote and to live in peace in Alabama.

Governor Wallace announced that the march could not go on. Dr. King thereupon went to Washington, D.C., for a meeting with President Lyndon Johnson, to ask his help. The marchers in Selma gathered without Dr. King, and on Sunday, March 7, 1965, they began the long walk to Montgomery.

What happened next is a very famous series of events that marked a major turning point in the civil rights movement and also electrified me in a very profound way. The marchers were attacked by numbers of Alabama state troopers as they crossed the Edmund Pettis Bridge trying to leave Selma. Using dogs and fire hoses, the troopers dispersed the marchers but not before being filmed by national television networks as they beat, terrorized, and injured a great many of the marchers, all of whom were unarmed.

I saw those television reports, and I was outraged. I had been collecting money to support the march, but when I saw those films, I knew I had to go myself. Bloody Sunday, as that day came to be called, provided a violent and disturbing view of what black people still had to overcome.

We learned that Dr. King was going to lead a second march to Montgomery a few weeks later, this one sanctioned by President Johnson himself. Watching television on March 21, Evadne and I saw Dr. King at the head of this new march starting in Selma, alongside other notables such as the celebrated black American statesman Ralph Bunche who, along with Dr. King, was also a recipient of the Nobel Peace Prize. I remembered that Dr. Bunche was from Los Angeles and my father often had spoken about him. Also at the head of the march was the Jewish theologian Rabbi Abraham Heschel and Rosa Parks. Show business people were present: Lena Horne, Harry Belafonte, Tony Bennett, Joan Baez, and the great Mahalia Jackson. Federal troops lined the fifty-four-mile route of the march, and the number of marchers grew as the march continued: from three thousand people at the beginning to twenty-five thousand as it approached Montgomery.

As I pondered going to Selma, an extraordinary gesture touched me profoundly. George Leonard's mother had moved to Marin County to be near him, his sister Julia, and their families. She was born in Georgia and prior to moving to Northern California had lived there her entire life. She was now well into her sixties. With her deep southern accent and syrupy ingratiating words, it was easy to think of her as an aging, quintessential southern belle. But before falling for a stereotype based on her words and manner, I discovered things about her that went much deeper. As we sat around discussing what was taking place in Alabama, she began talking about her life. Yes, she had been born in rural Georgia and at an early age became aware of the strict separation of blacks and whites. In her young adulthood she had thought frequently about her southern heritage and the abject racial hatred expressed all around her. She spoke freely of her awareness and discomfort with the attitudes and beliefs of her family and that of most of her circle of friends and acquaintances. As a result, she had determined long ago that this was a South that did not represent her and her true feelings. The events now being played out daily had touched her as they had most of us in our small circle.

Moving to Marin County had liberated her to now express her true feelings. Mrs. Leonard looked at me and said softly, "Price, if you go to Selma, I want to go with you." I was stunned. How could I possibly go to Selma with this elderly white lady in tow? I talked it over with Evadne and with George and decided that the risks were too great. As much as Mrs. Leonard wanted to go, to make a long-delayed definitive statement about her life, she would have to stay home.

I felt pummeled by the voices in my head telling me to go to Alabama. I longed to be there. I talked it over once again with Evadne. She sensed how important it was that I go. She gave me her immediate support but couched it in terms of caution. "Watch your step when you're there, Price. I was born in the South, and I know what can happen to you. I want you to go, but I just want you to be careful."

Armed with Evadne's loving and cautionary words, I flew to Montgomery.

•—◆—•

On Bloody Sunday men and women were knocked to the ground by water hoses, pursued by gnashing dogs and angry troopers, and thrust into paddy wagons by white troopers. The news that two white people—a minister from Boston named Reverend James Reeb and a union organizer from Detroit named Mrs. Viola Liuzzo—had been killed during those days in early March outraged thousands of people around the country. Not the least of them was President Johnson himself, who had introduced a voting rights bill before Congress on March 11.

Before now, I had been involved with civil rights only in a peripheral way. I had been to some meetings of the San Francisco chapter of the Congress of Racial Equality. I had met Ron Dellums prior to his election to the Berkeley City Council and subsequently to the U.S. House of Representatives. He and I had talked several times when I was on the board of the San Francisco chapter of the Urban League. But until then I had never put my body in the movement. Rather I was always in a support position to the real action that was taking place on the front lines. But Selma was to be a turning point for me. For the first time in my adult life, really, I stepped away from my professional concerns and took to the streets.

•—◆—•

I arrived in Montgomery early in the morning of March 25, 1965, the last day of the march. I noticed private and corporate jets at the airport. A lot of private and corporate jets. I hadn't been prepared for that, and I began to think that this might be an even bigger deal than I had originally thought. I took a taxi into Montgomery, though it was difficult to even get one at the airport. Taxi drivers were around, but a flood of people who had flown to Montgomery to join the march were keeping them occupied.

The march was being organized for that last day at the City of Saint Jude Catholic hospital, on West Fairview Avenue in Montgomery, where many of the marchers had slept the night before. Ironically, this complex was built on the site of the first black hospital in the United States. I arrived at the hospital grounds, dressed in a suit and tie. I had made my decision to come here so quickly that I had simply thrown an extra pair of underwear and an extra dress shirt, along with toiletries, in my briefcase. When I got to the march site itself, I felt a little out of place, because most of the marchers were far more casually dressed.

I'm wearing a suit and tie, I said to myself. My father would have worn a suit and tie. Warmed by the recollection, I headed for the march. So be it!

The walk that day was not very long, but it was extremely crowded. The black marchers were glad for those white people who had come to march with them, making it a truly multiracial alliance. I came up behind a group of white college professors, serious, cerebral-looking men, also dressed in suits and ties, who carried signs identifying them as members of the American Historical Society. Because of our similar dress, I began to think that some of the people walking around me thought that I too was a member of that society. The organizers wanted prominent people at the head of the march. So at one point I heard a large, deep, black voice come out of somewhere in the voluminous crowd. "Make way! Make way! For members of the American Historical Society. Bring 'em up in front! Bring 'em up!" Another brother, sweating profusely and not dressed in a suit and tie, yelled back. "The American Historical Society? A bunch of professors? Fuck the American Historical Society!"

There was an outburst of laughter among the blacks. Some thought: These white academics could not have suffered much from the travails of racism, so why should they be up in front? They looked about themselves, surprised and worried by the comedic conflict they had caused, prim in their suits and ties while all the other blacks within earshot, including me, just kept laughing.

The streets in Montgomery were lined with angry white people. There were catcalls, insults, and racial slurs the entire way to the capitol. People who had been marching all the way from Selma told me that the roads had been similarly lined at every step. Tight-faced, red-cheeked young white men and women screaming at us from behind the line of federal troops. "Niggers!" "Goddamned niggers!" "Fuckin' outsiders!" "Nigger go home!" These were not middle-class white people. Rather they were blue-collar whites, and I thought of them as the shock troops of the white South, and of white society in general. Looking into their eyes, I saw how much of their identity was taken over by hatred of black people and the desperate hope they had that, in the end, no matter what, they were superior to us. Without that sense of superiority, they were—and I felt that they must know it of themselves—simply underpaid, poorly educated, disadvantaged members of the white working class. Thugs, as well.

Looking at them and listening to the disrespect spilling from their mouths, I had some serious conflict within myself. I was a veteran, as were many, many of the other marchers. I wondered how many of these guys had served their country. I was exercising my rights as an American, an exhilarating exercise. And these people wanted to keep me from doing that. They wanted to take away my birthright as an American. It took a great deal of restraint and, for some, courage to remain calm, to keep walking and not retaliate against them. But we were under the spell of Dr. King and his message of Gandhian nonviolence. We knew how important it was that we remain in control of ourselves while these white goons discredited themselves for the six o'clock news cameras.

You could tell, just by looking at those people's faces, that somewhere in their souls they knew that an old order was passing. They were losing control. I had never seen hatred like that exhibited by the white people who lined the road. We were scared, but we had the federal government and the media watching. We had the American Historical Society! But most important we had ourselves, thousands of us for moral support.

I learned later that Branch Rickey, the man who had signed Jackie Robinson to the Brooklyn Dodgers eighteen years earlier, had been invited to participate in this march by Robinson himself. Eighty-three years old and wheelchair bound, Rickey had declined. But Robinson wrote back to him, "Please take care of yourself. We know where your heart is. We will take care of the Selma, Alabamas and do the job."

That last sentence carried the truth.

•—•

When we finally reached the shadow of the capitol, there was music from the various entertainers and the crowd itself. Speeches could be heard all day long from the capitol steps. Among all the women and men, the children holding a parent's hand, the local teenagers striding defiantly, among everyone marching that day was a sense that something monumental had been accomplished, truly and enormously.

I ran into all kinds of familiar people including Clarence Beverly, my classmate who had introduced me to Evadne. I encountered a woman from Montgomery. We introduced ourselves, and she was familiar with my name and turned out to have been a patient of my father. But what haunts me still is the speech I heard Dr. King deliver that day, March 25, 1965, from the capitol steps.

He asked the question, "How long . . . ?" "How long will it be before we see the new day?" "How long must we wait for justice to be done?" And the audience responded after each question, "Not long!" I remember being thrilled by the sound of his voice, asking such a question in the way that only Dr. King could ask it. "How long? How long?"

I've often thought, as the years have passed, that it's been longer, and will be longer still, than we thought it would be that day.

•—•

Afterward, I rode from Montgomery to Tuskegee with a black man from Birmingham who had participated in the march, Douglas Gill. There I was to spend the night with Evadne Davis, my wife's aunt for whom she had been named. Douglas was the husband of my cousin, Mattie, Uncle Sam's only child. By chance, we had seen each other at the march.

As we drove, we talked about our reactions to the march itself. There was a sense of triumph and exhilaration. Governor George Wallace, after all, who had stood for segregation his entire career, had in effect been defeated by this march. There was also a perception, really an illusion, that much more happened than actually did, that immediate and apocalyptic changes would occur. We had taken a quantum leap, we thought. As so often is the case, the passage of time was to show that, yes, we had taken some important steps, but we still had a very, very long journey. The reality of that journey's arduous path was clouded by our elation in the day or two just after the march.

I noticed as we were driving that Douglas was very carefully staying within the speed limit. When we came to a stop sign, he stopped. When the signal changed, he went ahead. If the speed limit was thirty-five, he drove at thirty, with great care, perhaps even overcautious care, I thought. This was far more than his being a "good driver."

I realized after some time that he was following a driving pattern which said "do not do anything to bring the notice of the cops your way."

Since Douglas had an Alabama driver's license, he was local. We were mindful of those white people who had been shouting at the marchers, their vitriol, their accusation that this march was just the work of a lot of outside agitators. I began to understand that for him, and black people like him who were citizens of Alabama, there was a burden that had come along with this march. People like me would get back on a plane in a day or two and fly away. But Douglas would remain in Alabama and be subject to the continued animosity of those white Alabamans who had so freely exhibited their hatred of black people during the march. He left me at the home of Evadne's relatives in Tuskegee, people who were closely connected with the staff and faculty of Tuskegee Institute.

As I walked up the stairs to the porch and rang the bell, I assumed that Evadne's relatives would be pleased as punch to see me, and that they'd be happy about my participation in the march. I'd flown all this way to show my solidarity with the marchers and with the ideas and ideals being displayed. I'd come all this way to soldier against segregation.

On one level they were elated to see me. Evadne was one of their favorite relatives, and she and her sister, Marion, had spent many summers in Tuskegee. They were educated people, immensely supportive of Dr. King's work and the movement. On another level, they were apprehensive about my being there. And ambivalent about the significance and consequences of the march.

What does this mean to us? They seemed to be asking. What will we be left to face once all of you have gone home?

"How long do you plan to stay, Price?" "You're leaving in the morning, isn't that right, Price?"

I was both surprised, and not surprised. These people were educated, professional blacks, so I knew that they were fundamentally interested in the issues of the march, the purposes of it, and so on. But in Alabama, bad and capricious things had happened to black people for centuries. And Tuskegee itself was a poor town, despite its being the location of the Tuskegee Institute. There were white "crackers" there, a lot of them. The family where I was staying overnight knew the Klan. They had seen Klan rallies. Indeed Tuskegee was a Klan enclave. So the price they paid for being in the circle of a black college in a poor Alabama town was that they had to stay in their place and not overstep their bounds with the white community.

They knew that they would have to face any consequences that the presence of all us marchers in Alabama could possibly bring once we were gone, once the bright light of national publicity had dimmed, once there was no one there to defend them. I had the distinct feeling that my hosts were worried that my presence in their home might bring real trouble their way.

•◆•

When I got back to San Francisco, I had much to tell Evadne. The march had caused a change in me, a kind of sea change.

I had lived in the South for four years. I had visited the South many times. I was very aware that the white South, with regard to racism against blacks, suffered a deeply ingrained hatred. But during that march, looking at the faces of those hecklers, I felt that I was finally, truly looking into the eyes of evil. Into the eyes of the Devil. A view like that can organize the mind quickly and decisively. It can spur action.

The march also allowed me to assimilate the truth of racism, to bring its reality into my consciousness, and to incorporate it into some of the things that I was thinking about professionally. Why were black people so angry? What made their emotional dysfunction at once the same and also different from that of other people?

The march made me realize that racism was still a fact. It was out there alive and well and potentially violent. After the march, I was able to see where I personally fit into all that. If one of the questions that could be asked at that time was "are you participating personally in the issues of your time?" I knew that from that moment on, my answer would be yes. There was to be no question about that. My participation was not to be on the periphery or extracurricular. I was not going to be just a psychiatrist, looking from afar at the issues of racism, rage, and violence. I knew that I had to integrate all these issues into one thoughtful consciousness, and to act upon them.

Evadne always had had an unerring eye for falsehood or pretense, for misplaced self-importance. She always anchored me in ways that kept me from too much expansiveness or self-aggrandizement. In this case, she realized when I got back that something undeniable had happened to me during that march. She nodded her head as I told her about it. She recognized that the gravity with which I told these stories was appropriate, and from that moment on, she was to support me wholeheartedly in everything I did.

• ◆ •

Dr. King himself made perhaps the most telling analysis of the events of Bloody Sunday, when he later wrote, "In the vicious maltreatment of defenseless citizens of Selma, where old women and young children were gassed and clubbed at random, we have witnessed an eruption of the disease of racism which seeks to destroy all America. No American is without responsibility."

Five months later, in August 1965, Congress passed the Voting Rights Act that put an end to voter discrimination against black people. On that day, there were 93,000 registered black voters in Alabama. Two years later that number had jumped to 250,000. The same pattern of meteoric expansion in the black voter rolls was seen in every state in the South.

• ◆ •

In 1967 I got a call from George Leonard, the same George Leonard who had arranged for the *Look* magazine article about the attack on our Westlake district home. He had been involved in the Esalen Institute south of Monterey, California, for some years and had been a vice president of the institute since 1966. Founded by Michael Murphy and Richard Price in 1962, Esalen was already known as the place for cutting-edge work in the behavioral sciences. It was established as an alternative educational center to explore what Aldous Huxley called "the human potential." Such people as Arnold Toynbee, Linus Pauling, Joseph Campbell, Buckminster Fuller, and many others regularly visited Esalen to hold seminars and workshops and pursue a new form of psychic exploration called "the confrontation group." Esalen has always been a very freewheeling place, where psychological experimentation is the norm. George was calling me with an idea for a new kind of confrontation group, one that even in the context of Esalen was to be truly revolutionary.

He suggested a racial confrontation group. It was clear to George that the issue of race was the issue in American culture. At the core of that issue was a pool of distrust, anger, and rage that kept blacks and whites apart. This was the most important element in the continuing legacy of slavery. If this element could not be exposed, talked about, and argued over by black people with white people, the separation would continue, no matter how many court cases, legislative reviews, marches on Washington, and think-tank white papers were produced in the future. George later wrote about this in his book *Education and Ecstasy*: "The traditional ways weren't working. The Black Power militants screamed their hurt, anger and hatred. By revealing themselves and voicing the truth, they begged for encounter. The white leaders responded with conventional language, revealing nothing of their own feelings. How could there be understanding without self-revelation? Didn't the whites feel outrage, fear, repressed prejudice? The measured, judicious response seemed a lie." I shared his sentiments.

Emotional confrontation was the way, and George was calling for help. As a black psychiatrist, a man who had had a number of racial confrontations and as someone who was actively thinking about these very questions, I would be essential to the planning and implementation of such an event.

I agreed. The group would meet on a weekend in July of 1967. We wrote the copy for a brochure, advertised the idea, and got a positive response from approximately thirty-five men and women. Blacks and whites and a few Asians.

Esalen was an unlikely place for a racial confrontation group. It is well over one hundred miles south of San Francisco and sits above the Pacific Ocean on twenty-seven acres of beautiful Big Sur coastline. The Santa Lucia Mountains are in the background. Its lodge, adjoining buildings, and swimming pool are on a cliff overlooking the water. While we were there, the constant pounding of the surf was heard day and night. It is a place of spectacular beauty and was a destination for many young people in the San Francisco Haight-Ashbury scene of the 1960s. The fabled Jack Kerouac had once visited there, and later someone wrote, "Every hippie eventually makes the scene at Esalen Institute."

In addition to the swimming pool there are baths fed by natural hot springs, and the catalog stated, "swimsuits are optional and nudity common." Oh God, I thought, what have I gotten myself into? Me, a conventional young black professional, raised to be respectable. The visions of long-haired hippies swimming nude made me wonder what my mother would have thought about us being there. But this is the place we had chosen, and what George and I were embarking on was certainly experimental, so Evadne and I drove off to Esalen with Price Priester and Renata in the backseat of our Dodge station wagon.

That weekend had a profound impact upon my life. Dressed in casual clothes, the participants arrived and eyed one another warily. In terms of how they looked, my fears were immediately dispelled. They all appeared to be the kind of people who attended seminars and lectures and were interested in something called "race relations." Several people were accompanied by spouses or close friends, while a few others came with colleagues from work. We gathered for the first session, and those who came together revealed their apprehension by clinging to one another. During the first day George and I arranged various exercises to unveil the participants' feelings about race and one another. At first everyone participated in physical exercises conducted by a Chinese guru. While he was a famous person for the Esalen regulars, until that day he was unknown to me. The exercises were the easy part. People could stretch, twist their bodies into various configurations, joke with one another, and generally work themselves into a festive mood.

Then we went inside into a large room. People sat around in typical seminar fashion—some in chairs, others lying against large pillows or simply sitting cross-legged on the floor. George and I were at the front of the room facing everyone. They were instructed to introduce themselves, share something about their background, and then state why they were there. Their initial statements exposed a mixture of boldness and fear.

A white schoolteacher from Los Angeles introduced herself. She started in a well-modulated voice and then almost shouted, "I'm here to try and find out what blacks really want?" It was obvious to me that she wanted to sound confident, almost strident, but her eyes stayed focused on the floor and her shoulders were slumped forward. Her body language spoke louder than her words. It was as if she didn't really want to know the answer to the question.

Another white person spoke up and gave particulars about himself— name, age, where he lived and worked—and then he finished by saying, "I've been a liberal all my life." With that he stopped and looked around, seemingly convinced that this declaration answered all questions about who he was and why he was there.

A black man started by talking about his many accomplishments. "I graduated from U.C. Berkeley, I play chess and tennis like many of you, and I still don't get any respect." Since no one had mentioned chess or tennis, it was obvious he wanted to identify with what he thought were the pursuits of the whites in the room. I stopped him and gently pointed this out. Although I didn't know he was going to be there, he was someone I had known at Cal. The number of black students in the early 1950s was small, so it was not unusual that we would know each other. Although we were never close friends, I wondered immediately how our past relationship might affect what would happen over the next two days.

The usual Esalen practice was to have people work in small groups. The intent was to provide a safer, more intimate setting where people could share their innermost thoughts and feelings. However, it was my idea to keep the group together. I had several reasons for this. One, I felt in this highly experimental and volatile group everyone needed to hear (and feel) everything at the same time. This would eliminate the need for third-party gossip and the sharing of tidbits about something said in another group. The other reason was that I wanted George and me to remain in the same room and be with the entire group. Without stating it, we would model our friendship, which by then was deep and solid.

As the first morning unfolded, long-suppressed feelings about race began to erupt. People began to offer up ideas and notions that they had never shared in any group, much less a mixed one. However, rather than heated discussions with whites and blacks talking about the racial gulf between them, the early out-and-out confrontations involved the black participants. I remembered with silent amusement my training as a leader in group psychotherapy sessions. In those, I could be laid-back and reflective, but here the demands were for engagement. George and I were not just quiet facilitators; we found ourselves actively participating in the conversations and arguments.

The black people present covered a spectrum of professions, educational levels, and abilities. They had all been making their way more or less successfully in their lives. These were not poor people; they were educated and middle-class. There was only one black woman. In the introductions and early discussions everyone almost casually mentioned the day-to-day discrimination they encountered.

A white man, who wanted to think he was speaking for others, interrupted and asked a question implying a black man was "too sensitive" or "that happens to me too." During his comments he was unfailingly polite and even charming, but it was apparent he didn't buy these black stories. Come on, he wanted to say, these things don't happen in Los Angeles or San Francisco.

As things heated up, I noted the black folks venting their frustrations and anger against one another. The brother I knew from Cal mentioned tennis again.

"Man, quit talking about that goddamn tennis, you're just trying to impress the white folks." This response came from one of the black men, who until this point had remained mostly silent.

While this comment startled the whites, most of the blacks immediately nodded their heads in agreement. Now the heat was turned up full blast and a one-upmanship developed among the black participants, in which each tried to "out-black" the other person. I was certainly not unfamiliar with this particular struggle around racial authenticity but was surprised it happened so quickly and in front of white folks too. These contests usually occurred in black groups out of the earshot of whites.

One man mentioned he would soon receive his doctorate at a major Los Angeles university. Before he could get the words out of his mouth, someone yelled back, "Is your wife white?"

Then the one-upmanship shifted to finger-pointing about who had marched, protested, or sat in. I looked out and saw a group of middle-class black folks, involved in their professional lives and attending a weekend gathering in a beautiful, bucolic setting. The truth was that few, if any, of them had actively participated in the "movement." The type of person of any color who responded to a brochure from the Esalen Institute was generally not at the front lines of racial protest. Yet I could see that their anger—and rage—was as real as any I had experienced from my days as a consultant with black prisoners or from the civil rights workers who came to my office for a sanity check.

It would not have been a discussion among blacks without someone being called an "Uncle Tom" or a "sellout," and I was not to be disappointed. Since several of the black men had arrived at Esalen with whites or were accompanied by a white woman, the targets were easy to find.

I saw an excruciating conflict about stating deeply held beliefs in the presence of whites. The blacks present had responded to something they thought might be useful, but there was a nagging guilt about talking so openly in front of white people. For me, it pointed out once again that most conversations about race stopped short of total disclosure. Even with "close" white friends, discussions about race involved events in the South, discrimination in housing or jobs, but they rarely touched on or exposed the deep personal anguish that most blacks felt daily.

For example, one person would call another "a racist" because the other person had not given enough of himself to "the cause."

"Yeah, well, you're nothing but an Uncle Tom yourself, thinking like that."

"A Tom!"

"Yeah. A fink, man. A fink! You work too much with the white man. Too close to him. So you must be a Tom racist, too!"

"Maybe so, but when they come at us with guns, my brother, are you gonna be for me or against me? You gonna be black or are you gonna be white?"

There were many more such exchanges, filled with hate and venom. I didn't know quite what to make of them. They were filled with anger and loathing for one another. I had thought that this racial confrontation group was to be a meeting of blacks versus whites. But here were black people excoriating one another, wounding one another, exposing a distaste they felt for one another and for themselves—in the open!

During an exchange about interracial sex, a black woman in the group suddenly addressed a very dark-skinned man who had been describing in detail how he would take one of the white women participants.

"You couldn't take me," the woman interjected. "And I'm going to tell you why. Because you're just a dirty little black nigger!"

The man was livid and had to exercise obvious control not to strike out at the woman. I quickly recalled my mother's color consciousness, her many words for different colors of skin, and the general belief among black people that the lighter-skinned black person was the more beautiful black person. What this woman had said was an even worse insult than it appeared to be on the surface. This man was dark. Much of our society presumed him ugly, and maybe he thought of himself as such, having been so dark all his life and reminded of it all his life. No wonder he was outraged!

But finally and inevitably, the confrontation for which we had ostensibly come to Esalen began to develop. The blacks turned away from attacking one another and began assailing the whites. They began telling the whites what racism is and how it feels to be on the receiving end, no holds barred. And it was here that I began to see the true depth of the rage that the black participants felt against the white participants.

"You think you have the right to say you've got problems?" a black woman shouted at a white woman who had been complaining of some difficulty she had experienced. "What do you know about having your kids called 'nigger' and there's nothing you can do about it? When's your kid ever been spit on because he was black?"

A white woman had asked for a black man's friendship.

"Fuck you!" he had replied. "And fuck your condescension! Fuck your pity!"

"Please! No!" she said. "Won't you help me?"

"No! You just feel what I feel!"

She broke into tears. "Please!"

"Cry those tears, bitch! Cry like I've cried all my life!"

Many of the white participants adopted a guilt-ridden attitude of shame for what they felt they had done personally in their lives and what they represented as the white oppressors of black people. They allowed themselves to be attacked. But some did not and lashed back at the pointed accusations of the blacks. Luckily, everyone honored the one rule that we had imposed, which was that physical violence would not be tolerated. But this was a boisterous, often angry, and quite confrontational series of meetings. The confrontation group went on for two full days, including one very stormy all-night session.

•◆•

The participants at this first black/white confrontation group learned so much about one another that weekend that few, if any of them, went home unaffected. Many friendships were formed. Some of the participants came away offended and upset. A few seemed shell-shocked.

I was amazed. I learned that weekend another dimension of black rage, how true a reality it represented, and how deeply it was felt.

In *Education and Ecstasy,* George Leonard quotes one of the white women as saying, "I had no idea it was this bad. I work with Negroes. That's my job. And I didn't realize. My best friend of fifteen years is a Negro, and I had no idea she felt these kinds of things. . . . I'm afraid to see my friend. I don't see how the race problem can ever be solved."

I would have agreed with her had I not myself become so aware of the rage that black people had been feeling for centuries. It now came as no surprise to me. But even I was surprised by the intensity of it.

I felt, though, that the race problem could be addressed, and that solutions could be sought. This weekend had given me the key. What that woman was so shocked to see had actually been a great service to her, to me, and to everyone at that Esalen group, because she had seen the truth of black rage.

•◆•

The Selma-to-Montgomery march had taught me many things about the obduracy of white resistance to the ascendance of black people to their proper place in American society. It showed how necessary it was to confront that resistance no matter the danger it represented. It showed me how ready black people were to make that confrontation, while at the same time reminding me of the caution that still existed among many black people, with good reason.

At the same time, the first racial confrontation group at Esalen revealed to me the true depth of black rage. Given the inexorable momentum and power of what was happening in government, the courts, and the streets in those times, I saw the importance of understanding that rage, explaining it to as many people as I could, and helping them learn how to manage it effectively.

I needed a way to do this—a forum, a channel. I found the vehicle for that when I met another black psychiatrist named William H. Grier.

CHAPTER THIRTEEN

When I met Bill Grier in the mid-1960s, he had just moved to San Francisco from Detroit, Michigan. He was newly divorced and hired to run the city's Child Psychiatric Clinic on Page Street. There were a couple of dozen black physicians in San Francisco at the time, and only one or two black psychiatrists, to be sure. So it was natural that we'd seek each other out, to see whether there'd be a possible friendship and a working relationship perhaps. I knew right away that Bill was a first-rate psychiatrist. His medical degree was from the University of Michigan, where he had also done his postgraduate study and residency, and he had done important psychiatric clinical work at the prestigious Menninger Clinic in Topeka, Kansas. His questions of me and his comments about patients and their social milieu let me know right away that his intellectual energy was firmly directed at the explosive racial issues of our times.

Like my father, Bill had an edge. He was direct. He didn't suffer fools. He was a man who understood clearly the psychological burden of a people who had been pushed to the outside, forced to stay there, and given very little room for moving from that exiled state of being. I'd seen that understanding in my father, and I could feel it in myself.

I had written an article that had appeared in the *Negro Digest* of July 1967 entitled "Journeys to Black Identity: Selma and Watts," in which I had spelled out the differences and similarities from an historical and psychological point of view, as I saw them, between the Selma-to-Montgomery march and the extraordinarily destructive Watts riots during the summer of 1965. The riots were one of the clearest demonstrations of unbridled rage that I had ever seen, and I expected more such events to come soon (as ultimately they did). Also, the Watts riots had a personal flavor. It occurred in my home town, and many of the buildings that were destroyed lined the streets, Central Avenue in particular, I had walked on as a boy in Los Angeles. Also, several people I knew well had their property burned to the ground.

The fact is, the country by this time was a powder keg. The prisoners at Duell had been one thing. But the black middle-class participants in the confrontation group at Esalen were quite another. Now I was seeing among my patients, on a regular basis, what I had observed during that weekend at Big Sur: angry black bank tellers, teachers furious with the way they perceived they were being treated, a lonely black airline pilot disgruntled with the task of flying the plane because he was so outraged by the slights he was receiving from his superiors. Many black professionals suffered from some unnameable anger. Many were ready to explode but not able to put a finger on why.

For example, many years later I knew a senior black executive of a major corporation, a rare species in American business at the time. The man was making fine money and had a great deal of responsibility. He had made it. He had even been invited to play golf with a few major white executives and the president of the United States! When he got to the golf course and was waiting for the president, one of the other executives asked him who he was caddying for. He wanted to deck the idiot.

These people, from young black managers, bus drivers, nurses, postmen, all the way up to this senior executive, were telling me how angry they were. If they were to complain about it, their managers or acquaintances—sometimes white, sometimes black—would respond, "Hell, man, you're doing fine. You've got a good job. You're getting promoted." In the case of the senior executive, they'd say, "You're playing golf with the president! What have you got to complain about when some fool makes a dumb mistake like that?"

Black people who were "doing fine" were still the same black people who had seen and experienced racism all their lives and kept pretty quiet about it. Up to this moment, keeping quiet about it had been a reasonable thing to do. But now riots were being emblazoned on the television screen almost every day, and those black people who were "doing fine" were discovering within themselves the personal outrage they had been feeling all along. These people were pissed! And now they were letting that fact be known to themselves . . . and others.

The question for many now became: "How can I *manage* this anger?" Up to now, for the most part, most black people tried to dance away from it, rationalize, ignore and deny it. I remember recalling at the time, "Sure, I marched at Selma, but that march could have taken place just as easily in San Francisco." An exaggeration, maybe, but I knew from my experiences in California and in the South that California's brand of racism was different from that of Alabama in degree only. The kind of anger it caused was the same no matter where you were.

Bill and I had our private-practice offices in the same San Francisco neighborhood, and we'd frequently get together over coffee at a restaurant on California Street to compare notes. We found that we had a great deal of experience and feeling in common. We also had patients with many common problems.

Bill admitted to me that he, like I, had been sensing a deep simmering anger not altogether under control. Bill told me that it was time for us to do something about all this. It was time, as he put it, "To get off the dime, Price."

We decided to collaborate on some kind of written project in which we'd present these issues and make an analysis of them. We wanted to acknowledge what we were hearing from our black patients and then try to provide some guidelines to understanding what they were feeling and how they were coping. The times were different, black people were marching in the streets, sometimes rioting. There was upheaval. Unrest. It was a time of real ferment, between, among, and inside black people. A time of profound questioning.

On hospital grand rounds, in clinic discussions, and often just in passing, many therapists had finally discovered race was somehow, somewhere, a factor, and they didn't know what to make of it. They sat down with a black patient, began taking a history, and then a line of inquiry would elicit unexpected answers and comments. Patients who had previously rarely mentioned their racial background now talked about little else. And the textbooks were bereft of material where one could go for answers. What little that had been written was frequently filled with the same stereotypes and pseudoscience as found anywhere else in our society. Suddenly the mental health field began searching for ways to understand, diagnose, and treat black patients. Our time was now, and we thought we could make a major contribution.

What does it mean as an American to have a slave name? What about the Black Muslims. What about Malcolm X? Bill and I wanted to write about that, the milieu in which our black patients were living. We discussed the rapidly developing and fracturing civil rights movement. What responsibility did each black person have for furthering the rights of all black people? Why are some black people made so angry by even being asked that question? Why did Dr. King and Malcolm seem so much at odds? Were they *really* at odds? Did we have to sacrifice ourselves for "The Movement"? Who were we? Were we still "colored people"? Were we "Negroes"? Or, given what was happening in the streets, were we something else?

This linguistic distinction was in itself very important. The shift in terminology was an historical one that had required a century or more to develop, and was coming to fruition even as Bill and I were talking. The term "colored" had come from the need for a defining term, in the early years after the Civil War, that took away the sting of the legacy of slavery, and that of slavery itself. It was intended to heal the emotional scars that accompanied the issue of skin pigmentation for black people in this country. It was much more formal than the word "black," which at that time was actually an insulting term to colored people. "Colored" implied a mixture of ethnicities, a good part of the mixture having been provided by whites. We weren't just black. We were colored, as indicated by the National Association for the Advancement of Colored People, founded in 1909.

Following upon the use of the word *colored,* "Negro" was an even *more* dignified term for black people. It was a capitalized word. It implied a formal place, assured value. In his time, my father was a Negro. Paul Robeson was a Negro. Marian Anderson was a Negro.

But in the mid-1960s both these terms seemed to have served their purpose. Now they felt like euphemisms that had been intended to defuse, in black people's minds, the identity they had as descendants of slaves, at being called "nigger" by white people, at their being on a tier of society very much outside and below that of the dominant culture. They were terms imposed on black people from outside, and so they took their meaning from these outside influences. They were terms that black people ostensibly used to give themselves dignity and worth, but they were primarily intended to turn the gaze aside from what he or she considered a shameful background, a background not to be viewed simply for what it was.

Many young black people made fun of the term "Negro." To be a Negro was, for a lot of the youth in the 1960s, to be an "Uncle Tom." People of my parents' generation suffered from this criticism, something that, no doubt, added to their rage.

Now everything seemed to have changed. A new term was to be used, one that under no circumstances was imposed upon us from the outside.

The first widespread use in public settings of the word *black* occurred in June 1966. The Meredith Mississippi March, led by James Meredith, the first black student at the University of Mississippi, was planned to go from Memphis, Tennessee, to Jackson, Mississippi. The purpose was to get African Americans to register and vote, and it was called a "march against fear." On the first day of the march, Meredith was wounded from a shotgun blast. The next day leaders of all the major civil rights groups announced the resumption of the march. Over the next several days, Stokely Carmichael, one of the leaders of SNCC, repeatedly shouted the words "Black Power" as he exhorted the marchers and reminded them of their mission. Whatever controversy might now ensue over the use of the word, it's time had come.

Prior to that, the word *black* had been a pejorative one. While scholars and Black Nationalists might freely use the word, it had no wide currency. Calling someone black had been one step short of calling him a nigger in anger. The fact that W. E. B. DuBois had used the term in the title of his great work *The Souls of Black Folk,* published in 1903, simply speaks to the prescience and clear-mindedness of his thinking. As Dr. King wrote, "There were few scholars who concerned themselves with honest study of the black man, and [DuBois] sought to fill this immense void."

I was in a meeting one evening in late 1967 or early 1968. I can't remember where the meeting was, or even what it was about, but I know it had something to do with civil rights. I do remember that whatever we were discussing was against a background of much sound and fury. People were accusatory. If you didn't agree with a suggested militant-sounding course of action, you were by definition a "sellout" or a "Saddity Negro." Then just as the counterpoint of shouting and responding became almost unbearable, someone uttered the phrase "Black is beautiful."

It was the first time I'd heard the word used as a way to calm a fractious, volatile meeting. There was a sudden silence among the participants, a pause, a holding of breath. You could have heard a pin drop. And then there was recognition among the people in that room that a change had taken place. Body language changed. Smiles appeared. Heads nodded in the affirmative. It was apparent to me as a psychiatrist, as an observer of the social milieu, and as a student of black people that we had somehow reached an epiphanous moment, and that we would not go back. We were, suddenly, no longer "Negroes" in that meeting. We were "blacks." And we were beautiful.

Psychologically we had moved in the same moment toward the legacy of slavery and away from it. Toward it in the sense that we were now embracing the legacy as part of our history, and away from it in that we would no longer accept that legacy as a set of irons that would continue to hobble us, a club in someone's hand that we had to run away from. We had finally embraced a self-definition, not one imposed from the outside.

It was a profound moment, the utterance of three simple words. "Black is beautiful." Just the sound of them formed a pivotal moment for everyone there that day. *Black* was the word that defined what and who we were. It was truth. The word *black* embraced a history that had been degraded and diminished in importance. By saying *black,* we were in effect turning that degraded history on its head.

"Say it loud!" as the great James Brown—surely one of the most prophetic observers of the times—was to observe. "I'm black and I'm proud!"

The ultimate bellwether for me in this change was my mother. She had always used the terms "colored" and "Negro" when she'd referred to black people. To her, the term "black" when referring to Negroes was a bad word. Soon after this meeting, though, I was speaking with my mother, and wondering to myself when she would use the term "black" in a nonpejorative, positive way. In the course of this conversation, she referred to the "black church" and its power for good within the community. Once I heard that, I knew that the term in its new context was now a permanent part of the lexicon. We had finally crossed over.

•◆•

The key thing for Bill Grier and me was that this coming of new ideas was a joyful union for us. We saw what was happening, and we had each other to talk with about it. We could share ideas and responses.

Bill and I never thought of our joint project as strictly an academic paper or a book-length endeavor for an academic press. We wanted the piece to be read, but we were also engaged in a balancing act. We wanted to write a guide for the treatment of black patients, taking into account the society in which they lived and the historical legacy accompanying them. In numerous case conferences, symposia, and clinic settings where we participated, psychotherapists and other clinicians were desperate for information so they could better understand and be more effective with black patients. We wanted our work to be read and deemed "acceptable" by our professional and academic peers, but we didn't want it loaded down with footnotes and references so that a wider audience would be driven away.

We toyed with titles. *Reflections on the Negro Psyche* was one that excited neither of us, although it was representative of our thinking in those first days. Titles like this didn't do much to identify the emotional pain that we were going to describe. But we still had the idea that this was going to be a scholarly work that would have to satisfy the expectations of the academic journals, and that it should have a similar tone to that of the books we had read in the field.

We had at our disposal innumerable case studies, anecdotal information, and a firsthand history from many, many patients that chronicled the anger that threatened to consume black people. Our feeling was that you had to expose that anger in order to understand it. You had to tell what it was. We saw the need to develop a new form of therapy to help these people. But even then we weren't sure quite what we were dealing with, and the first written effort we came up with fell short of what we wanted.

We had submitted our book to a major publisher, who had turned it down with a form rejection. When we got it back, we pored over the manuscript, trying to figure out what it lacked. What was missing? Why had so little attention been paid to it by the publisher? Had they even read the manuscript? Again and again we pondered the questions.

•◆•

It came to Bill and me almost simultaneously that, above all else, what we had written was lacking "the edge."

We were describing outright rage. But we were describing it as though it were a clinical condition that could be studied quietly in the light of academic reflection. What that rage really *was,* though, was a psychological condition that was causing pain to millions of black people and would ultimately lead to the incredible events that would destroy large sections of American cities (most notably, a year or so before the time of our writing, my own hometown of L.A.).

Our initial drafts were too reserved in tone. But what they described were open sores of negative emotion, extraordinarily violent personal responses, anger, hatred, and rage. And this rage was not only in our clients and patients, our friends and family, but in ourselves.

Looking over the first completed manuscript, we realized that the truth we had discovered was not being served by the way in which we were describing it. We needed a language that told that truth, in the way that it had been told to us by black people everywhere.

So we started a rewrite. We got rid of language that seemed too passive and academic. We looked carefully so we could cut out unnecessary psychiatric jargon yet remain true to our training and experiences. This was not to be a frivolous pop-culture exposé. It was an effort to reveal a deeply felt psychological reaction to very real conditions. We searched for a language that would tell the truth as we had been told, a language that would represent the actual words of the people we knew.

Rage had provided its own eloquence.

Several events from my own experience were helping to steer my part of the rewriting. Somewhere in the tone of the new writing, in the plain-spoken nature of it, in its raw feeling, was my reminiscence of the white kid across the street when I was six, calling me a nigger. Those fraternity boys and sorority girls at UCLA, causing me in effect to disappear even as I was redecorating their floats. That storekeeper tossing me out of the neighborhood market. The car salesman in Nashville. The white goons of Montgomery. The plight my mother had faced, dressed as a maid while checking out her new house. Our white Westlake neighbors. The outrage of my father having to see his patient in the hospital during visiting hours. All these things were in my heart, telling me how to write. I may not have had them specifically in mind as I was writing. But as much as such things existed in the tales I'd been told by my patients, so they existed in my soul, fueling my own rage.

Although we *were* writing about the clinical state of the Negro psyche, Bill and I were really describing exposed nerves, violently suppressed anger, teeth-grinding frustration and outrage on the part of black people from every level of society. So, keeping close to our sources, we decided that the title of our book had to tell the same kind of truth, directly and without equivocation.

We called it *Black Rage*.

•◆•

It took us less than a year to do the rewrite. We showed it to a colleague, Dr. Robert Wallerstein, an eminent psychiatrist and writer who was shortly to become the president of the American Psychoanalytic Association as well as the chairman of the Department of Psychiatry at the University of California, San Francisco. He thought we were on to something. His wife, Judith Wallerstein, was a psychologist writing books on the effects of divorce, particularly on children, that would become hallmark works in their own right. They suggested that we take the manuscript to Basic Books, a publisher of books on ideas and the intellect, with an interest in psychology, and Bob actually was the one to send it to them. To our great pleasure, we received a letter back from Basic Books, offering us an advance, and publication in June 1968.

George Leonard then introduced us to Sterling Lord, one of the premier literary agents in New York, and he took it from there. We were finally in business.

Bill and I congratulated each other and shared a bottle of champagne. We thanked the Wallersteins for their invaluable help, and I celebrated with Evadne and the kids. It was completely thrilling. I was finally a published writer, not just of an article but of a book! This was not a side profession, something to augment my work as a psychiatrist, but an endeavor to which I had always aspired in my secret heart. Our first effort would be a modest one, no doubt. We expected interest in academic and clinical circles and, with a little luck, modest sales among the general reading public.

But no one had any idea of the enormity of what was to happen when *Black Rage* finally came out.

· ◆ ·

Malcolm X had been assassinated at the hands of black men a few years before, on February 21, 1965, rival members of the Nation of Islam, during a speaking engagement in the Audubon Ballroom in Manhattan. Bill and I felt that he too had been a giant in the way that Dr. King had been. We had written about Malcolm in the final chapter of our manuscript that "if this black nobleman is a hero to black people in the United States and if his life reflects their aspirations, there can be no doubt of the universality of black rage."

Dr. King was assassinated on April 4, 1968. His murder in Memphis was of course a very great shock to me and my family, as it was to most people in the United States. If anyone were to stand as the symbol for the civil rights movement, it would have to be Dr. King. He had gathered the movement together, inspired the people who were leading and participating in it, and become the moral conscience of this nation. There was no way to diminish who he was or what he had done.

The death of Dr. King and the way he had died at the hands of a *white* assassin radically sharpened the urgency of our book's message. The murderous, enormously destructive riots in many of the major cities of the

United States that came in the immediate aftermath of his death were emblematic of exactly what we were talking about in the book. There was a compelling need to understand this and to write about it. But the book was in production, coming out in a month and a half, and we did not want to postpone the publication date. Nevertheless we contacted Basic Books the day after Dr. King was killed, insisting that we be allowed to add to the manuscript. To their credit, Basic Books understood this need and agreed right away to our revisions and additions.

We saw clearly how Dr. King's death would exacerbate the rage of black people. As we wrote: "To the extent that he stood in the way of bigotry, his life was in jeopardy, his saintly persuasion notwithstanding. To the extent that he was black and was calling America to account, his days were numbered by the nation he sought to save." If this man, whose life had been dedicated to the Gandhian notion of passive resistance and the Christian precepts of love for his fellow man and turning the other cheek, if a man like this could be cut down so violently, then the destruction of cities would seem to many a worthwhile act. Rage would flow.

We were able to address this in the book. Yet there was one more blow that was to come almost on the day of its publication, when Robert F. Kennedy was assassinated in Los Angeles. His death was nearly as big a shock to me as Dr. King's. I have thought a lot about the two murdered Kennedy men. I had admired John F. Kennedy a great deal, although I thought that his commitment to civil rights was more a matter of political necessity rather than coming from an intrinsic sense of right. He saw what was coming and reacted to it in accordance with its inevitability. So I've felt that he was a bit overrated with regard to his feelings for the civil rights of black people.

At the same time, I felt that Robert Kennedy was very underrated in these matters. I knew that he had served as an attorney on Joseph McCarthy's Senate Committee Army hearings. He'd been on the wrong side of many questions, as far as I could see. His reputation as a cold-blooded right-wing zealot was, early on, well deserved.

But I felt that his own brother's death had caused a transformation in Robert Kennedy. His soul had been seared by what had happened to

John Kennedy, and he seemed to have studied the rage that that must have caused in him, and to have decided on a different, more peace-seeking path toward achieving his own political goals. I no longer perceived, in Robert Kennedy's actions after the death of his brother, the calculation for which he had been known. Rather I felt his insistence on pursuing justice, especially for those who had been so marginalized as to have little recourse. I didn't doubt his sincerity.

When he spoke on the night of Dr. King's death, he had counseled black people: "For those of you who are black . . . you can be filled with bitterness, with hatred, and a desire for revenge. We can move in that direction as a country, in great polarization—black people amongst black, white people amongst white, filled with hatred toward one another. Or we can make an effort, as Martin Luther King did, to understand and to comprehend, and to replace that violence, that stain of bloodshed that has spread across our land, with an effort to understand, with compassion and love."

I believe he spoke from his soul's conviction that night. And he died for it.

But Dr. King had spoken for himself, in a way, as well as for Malcolm and the two Kennedys, when he had said, "The ultimate measure of a man is not where he stands in moments of comfort and convenience, but where he stands at times of challenge and controversy."

I felt that all of them had come up to that measure.

•◆•

Black Rage was an instant phenomenal success.

It received stellar reviews. *Time's* writer said, "For whites the book [is] basic education. . . . To blacks, [it] offers that hardest lesson of all: suspicion is justified, but paranoia is a disease." By this remark, the reviewer showed his understanding that the rage that black people were feeling had an explanation. I would have used a term different from "a disease," perhaps something like "an explainable condition," "a manageable condition." But basically he got it right.

A man whose own work I much admired, Robert Coles, wrote in *The New Republic*, "A book that takes account of the ambiguities in the psychological make-up of black people and, of course, all the rest of us."

Maybe the most intense appreciation of *Black Rage* came from the *Chicago Tribune*'s Thomas R. Frazier: "No book I have ever read so convincingly portrays the condition of black America. Even the intensely personal disclosures of Richard Wright, James Baldwin, John A. Williams and other novelists do not have its impact. . . . Remarkable."

I was personally touched by Mr. Frazier's praise because I so admired the work of the three writers he mentioned. All of these men wrote directly from the heart *about* black rage. As novelists, they had attempted to visit rage's deepest flames and study them for what they were.

Suddenly we had book tours, with radio and television interviews in most of the cities we visited. There were microphones. Television cameras. We were interviewed for newspaper articles and written about. Evadne and I went to Savannah to visit her family, and *Time* magazine asked us if they could send a writer and photographer along with us, to do a story.

The experience was heady in the extreme. But through all the excitement new ideas were churning. I sensed in black America a yearning for explanations beyond a fight for civil rights. People wanted to know more about themselves and the effect racism had on them personally. They were looking for a different voice to speak with authority about this phenomenon that we had uncovered. Dr. King was gone, as was Malcolm X, and to be sure neither Bill nor I had any illusions about our own importance by comparison. But I saw how what we had laid bare about black people had opened the possibility of revealing many more things about themselves.

Therapists—white, black, and all persuasions in between—thanked us for the clear explanations we had provided, the intense stories, the examples of rage they had been unaware of, that now gave them more insight and suggested methods of intervention.

I'm sure that active racists would not read a book like *Black Rage*. They don't care. But for the majority of white people, who had not done overt harm to anyone and really didn't intend to, whose own racism was nonetheless ingrained in them by the weight of so much history, so much intended and unintended prejudice and so much misguided law, our book was a revelation. Suddenly they were looking at themselves and asking what *their* responsibility was in all this. If the primary purpose of our book was to reveal black people to themselves, so they could deal in healthy ways with their rage, a secondary achievement of it was to reveal white people to themselves as well.

At these book tours and publicity events during the first months after publication, I was approached with all sorts of questions.

"Dr. Cobbs, I'm the first black branch manager at the bank I work for, and I can't seem to make headway with my boss, who's, you know, a white guy. Not a bad guy. Just a white guy."

"I have a son with epilepsy, and I'm wondering if you could help me with some ideas about how my wife and I can deal with this."

"My teenage girl is . . . well, we just can't seem to get along with her, and my wife's at her wits' end, and . . ."

There were others, not nearly so appreciative. A white psychiatric colleague of mine with whom I always had a dubious relationship gave me the opinion that "black intellectuals are on thin ice, Price. A lot of people are going to wonder if you've got what it takes to back up a theory like the one you've got in this book."

But we knew, based on the reactions that we were getting everywhere, that Bill and I had uncovered a unique truth, and that the results of it were to be of real value to many people.

•◆•

As always, Evadne was the repository of good sense while all this was happening. With adulation and fame at once real, imagined, and exaggerated coming my way, I was undoubtedly beginning to think of myself as someone quite special indeed. An important writer! A social scientist to be reckoned with! A commentator on the national scene! One evening, I was to speak at a convention of the American Association of Secondary School Principals, to a group of about two thousand people. While outwardly conveying the proper level of humility, I was full of myself and this newfound celebrity. I have to admit that I was celebrating it somewhat publicly, as though surely I deserved it. Even more exciting was the fact that the convention was being held at the Civic Center Auditorium in San Francisco, and there would be people in the audience whom I knew.

Evadne took me aside that evening as we were heading to the auditorium. "You're reading your own press, Price. You're starting to believe what they're saying about you."

She was absolutely right. It was sober advice and, as always with Evadne, direct. I listened to her when she told me such things. I was painfully aware of a certain attraction to fame and celebrity. That Evadne was so careful in reminding me that I shouldn't be *so* self-absorbed, that I was still, after all, just Price Cobbs, made these heady experiences even more valuable to me in the end. She kept me on the ground. She kept me balanced.

And as if to remind me of my own hubris and our human frailty, another event interceded in all this vainglory which changed our lives forever. At the height of the most dizzying moments after the publication of *Black Rage,* Evadne was to encounter a truly disastrous problem of her own. She discovered a lump in one breast and was shortly thereafter diagnosed with cancer. She was forty-four years old.

CHAPTER FOURTEEN

I never expected to see Evadne, so vibrant a woman, whose physical abilities had seemed so unstoppable, reduced to a point where she needed help just to get in and out of bed. She was too young for this. She was too alive!

After a mastectomy, she went into chemotherapy. The results were immediate: the gaining of weight, hair loss. She worried about these things, ever a woman, worried that somehow she was losing her attractiveness to me. I felt at a loss to help. I understood her concerns. She remained desirable to me no matter what, because I loved her and always would. Her illness was part of her, something none of us welcomed. But she was still very much Evadne, always pretty Evadne, always Evadne the fine dancer, the tennis player, the teacher, the young mother. I gave her as much love and assistance as I could, and made sure that our kids, Price and Renata, had as much access to her love as possible, so that she could benefit from their loving concern as well.

Evadne's struggle with her cancer was to go on for four years, through surgery, chemotherapy, apparent remissions, more surgery, and slow decline. I loved her throughout, marveling at how she was handling it. One often hears how brave someone has been while going through such a trial, how they've faced up to the difficulties, how they never complained. Evadne was such a person. She felt the pain she was in, but she seemed to accept it with a kind of shrug of the shoulders and the suggestion that we should all get on with things and not worry so much about this.

"I'm not afraid of death," she said to me once. "I just want to live!"

Even when she was quite ill, if she could go out she would. And when

I talked later to people who knew her only slightly—grocery clerks, mail delivery people—they'd express real surprise to learn that Evadne was suffering such illness and duress. To them she seemed unaffected by it. I admired her tremendously for that and loved her all the more.

I learned something about myself as well. I knew that Evadne was dying, and there were times when I descended into a silent self-pity. Why is this happening to us? It seemed so unfair. I don't think this is unusual for the family of someone with horrific medical problems, but I felt nonetheless that I had to take myself in hand and set myself straight.

I'm not the one dying here, I'd think to myself, and, like Evadne, I'd get on with things. But I think that family members have the right to suffer, nonetheless. It was Evadne herself, and her forthright bravery and continued affection, that helped me through those moments.

•◆•

I learned something about my profession too. One day, during a time when she was having significant difficulties, I had gone to the hospital at the University of California at San Francisco to visit her. We were sitting talking when an attending physician, followed by an entourage of interns and residents, walked into the room. There was no effort made at introductions, no niceties shared, no bedside manner. The doctor simply took Evadne's covers from her as all the others gathered round.

"O.K., Evadne, we need to take a look at you here, so would you mind . . ."

And the examination began. As with all such examinations of patients with serious problems, Evadne had to remain still while the physician talked about some very intimate issues. He continued to call her "Evadne" and refer to her as "Evadne" to all the others there. He had not even been polite enough to ask her permission to begin the examination.

She was embarrassed, and I was outraged.

"Pardon me, Doctor," I said, interrupting his examination and the instruction he was giving the others. He looked up at me surprised, a bit disgruntled at being interrupted. Although I was at the time on the medical school staff and clinical faculty at UCSF, I had not met this man.

"Her name is not Evadne. It's Mrs. Cobbs," I said.

"I see. And you, you're . . ."

I felt that this man's treatment of my wife had exposed her to embarrassment and stripped her of her dignity.

He tightened his lips. "You're Mr. Cobbs?"

"No. I'm Doctor Cobbs. I'm a physician, and I'm on the faculty here."

There was a pause as this man and the others regrouped, altering their assessment of this interloper and how he felt that he could intervene.

"You're a physician here," the doctor said.

"I am," I replied.

There was an apology, and the sudden appearance of a good deal more politesse. Evadne was able to cover herself, and she got an apology too.

I think racism had something to do with this physician's initial attitude. Like the white psychiatrists a few years earlier at Mendocino State Hospital, he may have felt in his heart that a black woman patient would have no avenue for complaint, and would *not* (or could *not*) complain about any kind of shoddy treatment.

The fact of the matter is, though, he probably didn't think about it at all, which is often how racism (and disrespect) works. It gets expressed thoughtlessly, seemingly without overt malice but with devastating power nonetheless.

But racism was only a part of what was wrong with this scene. As a physician myself, I hadn't realized to what low levels the concern for patients' dignity had sunk in hospital-care settings. This was in the early 1970s, well before the notion of patients' rights had come to the fore. In that era of faceless medical teams and the treatment of disease as an abstract puzzle to be solved without patient involvement, in that culture where privacy and dignity were ignored in the midst of real pain and suffering, just about *any* patient had to put up with what Evadne experienced. I came to understand that day how at least one part of the Hippocratic Oath was being violated. It was the early sentence that says "I will follow that system of regimen which, according to my ability and judgment, I consider for the benefit of my patients, and abstain from whatever is deleterious and mischievous."

• ❖ •

We sought counseling and went to see a psychoanalyst whom I knew named Norman Reider. Dr. Reider was well known in psychoanalytic circles as an expert in the psychodynamics of families, using the family system as a whole to understand both the individual and the family members' interrelationships. His work and mine had a similar thrust, in which the social group provides the essential vehicle for understanding the individual. So I felt he was intellectually right for the job of helping us. However, we went for the first visit less for his skills as a psychoanalyst, but rather because he was a trusted friend and colleague. Most important, Evadne and I just needed help dealing with her illness and pain.

We went together at first. But Evadne wanted more personal counseling. So after several sessions, she began to visit Dr. Reider by herself. Her responses to these sessions at first were quite negative.

"He doesn't know anything," Evadne once said, "about what it's like to be a black woman." She sometimes fulminated against him, so angry with him and his abrupt manner. Dr. Reider was, to be sure, Jewish and a white man. But as Evadne's therapy with Dr. Reider continued, as he got to know her and she got to know him, her tone slowly changed. Eventually she came to like and respect Dr. Reider immensely and even, as times got really rough for her, to depend on him. Despite his lack of experience of what it meant to be black and a woman, Dr. Reider remembered one thing that meant almost everything to Evadne and me. He respected and treated her like a true, thoughtful, intelligent woman whose emotional well-being was very worth protecting and asserting.

He was occasionally argumentative with her. With a mixture of bemusement and anger, she would occasionally tell me about a heated debate that had occurred. The important part of the story was that she liked and respected this man who treated her as a person not as a patient who was dying. He occasionally forced her to face bleak truths. He was not simply all kindness and warm feelings. He engaged her in the process of her own therapy and forced Evadne to face what she had to face, and to talk about it in real terms that spared nothing of the truth. So, death was a part of their conversation. Pain was a part of their conversation. Doubt and dismay. Despair. But because he was so direct and honest a man, she felt he was *truly* feeling of the difficulties she was in.

•◆•

At the same time, I was finding out about both the positive and negative aspects of what it's really like to be highly visible in the cultural or political arena. When you've written something extremely controversial, that directly affects many people's attitudes in what is a very volatile political question, you can come in for your share of lumps.

I was asked to appear on a television show with Malcolm Boyd, a well-known Episcopalian priest, whose book, *Are You Runnin' With Me, Jesus?*, had come out at approximately the same time as *Black Rage*. Before the broadcast, we were talking with each other, and Boyd complained about what he called the "humiliating hucksterism" that was involved in publicizing books. He found the process demeaning, he said. He was sure that I agreed that two such intelligent writers as he and I shouldn't have to submit ourselves to such used-car sales extravaganzas as this television show. We shouldn't have to preen and strut like that.

I agreed, of course.

When the cameras went on, however, Boyd quickly upstaged me, hogging the camera, and touting his book as though it were the only one being discussed. I sat quietly in my chair as he yammered at the camera. I learned in that moment that one had to maintain his vigilance when competing books were on the same stage.

Black Rage had some very important things going for it, though. There had been nothing like it before, and many of the reviews agreed, as did many of the audience who came to our readings or signings. We felt we had written with an authentic black voice that had authority and credibility. A great deal had been written about similar issues in the black experience. But little of it had the direct immediacy that fuels *Black Rage*.

This confidence helped me through a number of experiences that were not at all so congratulatory. This was the late 1960s and early 1970s when a new black identity was being forged. At universities, I often encountered black students who, as part of the politically explosive atmosphere on campus in those times, would deny their middle-class upbringings. They would chide me from the audience for not being "really" black because I was wearing a suit and tie, or because I was a physician or, even more so, a psychiatrist! I must have "sold out," as the derisive phrase went, tossed away my blackness in some onerous pact with the white man. A pact that gave me access, however limited, to the white man's schools, the white man's professions, the white man's manner of speech, etc. More than once I was asked from the audience at some appearance, "What do *you* really know about being black, man?"

At the many elite and expensive colleges and universities where I spoke, "being black" included the appearance of being poor, hip, cool, in short "a bad motherfucker." The most respected black people showing up on campus in those times were often the Black Panthers, who would be present and speaking at political rallies. There weren't a lot of college graduates in the Black Panthers, but they were deemed leaders. They were real. They were direct. They were from the streets. So who needed a psychiatrist in a suit?

In the face of such a question, I would look at the student who had asked it, and wonder, How in hell did *you* get here, man? It was very obvious to me that most of these students were from families like mine. Remember, this was before affirmative action programs. Their parents had found a way to become middle-class, so that they could send their children to college, surely a must for any middle-class family. So I felt a certain hypocrisy, however unknown to them, on the part of black students who would ask me that question and others like it.

I was sympathetic to them nonetheless. I knew they were asking that kind of question because of the rage that was boiling in them. I remembered the racial confrontation group at Esalen, which had begun with the black participants attacking one another before turning their attention to the white participants. The rage of these middle-class students was coming to the surface in the very words that they were using to castigate me, another black man.

My response to such questions was to ask them, first, if they'd read my book. If they said yes, then we'd talk some about what was in it, information that I felt was so directly *about* being black that it was undeniable. If they said no, they hadn't read it, then I'd suggest they do read it, so that they could *know* what they were talking about.

The truly surprising response I got came from some of these same black students when we'd go later for coffee or a meeting of a black student organization (where there were no white people present), and then they'd embrace *Black Rage*.

"You're telling it, man," such a student would say. "We're with you." In front of the white man, we confronted each other. Privately, we embraced. I realized how important that kind of public posturing must have been to those black students at that particular point in time.

There was another response, from another kind of person. A black psychiatrist I knew told me, "Price, you and Bill shouldn't do this. You're peeping our secrets."

I was well aware of the penchant among black people for keeping the details of our true feelings masked from white people. You played your emotional cards close to the vest if you were black and in the presence of white people, because an open declaration of those feelings, if they were negative, could get you into real trouble. So an open declaration like that of *Black Rage* (in the title *and* in the text) was problematic for many black people. This was too brazen, too revealing. I thought such feelings were part of the legacy of slavery playing itself out once more.

I didn't feel nearly as resentful, though, of these students confronting me in public or of my peers chastising me for revealing long-held secrets as I did of some of the white members of campus audiences where I spoke. In establishing their radical credentials, some university professors would speak disparagingly—and patronizingly—about why black people didn't really need a college education. Many of the Black Panthers, after all, hadn't had a college education, and they were being heard. For these white academics, a college education for blacks somehow wasn't "cool." It wasn't "black." It wasn't "hip." The education of the streets, of personal experience, of drugs and funky music and street smarts, of being knocked about by the cops and the welfare bureaucrats was deemed better, more pure, more true for black students.

I noticed that these white people did not say the same thing about white students. In their case, the education of the streets would be deemed a waste of valuable time, a loss of real opportunity, the expression of foolishness or laziness.

These white people had the idea that, because of black people's history, blacks were somehow born with deeper wisdom and more fully developed souls. I felt that this notion was based on some misguided romantic ideal and was racist in the extreme. It was like one of the comic images, so beloved by whites, that had come from the minstrel shows of the nineteenth century. The happy-go-lucky darkie had morphed into the soulful, bad street-smart black. As someone who had had the good fortune to benefit from a university education, and who was a black man who had grown up in segregated L.A., I knew that the school of hard knocks was worse for black people than it would ever be for white people, and that a college education was *more* essential to black people than it was to white people.

So I dismissed this idea—so often presented to me by white folks, especially by white professors on campus—as racist idiocy.

•◆•

During this time, I also became involved in more of the racial confrontation groups that George Leonard and I had pioneered at Esalen. There was a new chancellor at the University of California Medical School, Dr. Philip Lee, who was instrumental in developing studies at the school that were part of a program to reduce racism on the campus. Phil had been an assistant secretary of health under John Gardner in the administration of President Lyndon Johnson. He had read *Black Rage* and had told me that its revelations had changed the way he thought about race. I had spoken with him about the experiences George and I had had, and he asked me to put together a program that would sponsor such confrontation groups among faculty and students.

Dr. Lee, who was so helpful in putting together this program, went on from the chancellorship of UCSF to eventually return to Washington again as the assistant secretary of health and human services under Donna Shalala, in the Clinton administration.

We had many such groups, and every one of them featured the elements of confrontation, raucous back and forth, rough talk, truth telling, and confrontation that we had seen at Esalen. Indeed there were patterns to the conversations from group to group that made up a new patchwork that was making real sense to me. I was hearing things from different participants that could come only from people of a specific ethnic group, whether they were black, Hispanic, or Asian. This was most noticeable to me from black participants, of course, whose ethnicity I knew from bottom to top. They'd use these groups to vent every kind of pent-up racial resentment, every nuance of their own personal rage, all from a uniquely black perspective. It never failed.

Because of this, I was testing in my mind the concept of a new kind of therapy. I knew that the classic models of therapy that had been spelled out by the fathers of psychiatry—Freud, Jung, Otto Rank, Sullivan, and others—had been groundbreaking and essential, as far as they had gone. But none of them had discerned something that I was now seeing as obvious. Psychoanalysis had come from Western Europe early in the twentieth century. Other theoretical models and schools of psychotherapy followed this cultural path. They reflected first a western European, then a white American, bias that did not take into account the cases of potential patients who were not of that ethnic and racial mix.

So my advice about our black woman patient years before to the doctors at Mendocino had led to a new understanding on my part that the ethnicity of a patient was a very real factor in that patient's psychological makeup. A practitioner could not fully understand a patient's difficulties without a healthy knowledge of that patient's background.

In order to gain this knowledge about my patients, I developed new lines of inquiry. Did the person perceive himself to be a member of a group that had historically been devalued? How did this affect his view of himself? What negative experiences of unearned prejudice and discrimination were stored in the memory? What stories passed from generation to generation about the oppression and victimization of one's particular group were remembered? What were the scars an individual felt and how did they impact her behavior? These and many other questions led to disclosures, revelations, and insight. It was as if many people had been waiting for years to talk about what they lived with every day.

Many of my patients were decidedly not reasonably well-to-do white people. I already knew that a therapeutic model had to be altered and customized for every individual. What worked for one kind of patient would not necessarily work for a black machine-shop foreman born and raised in Biloxi, Mississippi, or for a Mexican-American bureaucrat at the Department of Motor Vehicles, for a Vietnamese refugee whose surprising business success in his new country may not have been accompanied by personal happiness, or for the white mother of three children whose father is black, and who's trying to understand why her children are having such troubles figuring out who they are. There had to be a therapy that kept that ethnicity in mind and used it to create a deeper understanding of a patient's issues.

I spoke about this with other professionals in the field, and remember particularly a conversation I had with Judith Weinstein Klein, a close friend and later an accomplished therapist who attended some of our confrontation groups. Judith said, "I'm Jewish, and we ought to be working in this way with our identity too! Because there are many similar issues: anger, self-hatred, and identity confusion. Intergroup issues. Intragroup issues. *Within* families." Judith became a protégée and went on to complete her Ph.D. dissertation on *Jewish Identity and Self-Esteem*. She saw how pertinent religion and ethnicity were to her work, particularly with Jewish patients.

"What is it about being a Jew that makes this patient's concerns particular to him?" she was asking. "And how does my knowledge of being a Jew help me treat him?"

It was a new approach to therapy. I saw it as being on the cutting edge of psychotherapy as well as being a way to describe a lot of the social and political difficulties that were rising up on the streets in this country. It opened an entire new way for me and many of my colleagues to look at patients and their difficulties, and we felt it needed a name. I called it Ethnotherapy.

• ◆ •

In the summer of 1972, I had a speaking engagement in Detroit. Because of the severity of Evadne's illness, I was unable to go. A close associate and protégé from San Francisco, Dr. Ron Brown, filled in for me. Ron was a thoughtful person and, as the son of a Baptist minister, an excellent speaker. As a result, his talk was received very well. In the audience were several managers from Procter & Gamble. One of them, Chip Henderson, flew out to San Francisco to talk further and then invited us to visit their company in Cincinnati. He wanted us to learn about some problems they were having with an influx of new entry-level managers who were black. There were integration problems of a sort. Not the integration per se of black people and white people. In this case, blacks were already in. But they weren't being understood by the white employees very well, and they themselves were having trouble understanding the corpo-

rate culture at P&G. P&G management had realized that there were issues that had not surfaced when only white men were being considered
for managerial positions.

I had never worked within a corporation. My experience outside of
private practice had been mainly in hospitals, mental health clinics, with
publicly funded projects or government programs. "Business" was a different matter altogether, I suspected. But I was too inexperienced with
the "business" mind to know how remarkably different it is from the
"public sector" mind. How corporations are organized, what's important
to people in corporations, what pressures they feel, how they work . . .
these were all new issues to me.

Ron was from Cincinnati and knew how important P&G is to that
city. Its corporate headquarters is there, and the company is of bench-
mark importance to Cincinnati's economy. When we received the invi-
tation, he was very excited by the prospect of working and consulting in
his hometown.

P&G was indeed hiring black engineers and business school graduates—a relatively new breed in the United States in 1973. But managers—black and white—were encountering things that neither group
knew quite how to deal with. For the blacks, entry to American corporate life was a milestone. P&G was the very essence of the kind of
corporation—enormous, with a monolithic and certainly white-faced
management force—that until now had been strictly off-limits to blacks.
Those black people who did work for such companies in the past were
kept in menial positions, which was the time-honored practice of almost
all American institutions, business or governmental.

Now things had changed. P&G had hired black people to become
mid- and, it was supposed, eventually upper-level managers and executives. Some of the white P&G managers were resistant to the very presence of blacks, a position that was also a time-honored American
institution. But not all of the whites felt this way. For others, the acceptance was there, but there were more subtle concerns: how basically to
treat the black managers; should it be different, and if so, how different;
how the white managers could (or should) deal with their own racism,
even though it might not be overt or necessarily intended; how to criti-

cize black managers when it was necessary; how to inquire whether the new black managers felt they were being treated fairly; how to handle situations when a black manager was in charge of a group of resistant white blue-collar workers; how to deal with difficult black managers; how to enable black managers to circumvent white managers who may be blocking their progress.

At the same time, the black managers themselves were looking for advice on how to make heads or tails of this corporate life, and of course (I knew) they would have issues of rage to deal with. So both sides, black and white, needed help.

I saw an entire field of endeavor possibly opening up to me and, most importantly, for the ideas I'd developed in my notion of Ethnotherapy. American business could be a proving ground where I could put the ideas of this kind of therapy to real work, in ways that could be rewarding for everyone involved. So off to P&G we went.

The contract I signed with them—under which I was to work with black and white managers to define and confront these new issues—was an experiment for me, just as coming to work for P&G was an experiment for the black managers. We were all on new ground together, and there was a certain irony in the fact that it was I who was supposed to advise and counsel these people. To be sure, I had a lot of experience as a therapist and a board-certified psychiatrist. I also had visibility as the coauthor of *Black Rage*. But as far as I could tell, there were *no* black management consultants. And, even if there were some, they had to adhere to the norm of "color blindness" in order to be accepted and go about their work. So I was to be part of that community that my father had joined so many years ago: that is, the community of "firsts."

There were several fundamental issues that I quickly realized had to be understood and dealt with effectively, or else we weren't going to get anywhere. The bromide that we had all learned was very much required, namely, that we all (and certainly me) had to work twice as hard. We knew that exemplary performance was an essential basic requirement.

Beyond that, the first thing I discerned was the most important lesson I ever learned about business. In business, the maintenance of the so-called bottom line is the ultimate concern. Without a healthy bottom line—good sales of good products, good cost containment, constant and healthy cash flow, and good profits—you haven't got a good business. In fact you eventually won't have any business at all.

The second revelation, which came hard upon the first, was that for individuals to affect this bottom line they had to attain power within the corporation. This discovery made me much more sensitive to the language and imagery of the organization. I would sit in on staff meetings and hear ambitious young managers talk about wanting to "add value" or "get more responsibility" or "gain more influence," but it became apparent to me that these were corporate euphemisms for wanting more power. I learned early that power itself is neither good nor bad. It can be used for good or bad purposes, but that depends upon the individual's will and value system. But power itself is morally neutral. Power is necessary in corporations, because without it, you cannot have much effect on the bottom line. So if these entry-level black managers were to rise through the company, to get to a place where they *could* affect that bottom line, they would have to understand how to gain power, how to maintain it, and how to use it effectively.

At P&G, senior management had acted in good faith to enable the program that I was implementing. There was immense pride in P&G being a well-managed company. They were giving me and the managers time to identify and impact these new challenges. But I knew that not all corporations would allow new black managers that luxury. Indeed, most corporations would more probably take a "sink or swim" attitude, that would simply throw new managers, black and white, into the competitive fray, to let them fight it out among themselves.

Once I learned the lesson—that the acquiring of power to enhance the bottom line was the way up the ladder in a corporation—I realized that black managers had additional challenges to overcome. It came as no surprise that most black managers were adverse to the very use of the word *power*. They were steeped in the notion that hard work and exemplary performance were the only ways to get ahead. Anything beyond that was devious, if not dishonest, or thought of as "too political." I certainly knew that hard work and exemplary performance were indeed important, but I could see that they were merely building blocks for moving up the corporate ladder. Whatever one's race, most corporate problems could best be handled by those who had acquired power and who could affect the bottom line. I could see that successful black managers could *also* use their superior performance to help expand the social consciousness of *all* the corporate employees. This was not to be integration through tokenism and appearance. This was to be integration through the use of the most real and direct of corporate priorities—profit.

The job of a consultant is to give advice and counsel, but at first I didn't know how to do that. This was not something I had experienced myself. So I couldn't very well tell the new black managers at P&G how to go about doing it. We had to learn together. I began to read avidly about power and suggested books for others to read. We talked. We strategized. We shared stories and checked with one another. We became a close-knit group helping one another out.

In so doing, we figured out that the way to power in a corporation begins in an understanding of how that corporation is organized. Everyone had to become a student of the culture of their corporation. Who's in charge formally and who's in charge behind the scene? How did they get to where they are? Who were their mentors and sponsors; who were their allies and who were their enemies? What were the parts of the organization that most lent themselves to upward mobility? What was personal power, and how did it differ from organizational power? Where did the lines blur and merge? What were the different forms of power in the organization and how were they utilized? Since power resides in the hands of those in charge of people, resources, and ideas, a good understanding of the subtleties of the organization, of the realms of authority, and especially, the personalities of the people currently occupying those realms, was central.

This was very different for me. In the work I'd done in the public sector, I'd found that power was only one of many factors affecting how people would fare in an organization. Most public organizations were not as tightly drawn as those of corporations. The lines of communication are often murky in the public sphere, and it is often difficult to determine exactly who's in charge. I had found that people who were successful in the public sector were more often than not those who had learned how to master the bureaucracy, that fabled tangle of red tape and the policies and procedures of governance.

The private sector idea of power as the essential requirement to affect the bottom line appears stark, maybe heartless, at first glance. But it is easier to understand and, most important, to effect in the private sector than in the public sector. You knew what you needed to do. The way to power is clear, though difficult. It is strewn with potholes, cracks in the road, dangers, and opportunities for missteps. But if understood and worked on diligently, it is the vehicle that can take you up the ladder.

When we figured this out, we set about devising strategies, talking to each other, and working in ways to get these new black managers to places where they could take some of that power. It was a heady experience for us. This was territory that none of us was familiar with, that in this venue had been explored by very, very few black people, if at all. I didn't realize then, in those times of experimentation, education, putting one foot in front of the other trying to find our way, that I was making some friendships that would mean an enormous amount to me both personally and professionally.

Most of these black managers were eager to move up the ladder. Most came to well understand this concept of gaining power and the maintenance of the bottom line. Many, many of them became very close friends. And a very few of those entry-level black managers would in time become senior executives and CEOs themselves of very large companies.

• ◆ •

Evadne's health began to deteriorate in a very drastic manner. She had lost weight and was growing weaker and weaker. We had entered that realm of caregiving in which you do give care but feel in the end powerless. You get to the point where you can simply watch as this person, with whom you've shared everything and built so much, must now suffer alone. You can hold her hand. Take her in your arms. You can tell her how much you love her and always have. Read to her. Protect her. But she is entering a place alone that only she can understand. And finally, on October 23, 1973, Evadne passed away. She was forty-eight years old.

Our kids—Price was now fourteen and Renata twelve—were devastated. Totally lost. I was the same and went through all of the worry and self-examination that ends with the inevitable question, What more could I have done to help her?

Her presence of course was everywhere in our house . . . photos of her and her family, pieces of furniture that she and I had so enjoyed contemplating before buying, the curtains she had designed, the sets of dishes and glassware she had loved, the garden she had maintained. The sound of her voice, in the advice she had given me so often, always direct, grounding, laced with loving humor and, I am glad to say, always excellent and well intended, came back to me time and again.

The love she had given us was still there, in the very air we breathed in that house. But Evadne herself was gone.

CHAPTER FIFTEEN

We were alone.

My children and I missed Evadne desperately. We were struggling to maintain ourselves as a family. I had never imagined in my wildest imagination that I would be a single dad to a twelve-year-old girl and a fourteen-year-old boy. I began to realize just how much emotional sustenance Evadne had provided the kids, once the task fell entirely on me.

We worked on this. One thing I did was to get the kids involved with the Jack and Jill of America organization. This was at Evadne's suggestion from some months before her death, and Jack and Jill turned out to be extremely beneficial and benevolent to me, Price, and Renata. The decision to join was made after several, sometimes heated, discussions between Evadne and me. Parents everywhere face challenges, but black parents in America face unique ones, and sometimes a healthy black identity for one's children is hard to come by. We wanted Price and Renata to know other black kids from comparable backgrounds, but I also had concerns that the group might be too snobbish, or "hincty," as my mother might say. We debated the pros and cons, but in her usual unflinching way Evadne cut to the heart of the issue, and the decision was made.

Founded in 1938, Jack and Jill is the oldest African American family organization in the country and has as its stated goal the wish to provide constructive educational, cultural, civic, health, recreational, and social programs for children. The San Francisco chapter was a place for my kids to meet other kids, where there were all sorts of safe activities for them.

Our experiences there were invaluable, and in my case sometimes even humorous.

As a good dad, I attended parents meetings where, usually, I was the only man. Even though Jack and Jill was ostensibly a family organization, in fact it was a club for mothers and their children. In attending meetings I would walk into a room filled with women. At my first few meetings, there would be a moment of silent surprise with the unspoken but quite clear question being asked: Why is he here? But I persisted, surrounded by feminine energy. Maybe I was a little bumbling, a little nervous, a little too much like a man in these meetings. But the women treated me with kindness, especially once they understood that I was a single dad. They understood the burden, and they helped me.

•◆•

My own financial situation had improved. *Black Rage* was still doing well. Because of its success, my patient load had increased and I was doing an increased number of consultations. Bill Grier and I had received a very nice advance for our next book. Also, as an entrepreneurial undertaking some time before, I had founded a "board and care" home in San Francisco.

The term "board and care" is a professional and legal term that refers to an establishment where people who have just been released from a mental institution live for a time and reacquaint themselves with life on the outside. It's a place in which a patient's basic needs are taken care of, with the goal of an eventual return to a life in which they can be responsible for themselves. That eventuality may or may not actually take place, of course, depending upon how they do at this first stage.

A "board and care" precedes a "halfway house," where a person would go who was really on his or her way to a full return to the community. My own board and care home was located in a modest, mostly working-class San Francisco family neighborhood called Excelsior, and soon it too was doing well.

All in all, my business life was proceeding apace, so I felt that I could splurge on a new automobile. I chose a Mercedes-Benz.

The people living in the board and care were patients who needed therapy, whose medications were distributed and supervised by me and my staff, for whose welfare I and my company were responsible. I was there every day, and I would come and go, driving my new car to the board and care home, and parking in front of my business.

A Mercedes was conspicuous in those times. It bespoke a certain style, a certain wealth, that I may or may not have actually had. But it *was* conspicuous. And I was a black man who would arrive every day at the board and care in this flashy new vehicle. In this mostly white neighborhood of hard-working people, I undoubtedly represented someone ripping off the system. I now know that choosing a Mercedes represented a level of hubris and arrogance for which I ultimately paid a heavy price.

A new patient had been referred to the board and care home from San Francisco General Hospital, where he had been under treatment for a period of time. He had responded well to their treatment, and they had concluded that he could be safely referred to my establishment. So, based on that judgment, we had accepted him. One week after Evadne's death, when the patient was out walking in the neighborhood, a woman on roller skates, no doubt enjoying some harmless recreation, came skating toward him. He yelled at her, then attacked and ultimately killed her.

When I heard about it, I immediately felt a great sinking in my heart. This poor innocent woman had been killed by a certifiable madman. I was not responsible for his madness. But of course I repeatedly asked myself, What was my responsibility in this terrible act he had committed? Shouldn't I have known more about this man's madness? Shouldn't I have monitored the case more carefully? Couldn't I have spent more time with him? I should have been able to see in his case history the possibilities for such violent reactions. His medication regimen may have told me something more about him. Why hadn't I studied it more carefully?

There was a furor in the community. The newspapers reported on the event, and a week later there began an investigation of my board and care by the State of California. My records were subpoenaed and studied. To my surprise and great embarrassment, the investigation turned up evidence that I had overcharged a number of patients for a total of about nine thousand dollars for services rendered. I was indicted for MediCal fraud as a result.

The subsequent trial and defense, which went on for years, required my hiring an attorney, appearing in court many times, defending my business practices, my honor, and my reputation. The newspaper articles about the situation added greatly to my troubles because they contained quotes from the neighbors, some of them seriously outraged by the madman's assault on the woman, about this "fat cat" doctor, author, and self-declared authority driving around in his luxury Mercedes. He had obviously been exploiting the system and the misery of these mental patients for his own good. So I was painted as an opportunist and victimizer.

My wife had just died after a terrible illness. My kids were in mourning, and I was trying to deal with their situation. I felt a significant degree of responsibility for the death of this woman at the hands of a resident of the home, which led to my questioning my personal judgment, my medical acumen, and my own emotional worth.

These events all gathered together to frame the lowest point of my life. The most significant personal difficulty was my own sense of personal responsibility and worry that, somehow, I may have actually become what the newspapers were portraying me as being. Was I an inadequate doctor? Was I a dishonest businessman? Was I a man given only to self-aggrandizement? Had the success of *Black Rage* clouded my judgment? Had I been reading my press clippings and forgotten that I was supposed to be responsible for my actions?

A court decision after three years exonerated me from the medical fraud charges. The judge ruled that the overcharging had been the result of a technical accounting error. The state, though, appealed the lower court decision successfully, and we had to go back to trial.

I realized that, as the owner of that board and care, I was responsible for any accounting errors that had been made, and I was sorry for them. But I was innocent of a crime. Once the judge threw the case out of court, I felt that the issue had been properly adjudicated. That we had to go back to court made me wonder if race might be an issue in this. Was this a case of selective prosecution? It seemed possible to me, since the amount of money being discussed was so small, and it had been decided by a perfectly competent judge in a court of law that the overcharging had been a simple accounting error.

I was still bereaved yet saw another long trial ahead of me, of more attorneys, more court appearances, and mounting expenses. The legal expenses were already almost more than I could bear. And there was the damage that this could possibly be doing to my kids. To avoid all that, I pleaded nolo contendere and was put on probation for one year. The fact is, I just wanted to get rid of this burden so that I could get on with my life.

But then, because of the fraud issue and the circumstances surrounding the board and care, my medical license was called into question. There were hearings before the state medical licensing board, all of them torturous to me and well publicized. Eventually, to my great relief, the board decided that my license would remain intact.

• ◆ •

These events and their aftermath came as staggering blows, a series of traumatic occurrences. So close on the heels of Evadne's death, they could not have come at a worse time. And the results of the events actually took five years to play themselves out, from the day the resident killed the woman in the street in 1973, through my indictment for Medi-Cal fraud and the subsequent efforts to clear myself, to the day in 1978 on which I was told that I would not lose my medical license. So I had quite a long time to think about this.

I was extremely embarrassed. I felt humiliated. I was angry at myself. I was angry at my board and care neighbors who had painted the picture of me—for my unhappy decision to buy a Mercedes—of self-serving, almost criminal-seeming venality. I knew I was controversial because of the books I had co-written. I felt that much of the criticism I was getting was a result of that and other successes, all of them symbolized by the Mercedes-Benz.

But more than all that, I was angry at the failings in my judgment that were part of what had happened. I could see the doubt on the faces of my colleagues, wondering about whether I had acted honorably. Whether I could be trusted. Whether I was a good physician and psychiatrist.

I recognized then that I had a responsibility to be much more careful about what I was doing with my life, because I was trying to be something special. I could have played the part of the humble-pie regular guy who is just living his life and then stumbles. But I realized that I was at-tempting to do things that few had done before me, and that I was vul-nerable because of it.

All this had occurred when my greatest confidante was dead. The one person with whom I could have shared these experiences, from whom I could have gotten sound advice, on whose shoulder I could have cried, was gone.

So I had to change how I was living my life. There was much to be learned. I had to understand that I must comport myself differently. I had to protect myself, be judiciously cautious. Most important, I had to know what I was doing, and be aware of the consequences.

There was something else I had learned. I had studied and written about black rage, and had thought in depth about what that was, where it came from, and, above all, to what it could lead. Meanwhile I knew that I had my own rage. Every black person does. I asked myself what those sad events in my personal and professional life could reveal about my own personal rage. Or what could my black rage reveal about where I may have gone wrong in how I conducted my life? What had added fuel to the self-castigation that I inherited from the legacy of slavery? What did that legacy have to do with my personal lapses in judgment?

The breakthrough for me came when I realized that one of the ques-tions that was gnawing at me was in fact the most wrong of questions: How can I escape this? The real question was: How can I *use* this anger and rage to set the situation right, and to set my own soul right?

I couldn't just sit around and be mad at myself, obsessed and self-accusatory. I couldn't just conclude that what had happened to me was the result of some perceived racism on the part of angry white neighbors and aggressive white newspaper reporters. I had to make adjustments to my own judgment, and to exercise better judgment. I'd have to use that rage as a vehicle for self-understanding.

I looked at myself for quite some time and came up with some con-clusions. Price, I said to myself, don't cut corners, professionally or per-sonally. Be careful of people, especially those who may wish to do you harm. But also, care for people. Worry about them and their welfare. Be a stand-up guy and take responsibility. Be accountable. Be who you are, but be *intelligent* about who you are. Be cautious (although not neurotically cautious so that you don't take action). Be authentic. Stand for something, and acknowledge to yourself that you stand for something.

All these instructions to myself may appear to be self-evident lessons and pieces of advice that anyone would acknowledge as sound. But I saw that I had not consciously enough held them as principles on a day-to-day basis. So I had to work to keep these prescriptions for personal action clearly in front of me every day.

I had begun to realize that I must manage my rage in such a way that it could lead to personal understanding and personal principles. Then I had to forge those principles into considered and real action.

•—•—•

The reader may have wondered about the family of the woman who was killed. I was sued by them for medical malpractice, and my insurance company negotiated a settlement. But no amount of "negotiations" by an insurance company can ease the hurt caused by those events. A husband had lost a wife. Children had lost a mother.

A few years ago, I was walking from my office in San Francisco toward California Street, where there is a small shopping center. I looked up and saw the husband of the woman who had been killed, walking toward me in the opposite direction. He saw me at almost the same moment.

We stopped and talked a few minutes. I asked after his family. He asked after mine. We talked about the terrible events, all of which raced through my mind in the brief moment of our conversation. I'm sure it was the same for him. Probably worse. The pain, the cruelty of the circumstance, the loss of a loved one so violently and quickly, so without reason. We shook hands. Then, briefly, we embraced, two men who had been brought together years before in a terrible way by chance.

I hoped from that embrace that this man had forgiven me.

•—•—•

Despite the considerable legal difficulties I was facing from 1973 through 1978, I was able to continue my career and widen the scope of work I was beginning to do for corporations. As often happens, one finds relief and solace in hard work. In my case, the continuing applications of my ideas about Ethnotherapy offered me an opportunity to regain balance and stability in my emotional and professional lives. The opportunity was a godsend.

CHAPTER SIXTEEN

Someone was to come into my personal life, someone whom I had actually known for years. Evadne and I met Frederica Maxwell Tipton in 1958 in San Francisco, just after we had come out to the West Coast from Meharry. Freddie's husband was in the last year of medical school then. The four of us went out now and then to dinner, and we developed a friendship.

Later, when Evadne was ill, Freddie came to visit her many times, in the hospital and in our home, something that both Evadne and I very much appreciated. By that time Freddie was divorced. After Evadne died, Freddie and I didn't see much of each other for many years. But one day in 1983, I was standing in the driveway in front of my home in San Francisco, and a car driving up the street stopped in front of the house, a hand came out of the window to wave, and I recognized Freddie Tipton behind the wheel. We talked for a few minutes, to catch up with each other and our kids. I thought to myself afterward that that had been a very pleasant couple of minutes. . . .

I had been involved for a while in what I'll call the middle-aged dating scene, a scene that hadn't been the most enjoyable experience. I was traveling a lot and had grown tired of the back-and-forth of a date with some perfectly nice woman in Washington, D.C., dinner with someone I liked in Tulsa, a drink after work with a woman I knew in New York.

During my time as a single father, it was O.K. with my kids if I dated. While they had negative views about several unfortunate choices, this was discussed between them and I was left out of the loop. Above all, they wanted me to be happy, so they were interested in any woman with whom I spent enough time for them to meet. But the scene was fizzling out, and after a string of unsuccessful relationships I soon stopped this perfunctory dating. For the first time in my life, I began carving out an existence on my own, which was difficult, because I am normally pretty gregarious. I tend to seek the company of others, and this solitary life was truly a new experience.

A few weeks after the conversation in front of my house, I ran into Freddie in a store in Palo Alto while buying a suit for Price, whose birthday was coming soon. Price was a student at Stanford University, while Renata had graduated from Spelman College in Atlanta with a degree in drama. Freddie and I had another pleasant talk. She was delighted to see Price, with whom she had not spoken for some time, when he and Renata saw Freddie's two daughters at a Jack and Jill function in San Francisco.

Coincidentally, a mutual friend of ours invited Freddie and me to a surprise birthday party several weeks after our conversation in the clothing store. We both arrived alone and spent the evening talking, and I left the party that night definitely interested in seeing her again. It was a comforting prospect because I already knew her, and knew her to be a woman of quality. I had sensed in our conversation at the party a real compatibility between us. I was attracted to Freddie. I wanted to go out with her.

We starting dating and found we had quite a lot to talk about. Freddie graduated from Sacramento State University and was an elementary school teacher. The former wife of a physician, she had two daughters. We had similar middle-class upbringings and values. Freddie was the daughter of a career Army Air Corps sergeant who had gone to law school. One of his brothers was a school principal whose wife was also a school principal. Another of Freddie's uncles was a pharmacist. On her mother's side there were a couple of lawyers, one of whom was Judge Raymond Reynolds, who served many years on the San Francisco Municipal Court bench. Not coincidentally, Freddie was also from a family of "firsts."

I became quite, make that intensely, interested in Freddie, and I wanted to give her insight into what I did for a living, since my profession as a psychiatrist had taken some unusual turns. Once we started going out in earnest, I invited her to join me on a few business trips. I wanted her to fill in the blanks about what I did and why I did it because I had been quizzed so often by people about my work. Yes, I was a physician, but I didn't seem to practice medicine. Well yes, I was a psychiatrist, but I didn't see patients in my office for traditional fifty-minute-hour sessions. There was often a variation on the theme of, "Oh, Dr. Cobbs, I see that you're black. You're in something having to do with race relations, isn't that right?" Or, "You make a lot of speeches, don't you?" Or, especially from a few black friends, "What do you do, Price, jack up white folks? And they give you money for it?" The last question was usually accompanied by a sly grin, as if I had discovered a formula for how to capitalize on white guilt.

I wanted Freddie to know that what I did for a living was quite a bit more than that. So one of the trips we took together was an extensive visit to Digital Equipment Corporation in Massachusetts. I had a long history consulting with the company, and I knew many of the managers and executives. Freddie sat in on several groups that I led, listened to the give-and-take among the managers in those groups, and witnessed some coaching sessions. She also attended a keynote speech I gave in Boston at a dinner for community organizations that sponsored and advised halfway houses for adults and young people with social, drug, or education problems. This was somewhat outside my main work with corporations, a bit of a throwback to my previous work as a psychiatrist with public organizations and owner of a board and care home. But I wanted Freddie to be there because I was to be introduced by Michael Dukakis, who was then the governor of Massachusetts.

I recall how Governor Dukakis introduced himself as being a citizen of what he called the "People's Republic of Massachusetts." It was obviously a tongue-in-cheek reference to the very liberal agenda that he had in place as governor. But that particular phrase was one I'd heard previously in reference only to Berkeley, California, and that city's unique blend of political radicalism and unusual government. It seemed a curious phrase and didn't strike me as appropriate to a national audience, which he would face were he to run for president, as it was suspected at the time he would. When we were hurriedly introduced before my speech, there was little eye contact and even the feigned connection most politicians exuded was lacking. I mentioned that I was from San Francisco and a friend of Willie Brown, the powerful speaker of the California Assembly, and even this reference elicited no response. As he spoke, I got a sense of liberal cockiness, of intellectual superiority, as though the governor believed he had everything he needed, all his knowledge between his ears, so that outside advice would not be necessary. As he finished the introduction, Freddie leaned over to me and said, "I know he may get the Democratic nomination, but he'll never win the election."

Freddie was very interested in all the corporate work she saw me do on these trips, never having seen the workings of corporate life firsthand and up close. She had many questions, many observations. I saw right then that she was very smart, insightful, and articulate about these matters and could be a helpmate to me, as I hoped I could be to her. Despite my often gregarious personality, there was still a place within me of isolation and solitude. The isolation had been alleviated by Evadne and the children. But in the years since Evadne had died, during which the kids had done a lot of growing and developing a life of their own, that sense of isolation had become prominent once again.

In the most recent years, in fact, loneliness had become a major issue. I was saddened by it, sometimes at odds with myself because of it. I had tried several relationships and even a brief, failed marriage, but nothing helped. But when I met Freddie, there was a chemical spark between us. I felt it immediately and wanted to be with her so that I could feel it again. Beyond that, I realized that we had the capacity to be friends. That capacity was to me, in my mid-fifties, as important a factor as anything else. We could share things. We could talk. For me—a person for whom talk and conversation is very important—Freddie brought directness to the conversation that was very helpful. I tend to overcomplicate things in my talk, and Freddie keeps me focused by getting to the heart of the matter.

We continued seeing each other. Love came quickly. And our friendship deepened that love.

I soon asked Freddie to marry me. She consented, and in May 1985, we became husband and wife.

⋆—⋆—⋆

My new happiness with Freddie was to sustain me through the loss of my mother four years later. In the twenty-nine years since my father's passing, my relationship with my mother had gone from that of being a dutiful and loving son to one of very close friendship. The conversations to which I had been looking forward with my father when he was so suddenly taken away had found their replacement in the many talks that my mother and I had together. For years I was able to ask her advice on just about any subject, and could depend upon receiving an answer that was considerate, thoughtful, and above all, acutely sensitive to my own emotional needs. I always felt quite loved by her, and I think she was especially happy that I had become a physician. If I could not become a bishop in the CME church, medicine was, for my mother, the highest of callings.

Mother always had a great sense of humor and took to Freddie right away, but with several important reservations. On a visit shortly before our marriage, with a twinkle in her eye she insisted that we sleep in separate bedrooms, "until it's legal."

"But mother," I replied, "I'm in my mid-fifties."

She stood up and adopted a pose of mock indignation. "You may be in your mid-fifties, but you're still under my roof."

In the numerous telephone conversations with mother after our marriage, I always referred to Freddie as "my bride." Finally, on a visit to Los Angeles several years after we got married, mother had had enough. She looked at both of us and said, "When does one stop being a bride and become a wife?"

In 1988 mother had a stroke, and we decided to place her in a convalescent hospital. It had been a debilitating stroke and had left us all in a quandary. My mother had always been so independent a person that going to such a hospital was not her first choice—or ours. But she needed constant care, and none of us was able to offer her that.

My brother, Prince, had been married for over two decades to his wife, Veronica, while working as an L.A. County probation officer. Our mother had been living in a duplex apartment for a year or so in the same building as my sister Marcelyn's home, and Marcelyn had been handling the lion's share of her care and companionship. But once mother had the stroke, daily care became a twenty-four-hour matter. She was mobile. She could speak and get along. But she was eighty-nine years old and needed to be cared for constantly.

We had all talked this over, including our mother, of course, and decided that the convalescent hospital was the one place where she'd get the care she needed. Marcelyn visited mother there twice a day. Prince and Veronica went to see her once a day, and I flew to L.A. very frequently to visit her. There were few blacks in the hospital, and mother had no problems with the fact that the patients were mostly white. All her life she had been a staunch integrationist. So, at first, the convalescent hospital seemed to be a workable solution for us all. Despite a stroke and an abrupt change from home to the hospital, her humor remained intact. When my visits were occasionally shortened by a business appointment, mother would smile broadly and state, "Oh, so now I'm reduced to just an executive visit, am I?"

But as the months went by, we saw that mother badly wanted to be at home. Or at least among black people with whom she felt more of a social and cultural affinity. It was simply a matter of her wanting surroundings with which she was comfortable and people with whom she could talk. She didn't complain much, but we saw that mother would prefer to be in her own home, to sleep in her own bed, to receive her visitors in the privacy of her own living room. There wasn't much we could do to provide that. Mother needed proper care, twenty-four hours a day constantly, and she wouldn't get it if she were at home, especially since Marcelyn would have to take the principal burden of providing that care. No single family member could provide such attention.

Marcelyn had married and had two children. After a divorce, she had become a teacher at Jacob Riis High School in Los Angeles, working with disadvantaged kids and others with significant problems. Later she'd gone on to work for a business magazine published by McGraw-Hill. During all this time she had still been having occasional severe mental health issues. She was frequently on medication and over the years was hospitalized several times. As with many people, her problems with chronic schizophrenia might wax and wane but they never really went away.

But what she did was to deal with them in very brave and admirable ways. That she was able to carry on such a career at all was an affirmation of the resiliency of the human spirit. That she did so with such distinction as a teacher and an editor caused me to admire her very much. She added to those career distinctions a caregiving relationship with our mother that was part of a symbiotic exchange between them, in which mother helped Marcelyn manage her emotional difficulties while Marcelyn helped mother with companionship, a great deal of love, and as mother grew elderly, real day-to-day help with just the business of living.

Several days after Christmas Day in 1988, Marcelyn picked mother up to bring her to a party at Prince and Veronica's home in Woodland Hills, a suburb of Los Angeles. The occasion was the celebration of the twenty-fifth anniversary of their marriage. It was also during the Christmas holidays, so Prince's home was richly decorated for the season.

When the time came for my mother to return to the convalescent hospital, she refused. On the way to the car, she stopped, pulled away from Marcelyn and me, and began swearing.

"Godammit, don't take me back."

It was one of the few times in my life that I ever heard my mother use profanity. She shouted that she did not want to go back to the hospital, and she literally held her hands against the side of the car to keep herself from being placed inside it. Her voice rose, and the emotional pain that she felt from her own infirmities and the fact that she could not care for herself was clearly etched in the sound of her voice.

Prince came out of the house and we were all worried about this. My mother was embarrassed. We commiserated with her, upset with the situation, and sad that she had to go back to the hospital. But there was nothing we could do. Mother had to go back. She needed the care the hospital gave her. Ultimately she agreed to enter the car. As Marcelyn drove away, I stood on the curb watching the car, weeping at the thought of my mother's being unable to care for herself and at her children's inability to give her what she wanted.

She was not to stay in the convalescent hospital much longer. In February 1989, a few weeks short of her ninetieth birthday, my mother, Rosa Mashaw Cobbs, passed away. I had talked with her about death. She had told me that she was prepared for it and would go gladly when the moment came. I think now that part of her protest after the party was based on the fact that she knew death was near. She understood that she had led a notable life, both as a wife, but also on her own as a mother, a church leader, an accomplished woman. But I also believe in my heart that she was preparing herself for her passing, and that she did not want to die away from her own home and family. She wished to spend her last days in comfortable surroundings, with the photos of my father and their children, with the many things she had collected over the years, the mementos of their marriage, of our childhood, of her own parents and of her religious beliefs, confident that she had led a good life and that God would welcome her.

I've had many friends, many mentors, and many helpmates in my life. But I could not have asked for a friend more loving and concerned for my well-being than was my mother. I'm certain that God did welcome her with open arms.

Epilogue

In the thirty-plus years since *Black Rage* was published, a great deal has happened. The civil rights movement greatly accelerated the process of knocking down the Jim Crow laws that had endured into the 1970s and making discriminatory practices in hiring, bank loans, real estate sales, university admission, and all manner of other things illegal. Building on the legacies of Martin Luther King Jr. and Malcolm X, many black people have engaged in a very self-conscious examination of themselves, the legacy of slavery, and the meaning of being black in America. They have seen very real changes in laws that long resisted change. Many have availed themselves of the educational opportunities now open to them in the same way that they were previously open to other citizens.

This process will extend well into the present century, I'm sure, because it has really only just begun. Yes, the racist laws that kept black people out have been struck down. Yes, there has been much very positive change. But many of the realities of racism still exist and must be dealt with. While much eroded, the historical paradigm of presumed white superiority and assumed black inferiority has yet to be extruded from the minds of too many Americans of all backgrounds.

Today's black American has a new attitude. The long era where we were grateful just to be partially let in, or to accept a few scraps from the table, is now over. Blacks don't have to settle for those few fields that were available to my father and mother or, for that matter, to me. The ledge to which I've referred, on which all black people stand, has widened, so it now allows for a more enjoyable view toward the horizon, rather than a frightened consideration of the possibility of falling.

True as this is, there remain millions of black people who have not yet been able to take advantage of the change. Some are trapped in the vicious cycle of poor schools, lousy housing, lack of employment, poverty, and low expectations. Others remain shackled to a mentality and lifestyle that contributes to too many fatherless homes and rootless children. They continue to feel the rage we initially identified in the late 1960s. Indeed it is still very much with them and a part of them. At bottom, they have unwittingly incorporated a sense of themselves as victims. As a result, whatever else may impact them, the legacy of slavery maintains a grip on their psyche. Life continues to deal them a bad hand, and they're damned mad about it

In thinking back over our many centuries in this country, I am aware that every generation of black Americans has had to try mightily to identify the obstacles to be overcome. Looking through the rearview mirror of history, the obstacles seemed more clear years ago and are more amorphous in today's world. Oppressed people are always doing a balancing act, struggling to remove externally imposed barriers while also trying to resolve those that reside inside themselves. This is no less true of the current generation. They need to understand their own rage. They need to manage it, by educating themselves about themselves and the history of how they came to be. Through this they will discover that they need not be victims, that they need not be hobbled. They need to understand that they are entitled to full citizenship and entitled to be who they wish to be. It's a difficult undertaking, one fraught with pitfalls and dangers. Any self-examination is so, especially that which is undertaken by people who have in fact been historically victimized. But many black people have negotiated those pitfalls and dangers because they have understood their rage and have then used this knowledge to fuel their intellect and claim their own entitlement.

The entitlement of which I have continued to speak is an internal issue of the soul and a state of being. It's a way of looking at yourself so that you can claim what you desire as a human being and as a citizen of this country and the world. Entitlement is about having a sense of your own place, of your own ability, of taking charge of your destiny and of the quality of your own life.

As my life's odyssey transported me from rage to entitlement, I came to realize that the themes of my personal journey were not unique to me.

I was always aware that the struggles of my life were intertwined with the history of my people. After years of wrenching introspection and often painful insight, I came to understand that the rage felt by me and others was justified. Yet, I also understood that however justified a complicated set of feelings may be—whether rage, revenge, or even hatred—if not understood and effectively managed, the person in whom they are felt is ultimately consumed. I found out successes in life and years of psychotherapy might make many issues more understandable, but something more was needed. Managing my own rage meant confronting the demons within me and figuring out what parts were useful for effective functioning and what others caused dysfunction and needed to be discarded.

The entitlement I came to recognize as lacking in me and others was an *innate entitlement,* an unconstrained, essentially healthy set of deep-rooted feelings that are essential to one's sense of self-worth. Once discovered and claimed as one's own they leave a person free to pursue and to possess whatever bounties that life has to offer. They create an unwavering internal sense, not that one is owed something, but rather that one is entitled to something. I now have come to see that for black Americans only by embracing this innate entitlement can the accumulation of centuries of internal shackles be identified and removed. Only then can individuals be free to focus their rage externally where it belongs and not internally where it cripples.

INDEX